Maria Petmesidou, Enrique Delamónica,
Christos Papatheodorou, Aldrie Henry-Lee (Eds.)

Child Poverty, Youth (Un)Employment, and Social Inclusion

CROP International Poverty Studies

Edited by Thomas Pogge

1   *Maria Petmesidou, Enrique Delamónica, Christos Papatheodorou, and Aldrie Henry-Lee (Eds.)*
      Child Poverty, Youth (Un)Employment, and Social Inclusion
      ISBN 978-3-8382-0912-8

Maria Petmesidou, Enrique Delamónica,
Christos Papatheodorou, Aldrie Henry-Lee (Eds.)

CHILD POVERTY, YOUTH (UN)EMPLOYMENT, AND SOCIAL INCLUSION

ibidem-Verlag
Stuttgart

Bibliografische Information der Deutschen Nationalbibliothek
Die Deutsche Nationalbibliothek verzeichnet diese Publikation in der Deutschen Nationalbibliografie; detaillierte bibliografische Daten sind im Internet über http://dnb.d-nb.de abrufbar.

Bibliographic information published by the Deutsche Nationalbibliothek
Die Deutsche Nationalbibliothek lists this publication in the Deutsche Nationalbibliografie; detailed bibliographic data are available in the Internet at http://dnb.d-nb.de.

Cover picture: © Roman Bodnarchuk - Fotolia.com

∞
Gedruckt auf alterungsbeständigem, säurefreien Papier
Printed on acid-free paper

ISBN-13: 978-3-8382-0912-8

© *ibidem*-Verlag
Stuttgart 2016

Alle Rechte vorbehalten

Das Werk einschließlich aller seiner Teile ist urheberrechtlich geschützt. Jede Verwertung außerhalb der engen Grenzen des Urheberrechtsgesetzes ist ohne Zustimmung des Verlages unzulässig und strafbar. Dies gilt insbesondere für Vervielfältigungen, Übersetzungen, Mikroverfilmungen und elektronische Speicherformen sowie die Einspeicherung und Verarbeitung in elektronischen Systemen.

All rights reserved. No part of this publication may be reproduced, stored in or introduced into a retrieval system, or transmitted, in any form, or by any means (electronic, mechanical, photocopying, recording or otherwise) without the prior written permission of the publisher. Any person who does any unauthorized act in relation to this publication may be liable to criminal prosecution and civil claims for damages.

Printed in the EU

Table of contents

List of Abbreviations 7

Note on contributors 11

Acknowledgements 13

Maria Petmesidou, Enrique Delamónica, Christos Papatheodorou,
and Aldrie Henry-Lee
INTRODUCTION 15

PART I:
CHILD AND YOUTH POVERTY, RIGHTS AND SOCIAL PROTECTION 39

Amélia Bastos
A REVIEW OF CHILD POVERTY APPROACHES:
The European Union Experience 41

Stefanos Papanastasiou, Christos Papatheodorou, and Maria Petmesidou
CHILD POVERTY AND INTERGENERATIONAL
POVERTY TRANSMISSION IN THE EU:
What is the impact of social protection policies and institutions? 67

Aldrie Henry-Lee
CHILD POVERTY, CHILD RIGHTS IN SMALL ISLAND DEVELOPING
STATES (SIDS): The Case of the Caribbean 91

PART II:
YOUTH (UN)EMPLOYMENT AND SOCIAL EXCLUSION:
TRENDS AND POLICY ISSUES 119

Alberto Minujín, Diego Born, María Laura Lombardía, and Enrique
Delamónica
UNPACKING THE NEETs OF LATIN AMERICA AND THE CARIBBEAN:
Methodological challenges and surprising results 121

Luis Garrido, Rodolfo Gutiérrez, and Ana M. Guillén
"BIOGRAPHICAL DUALISM":
Youth employment and poverty patterns in Spain 157

Apostolos Dedoussopoulos and Eva Maria Papachristopoulou
YOUTH IN THE GREEK LABOR MARKET 181

Sofia Adam
SOCIAL ENTERPRISES, SOCIAL AND SOLIDARITY ECONOMY,
AND YOUTH: What is the role for policy-making? 223

Catherina J. Schenck, Phillip F. Blaauw, and Jacoba M.M. Viljoen
"GENERATION NOWHERE": The youth in South Africa's informal
economy—the case of day laborers and waste pickers 243

I-Chieh Fang
"INDEPENDENT, YET NOT GROWN UP": Young migrant workers' journeys
in post-Mao China 273

Aldrie Henry-Lee, Christos Papatheodorou, Maria Petmesidou,
and Enrique Delamónica
CONCLUSION 303

List of Abbreviations

A&Y	Adolescents and Youngsters
ACP	African Caribbean and Pacific Group of States
AREPS	Agenda de la Revolución de la Economía Popular y Solidaria
AT	Austria
BBCs	Buy-back Centers
BE	Belgium
CCF	Christian Children's Fund
CCT	Conditional Cash Transfer Program
CPA	Country Poverty Assessment
CRC	Convention on the Rights of the Child
DE	Germany
DK	Denmark
ECLAC	Economic Commission for Latin America and the Caribbean
EL	Greece
EPIC	European Platform for Investing in Children
ES	Spain
EU	European Union
EUROSTAT	European Statistics
EU-SILC	European Statistics on Income and Living Conditions
FBES	Fórum Brasileiro de Economia Solidária
FI	Finland
FR	France
GDP	Gross Domestic Product
HDAs	Household Development Agents
HDI	Human Development Indicator
HH	Households
HHS	Household Survey
HIV/AIDS	The Human Immunodeficiency Virus/ Acquired Immunodeficiency Syndrome

IE	Ireland
IIPE	Instituto Internacional de Planeamiento de la Educación
ILO	International Labour Organization
IMJUVE	Instituto Mexicano de la Juventud
INE	Instituto Nacional de Estadística (Spain)
IT	Italy
JCF	Jamaica Constabulary Force
LFS	Labour Force Survey
LU	Luxembourg
MDGs	Millennium Development Goals
MENA	Middle-East and North Africa
NBER	National Bureau of Economic Research (Cambridge, MA, USA)
NEET	Not in Employment, Education or Training
NGOs	Non-governmental Organizations
NL	Netherlands
NPC	South Africa's National Planning Commission
NPOs	Nonprofit Organizations
OAED	Greek Manpower Organization
OECD	Organization for Economic Cooperation and Development
OIJ	Organización Iberoamericana de Juventud
PPS	Purchasing Power Standards
PT	Portugal
SCEs	Social Cooperative Enterprises
SDGs	Sustainable Development Goals
SE	Sweden
SEZ	Shenzhen's Special Economic Zone
SIDS	Small Island Developing States
SITEAL/UNESCO	Sistema de Información de Tendencias Educativas en América Latina/United Nations Educational, Scientific and Cultural Organization
STW	School-to-Work Transition
TVE	Township–Village Enterprise

UK	United Kingdom
UNDESA	United Nations Department of Social and Economic Affairs
UNDP	United Nations Development Programme
UNESCO	United Nations Educational, Scientific and Cultural Organization
UNICEF	United Nations International Children's Emergency Fund
VEL	Vulnerability in Education and Labor
ZAR (R)	The Rand (the Currency of South Africa)

Note on contributors

Sofia Adam, Ph.D. in Social Policy, Adjunct Lecturer at Democritus University of Thrace (Greece) and Independent Researcher.

Amélia Bastos, Ph.D. in Economics, Assistant Professor at Lisbon School of Economics and Management, Universidade de Lisboa and CEMAPRE, Portugal.

Phillip F. Blaauw, Doctoral Degree (DCom) in Economics, Professor in the School of Economics, North-West University (Potchefstroom Campus), South Africa.

Diego Born, MA in Social Sciences, UNICEF consultant, formerly at the National Institute of Statistics and Census, Argentina.

Apostolos Dedoussopoulos, Professor in Labour Economics at Panteion University, Greece.

Enrique Delamónica, Ph. D. Economics, Chief of Social Policy and Gender Equality at UNICEF Nigeria and Fellow of the Comparative Research Programme on Poverty.

I-Chieh Fang, Ph.D (LSE), Assistant Professor at the National Tsing Hua University, Taiwan.

Luis Garrido, Ph.D in Sociology, Full Professor at Universidad Nacional de Educación a Distancia (UNED), Spain.

Ana M. Guillén, Full Professor of Sociology and Head of the Department of Sociology at the University of Oviedo, Spain.

Rodolfo Gutiérrez, Ph.D. in Sociology, Full Professor at the University of Oviedo, Spain.

Aldrie Henry-Lee, Ph.D. in Sociology, Senior Research Fellow, Acting Director, Sir Arthur Lewis Institute of Social and Economic Studies, University of the West Indies (UWI), Mona Campus, Jamaica.

María Laura Lombardía, MA in Social Policies, UNICEF consultant, formerly at the National Institute of Statistics and Census, Argentina.

Alberto Minujín, Mathematician with postgraduate studies in Applied Statistics and Demography, teaches at the Graduate Program in International Affairs, New School University, Director of Equity for Children.

Eva Maria Papachristopoulou, Ph.D. candidate in Labour Economics, Panteion University, Greece.

Stefanos Papanastasiou, Ph.D. in Social Policy, Adjunct Lecturer at Democritus University of Thrace (Greece) and researcher at the Observatory on Economic and Social Developments, Labour Institute, Greek General Confederation of Labour.

Christos Papatheodorou, Ph.D. (LSE), Professor of Social Policy at Panteion University (Greece), and Head of the Research Unit "Social Policy, Poverty and Inequalities", Labour Institute, Greek General Confederation of Labour.

Maria Petmesidou, Ph.D. (Oxford University), Professor of Social Policy at Democritus University of Thrace (Greece) and Fellow of the Comparative Research Programme on Poverty.

Catherina J. Schenck, D.Phil. in Social Work, Professor and Head of the Department of Social Work, University of the Western Cape, South Africa.

Jacoba M.M. Viljoen, Ph.D. in Economics, Senior Lecturer in the Department of Economics and Econometrics, University of Johannesburg, South Africa.

Acknowledgements

The origin of this book was an international, interdisciplinary workshop that took place in Athens, in November 2014. It was jointly organized by CROP, the Observatory on Economic and Social Developments at the Labour Institute of the Greek General Confederation of Labour, and Democritus University of Thrace (Greece). The initial versions of the contributions contained in this book were presented and discussed in this workshop. They have benefited from the stimulating, critical discussions on child poverty and youth (un)employment and social inclusion, and for this we would like to thank all the participants in the workshop.

As always a collaborative endeavour such as this would not be feasible without institutional and financial support. We would like to thank for this CROP. The financial support by the Labour Institute of the Greek General Confederation of Labour for covering part of the costs of the workshop is also acknowledged. Our gratitude goes particularly to the director of CROP, Alberto Cimadamore, for his constant and whole hearted encouragement and insightful suggestions. Special thanks are also addressed to Thomas Pogge (editor of the CROP book series) and an anonymous referee for their valuable comments and suggestions on the draft manuscript, which have greatly improved the final outcome. Charlotte Lillefjaere-Tertnaes and other members of staff at the CROP secretariat as well as Jakob Horstmann have provided administrative support and we would like to thank them for helping us to navigate through all the stages of this endeavour. We also thank Ibidem for the final production of the book. Last, but not least, we thank the authors for their excellent collaboration.

Maria Petmesidou
Enrique Delamónica
Christos Papatheodorou
Aldrie Henry-Lee

INTRODUCTION

Maria Petmesidou, Enrique Delamónica, Christos Papatheodorou, and Aldrie Henry-Lee

Poverty reduction has been high on the international agenda since the start of the millennium.[1] Worldwide progress, however, has been slow and limited. Social protection responses to the 2008–09 crisis have either been marginal or produced mixed results in developing countries, while poverty and social exclusion have exacerbated in many developed ones. Within this context, this book critically examines the major structural causes and life-cycle processes connecting poverty and disadvantage in childhood, adolescence, and early adulthood. It raises the question of what policy strategies can break the vicious cycle of intergenerational poverty transmission.

According to data provided by international organizations (UNICEF, ILO) about half of the world's children live in poverty (suffering from multiple deprivations and violations of human rights constitutive of poverty), while the number of unemployed youth has risen to over 70 million people worldwide. Highly alarming is also the number of youth broadly classified as NEETs (not in employment, education, or training), as well as the persistently large proportion of young people trapped in conditions of working poverty across developed and developing countries (with Africa exhibiting the highest rate globally). As stressed recently by the Director-General of the International Labour Organization (ILO) at the UN 2016 Youth Forum, "the trap of working poverty affects as many as 169 million young people at working age."[2] Such a level of child and youth deprivation

---

1   During the 1960s and until the early 1970s it had also been very prominent (e.g., McNamara, 1973, Chenery et al., 1974). However, the oil crises, the external debt crises of developing countries, the period of structural adjustment, and other factors moved it out of the central stage.
2   See http://www.un.org/apps/news/story.asp?NewsID=53138#.VtsXa6R f2xD

has not been effectively discussed in the growing international dialogue on combating poverty.[3]

While there is currently a substantial body of research that analyses child poverty and the difficulties faced by youth in the labor market, there are fewer studies focusing on the long-term consequences of growing up poor, the close linkages between the two phenomena and the effects of early labor market entry on the future career. The contributions to this volume aim to evaluate the knowledge on the structural causes of child poverty and its short- and long-term consequences; examine the interrelationships between child poverty and the unsatisfactory (sometimes illegal) insertion of children and adolescents in the labor market; study the long-standing effect of youth unemployment and informality; and draw lessons and discuss advances and future challenges in policies targeting child poverty and youth unemployment, as well as youth employment precariousness.

Thus, the aim of the book is to enrich the comparative debate on these issues, in theoretical and empirical terms, and to set out the key policy challenges in effectively addressing child and youth poverty, disengagement, and exclusion. The analyses carried out by the authors attempt to constructively link various strands of study, research methods, and disciplines to child and youth deprivation—namely, as a violation of human rights; as a staggering cost on society, economy, healthcare, and criminal justice; and as inability to achieve an adequate level of personal development and social integration. They trace the negative impact of poverty and disadvantage on the long-term well-being of children, particularly if they remain in this situation for a protracted period of time. Inadequate nutrition, homelessness, barriers to accessing education, healthcare, and good quality care services create a vicious cycle in which the disadvantages faced in the early stages of life significantly limit the possibilities of obtaining a decent job that would provide young people with sufficient incomes to escape poverty, marginalization, and exclusion.

---

3   Among the most prominent few working on these issues, Brooks-Gunn, J. and G.J. Duncan (1997), UNICEF (2000), Gordon et al. (2003), UNICEF (2007), Minujin and Nandy (2012), and Minujin et al. (2014).

Child and youth poverty and labor force participation: Main challenges in the new era of the Sustainable Development Goals

A precarious entry into labor market is one of the channels through which these socioeconomic difficulties extend into adulthood, whether children start work early in their childhood or later on in their youth. One particularly problematic component of this vicious cycle is that adolescents and young adults living in monetary poor households enter the labor market at very early ages driven by the need to contribute to household incomes. Empirical evidence suggests that child and adolescent labor force participation leads to early school leaving, on the one hand, and results in lower family incomes, on the other.

Child poverty and child labor

These results are not contradictory at all. To disentangle these seemingly paradoxical statements, both the concept and the incidence of child poverty and child labor should be explored. While lack of income is a fundamental aspect of poverty for adults, children live and experience poverty differently (CCF, 2005). In order to understand child poverty, we have to explore the actual deprivations children suffer, independently of the parents' income. These deprivations are related to specific rights, which when not fulfilled or satisfied constitute poverty (such as education, health, nutrition, etc.). About half of the children in developing countries are poor. There is, of course, wide regional variation. The lowest incidence of child poverty is found in East Asia while the highest is in South Asia and in sub-Saharan Africa. The former is roughly a third of the latter. Within countries there are large variations too. In Latin America urban child poverty is about 20 percentage points higher than in rural areas. Nevertheless, in a few countries, there is no statistically significant difference between urban and rural child poverty, while in others there is a slightly lower incidence in rural areas (ECLAC and UNICEF, 2010).

Consequently, when low household income forces children to go out and work in order to increase their family's earnings, children have difficulties attending school. Even if they manage to stay in school,[4] they

---

4   A few years ago it was estimated that about 20% of children in developing countries combine schooling with labor (Gibbons et al., 2005).

have limited time for studying and homework, which increases the chances of repetition and, eventually, dropping out. Thus, although the family income may increase in the short term (perhaps even lifting the household out of monetary poverty), it is at the expense of child rights and an increase of child poverty (determined by the deprivation of the right to education).

Moreover, lack of schooling is one of the major impediments to obtain good, well-paying jobs for young adults. As a result, the medium- to long-term prospects of household income (in spite of a short spurt when children enter the labor force) are limited and lower than average for the rest of the population. Thus, child labor implies a double jeopardy for children and adolescents: First it robs them of their childhood and the possibility of schooling in the short term and then it hinders their future potential earnings.

According to the ILO estimates, in 2012 about 170 million children worldwide were in child labor (60% of them being boys[5]). Although this is a reduction of about 30% since the turn of the century, this number amounts to 11% of the child population as a whole. These are not all the children that work[6] but *only* those who are involved in work when they are too young (under 12 years of age), in work that is too heavy or onerous for them (at ages 12–14 years), or engaged in the worst forms of labor (enslaved, prostituted, participating in illegal activities, or victims of trafficking and forced recruitment). Half of all child laborers (5–17 years), namely about 85 million in absolute terms, work under hazardous conditions for their health, safety, and moral development (ILO, 2013: 3–5). About a third of child laborers are in sub-Saharan Africa and a significant number of them are in hazardous occupations.

While many children work in manufacturing export industries, most of them work in the informal sector. This includes children working in the agricultural sector, street-peddling, or household servants. The latter not only affects primarily girls but also it takes the form of debt bondage and other forms of slavery.

---

5   Clearly, due to gender discrimination, boys and girls made to work too early in their lives tend to be clustered in different sectors and activities.
6   The distinction between child labor and children who work is presented in the ILO Conventions 138 (1973) and 182 (1999). The precursor to Convention 138 (1973) is the ILO Minimum Age Convention of 1919.

Clearly, not all child labor falls into this category. Nevertheless, whether legally or illegally, child laborers are paid less than adult workers. This undermines efforts by adults to find well-paying jobs. Thus, a link exists between child rights and labor rights. Fully implementing the Decent Work Agenda (i.e., labor policies that ensure a minimum living wage, safe working environments for men and women, pensions, job security, equal pay for equal work for men and women, formal employment, sustainable livelihoods, etc.; ILO, 1999) greatly contributes to eliminating child labor. Similarly, promoting free and compulsive education[7] (which prevents or delays children from entering the labor market) and legislation to prohibit child labor help to strengthen the bargaining power of unions and adult workers.[8]

The worldwide youth job crisis

Global youth unemployment is almost three times higher than unemployment among prime age workers. Adolescents and young adults of poor households constitute a high-risk group, as they face the greatest difficulties to get a job. In the developing world, the quality rather than the quantity of jobs is the most important challenge for improving labor market integration of young people, as the jobs provided to a large proportion of youngsters hardly assure them a subsistence income. High entry flows to informal jobs that offer low remuneration, the incidence of transitions between informal occupations and unemployment, and the absence or low coverage of (any available) social protection policies, like unemployment benefits or transfer programs to poor households, create a vicious circle between low pay, insecurity, and lack of income.

In both the developed and developing countries, going through unemployment spells at a young age can lead to "scarring" effects thus producing a long-standing impact on future employment prospects. Early school leaving and other intertwined aspects such as gender, race, and ethnicity also decisively influence the paths of transition into the labor market by adolescents and young adults.

---

7   This policy also reduces the incidence and depth of child poverty directly by addressing one of the dimensions (constitutive right) that defines child poverty.
8   Not surprisingly, the earliest laws attempting to restrict child labour (in the first half of the 1800s) where promoted, among others, by trade unions (Cunningham, 1996).

The demographic phenomenon known as the "youth bulge" in developing countries, namely the rising share of persons aged 15 to 24 years in the population, is a crucial dimension of the youth employment problem. According to UN data,[9] more than two-thirds of the world's one billion youth live in developing countries. This demographic characteristic also propels the shift toward cities (e.g., in Africa, where a fifth of the world's one billion youth live). As the weak economies of these countries cannot create enough jobs for the rapidly increasing youth population, a large percentage of youth are unemployed, underemployed, or inactive (see on this point Ortiz & Cummins, 2012 and UNICEF, 2014).[10]

Even before the global financial turmoil, the worldwide youth unemployment rate stood at 12.3%. The highest rates were exhibited in the Middle-East and North Africa (MENA), but double-digit rates also characterized high-income countries. As Table 1 shows, nearly one in three young people in the MENA region are unable to find work, while the gender gap is very high as the unemployment rate among women is over 40% (compared to about 25% among men; ILO, 2014: 11). With the exception of the MENA countries, the youth unemployment rate in the developing regions is not very high, compared to some high-income countries (see Figure 1), but job precariousness and in-work poverty remain high. Thus, the proportion of people who are working but are unable to lift themselves from monetary poverty is comparatively large (see Table 1). Moreover, the high concentration of unemployed (and marginalized) youth in the growing urban centers of developing countries (e.g., in the cities of the Middle-East, North Africa and sub-Saharan Africa, but also in the cities of Latin America and the Caribbean) creates explosive conditions triggering social unrest, crisis, and instability (Ali, 2014).

---

9   Accessed at http://www.undp.org/content/undp/en/home/librarypage/democratic-governance/youthstrategy.html
10   The ILO estimates that 200 million new jobs will be needed over the next five years, in order for emerging and developing economies to keep pace with the growing working-age population (ILO, 2014: xx).

Table 1: Average youth unemployment rate and the share of the working poor (in the total working population) in the world regions (%)

	2007	2009	2012	2013	2014	2017 (projection)
World	11.7 (33.2)*	12.8	12.6	13.0	-	-
Developed economies and EU	12.5	17.3	18.0	17.7	16.7	15.5
Central and South-Eastern Europe (non-EU) and CIS	17.6 (5.5)	20.0	17.4 (8.8)**	16.8	16.8	17.1
East Asia	8.0 (25.6)	9.4	9.7***	10.1	10.5	11.4
South-East Asia and the Pacific	14.9 (38.3)	14.0	12.7	13.6	13.6	13.6
South Asia	8.6 (70.8)	9.8	9.9 (73.9)	9.9	10.0	10.2
Latin America and the Caribbean	14.1 (10.4)	15.5	13.5 (17.0)	13.3	13.8	14.1
Middle East and North Africa	25.3 (Middle East: 8.0; North Africa: 28.4)	24.0	28.7 (17.2)	29.1	29.5	29.9
Sub-Saharan Africa	12.8 (67.0)	12.5	12.3 (72.9)	11.8	11.8	11.8

Source: ILO 2012 & 2015
*In parenthesis: the rate of the working poor (in the total working population).
**Data refer to 2011.
***The combined rate of the working poor for East Asia and South-East Asia & the Pacific was 38.7 in 2011.

The global economic crisis further increased the global youth unemployment rate to 13% in 2014 (projections through 2018 show a slight rise in 2015 and a further slight jump in 2018; ILO, 2015a: 17).[11] According to the ILO estimates, youth make up 25% of the total working population but young people are three times more likely to be unemployed than prime age workers. Gender differences are also pronounced: as compared to young men, young women are disproportionally affected by unemployment across all regions of the world (ibid.: 7). The share of young people in the 15–29 age group who are neither in employment, education, or training (the so-called NEETs) rose in 30 of the 40 countries for which data was available in 2013. Two-thirds of youth in developing economies were out of work, not studying, or engaged in regular or informal employment. Also, in the developing world more than a third of employed youth (aged 15–24) struggle to survive on less than PPP-US $2 a day, and about 300 million on less than PPP-US $4 per day (UNDP data accessed at http://bit.ly/1KdkY7u; ILO, 2015a: 51).

Moreover, the economic slowdown in some middle-income and developing economies is expected to significantly reduce the pace of improvement in terms of the overall inequalities and the global poverty rate. After a period of employment growth in a number of middle-income and developing regions (Latin America, China, the Russian Federation, and a number of Arab countries), the situation is deteriorating. No major improvement in terms of employment has been recorded in sub-Saharan Africa, while in most of the aforementioned countries "underemployment and informal employment are expected to remain stubbornly high over the next five years" (ILO, 2015b: 11).[12] What is equally worrying is the fact that youth joblessness, underemployment, and precarious employment persist despite the fact that considerable improvements in average educational attainment can be observed among youth cohorts in a number of developing countries (ibid.). In other words, important as education is, it needs to be complemented with economic policies to promote and ensure full employment.

---

11   The ILO estimates the highest increases of youth unemployment in the coming years in the Middle East and East Asia (ILO, 2015: 19).
12   In sub-Saharan Africa, more than 40% of young workers are unpaid [UNDP, Empowered Youth Sustainable Future, http://bit.ly/1NgLyLt]

Figure 1: Youth unemployment rate in the OECD countries by gender (15–24 years), 2014

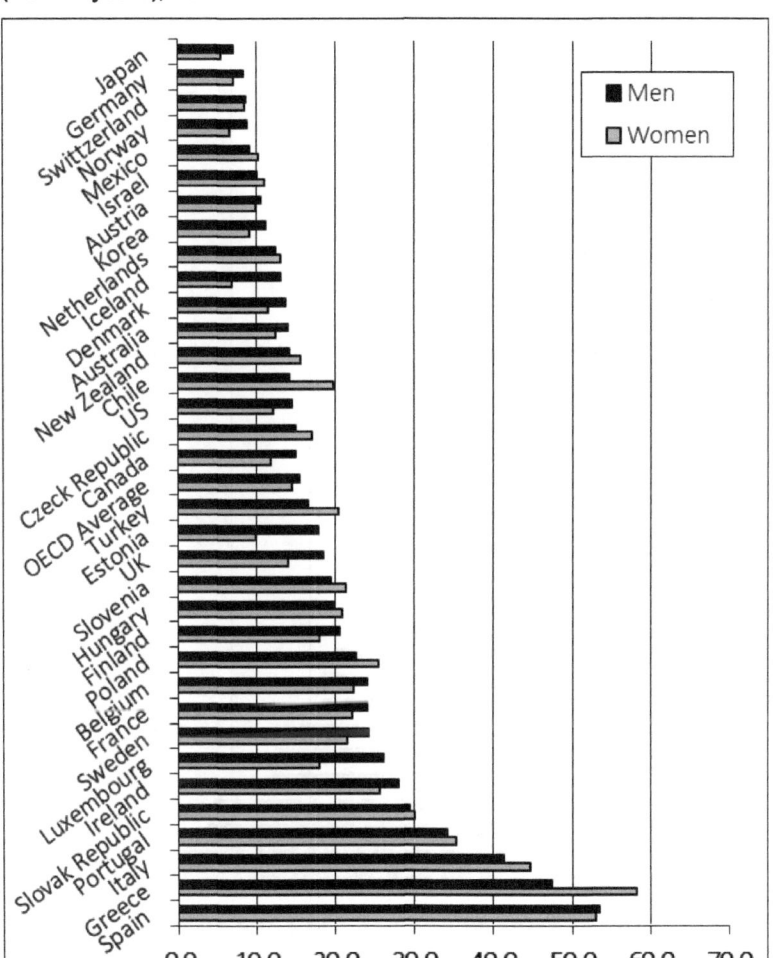

Source: Figure drawn by the authors on the basis of the OECD data accessed at http://stats.oecd.org

Figure 2: The NEETs rate (15–29 years), 2014

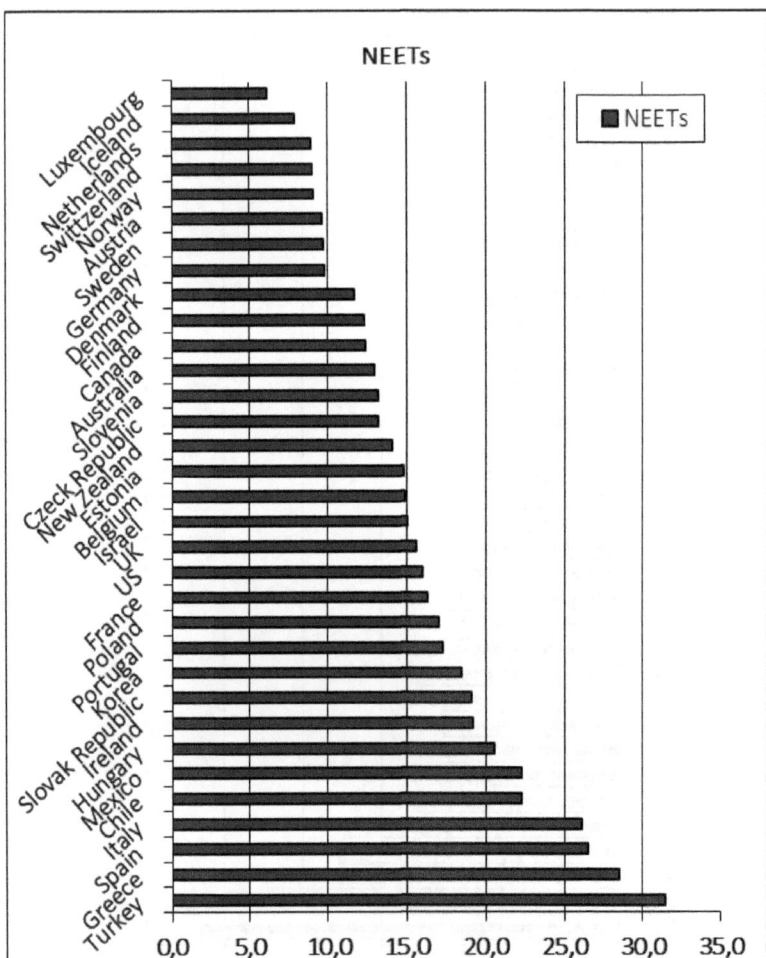

Source: Figure drawn by the authors on the basis of the OECD data accessed at https://data.oecd.org/youthinac/youth-not-in-employment-education-or-training-neet.htm

In the countries of the European Union most badly hit by the financial crisis (i.e., South Europe and Ireland) youth unemployment has reached record high levels (e.g., a little over 50% in Spain among young men and women, and even higher among females in Greece). Equally high is the number of young people who are not in education, employment, or training (15–29 years of age): close to 30% in Greece and a little lower than

25% in Spain and Italy. South European countries, together with Ireland and some of the countries of the most recent EU enlargements (Cyprus, Hungary, Bulgaria, and Romania), exhibit comparatively high rates of NEETs and also very high poverty rates among young people of the same age group (see Figure 3). Among EU countries, we can easily discern a close relationship between the rate of youth who are not in education, employment and/or training, and the poverty and social exclusion risk faced by young people. The EU countries depicted in Figure 3 seem to cluster into two groups. On the bottom left quadrant are the countries with comparatively low rates regarding both of these dimensions of the youth problem (the Netherlands and Austria are the countries where the NEET and at-risk-of-poverty phenomena among youth are the least acute), while the top-right quadrant comprises the countries with rates well above the EU-28 average (Greece is at the highest extreme).

By and large, in the advanced economies structural factors (such as the progressive polarization of the labor market resulting in fewer intermediate jobs and increasing job flexibilization and precariousness) are tending to make school-to-work transitions lengthier and more uncertain (Petmesidou and González, 2015). Young people are increasingly trapped in nonstandard jobs and opportunities for progression beyond entry level are diminishing. As shown by comparative studies (among others, see Iacovou and Aassve, 2007, Walther and Pohl, 2005; Ayllón, 2009; Eichhorst and Neder, 2014), youth unemployment, disengagement, and poverty can have "scarring" effects among the youngsters in the advanced economies facing a serious youth job crisis. Moreover, the available literature (see among others Bell and Blanchflower, 2009; Sullivan and von Wachter, 2009) points to health effects even 20 years after the experience of unemployment, while Helgesson et al. (2013) provide evidence of health and income consequences of even relatively short periods of unemployment.

Figure 3: The severity of the 'Youth Problem' among EU countries (as indicated by the NEETs rate and the At-Risk-of-Poverty and/or Social Exclusion Rate, 15–29 years)

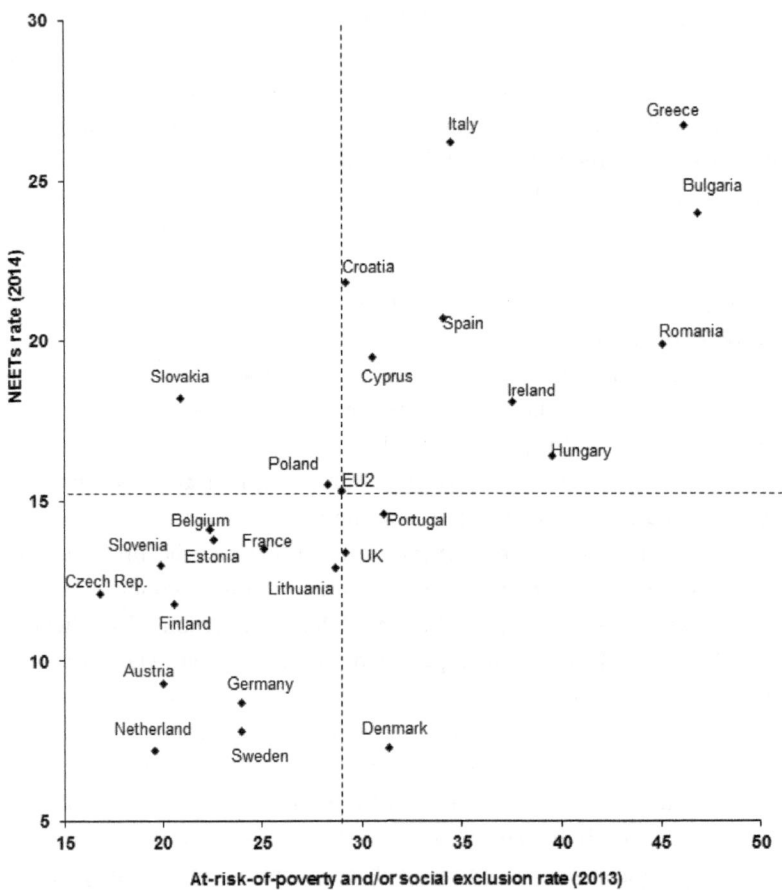

Source: Figure drawn by the authors on the basis of the YOUTH data of Eurostat. The dotted lines indicate the EU-28 average rates.

In the developing countries, the youth employment challenges are closely linked with the main objectives of the development perspective, namely the reduction of poverty and the improvement of the quality of jobs provided, as large groups of youth are trapped in informal jobs with incomes even below subsistence and lack of protection from social, economic, and environmental risks.

Besides the highly negative impacts that poverty, child labor, and youth unemployment have on those directly affected by them, these phenomena also entail serious negative social and economic externalities. According to a recent estimate by the European Foundation for the Improvement of Living and Working Conditions (Eurofound, 2013), in the EU countries youth unemployment causes costs of about 153 billion euros annually. They also lead to a higher incidence of youth disengagement and higher political and social tensions.

Hence, developing a long-term strategy to tackle the intergenerational transmission of disadvantages requires new approaches and the articulation of a wide and comprehensive set of policies aimed at reducing the structural causes of child poverty, promoting sustainable development that provides decent and productive jobs, improving education and skills of youth, and assuring universal access to basic social services to all citizens.

The challenge of employment generation was not given much attention in the initial formulation of the Millennium Development Goals (MDGs). Yet it is of central importance for the "North" and the "South." Unfettered globalization, the global financial crisis of 2008–09, and the ensuing sovereign debt problems in Europe are serious causes of the sharp rise of unemployment, deteriorating working conditions, and increasing employment insecurity in various geographical regions. Given the new agenda on the Sustainable Development Goals (SDGs) for the next 14 years, which aims to increase global awareness about poverty, hunger, inequality, and the need for sustainable development on a world scale, it seems an opportune moment to evaluate the progress made in terms of child poverty reduction and the improvement of access to decent labor conditions for youth. It is also important to discuss new theoretical approaches on both the short- and long-term causes and consequences of child poverty, with a particular emphasis on the relationships with labor market integration of the young population in developing and developed countries.

Both groups of countries face interconnected challenges regarding child poverty and youth unemployment. The financial turmoil and the ensuing sovereign debt crisis in several developed countries have disproportionally hit young men and women, as youth unemployment reached unprecedented levels. High (and long-term) youth unemployment tends to leave a permanent imprint on individual life course, contributes to the transmission of disadvantage to the children raised in the families of young people, and leads to a waste of potential human resources. In many developed countries, the harsh austerity regime put in place intensified poverty and disadvantage among children and youth. In this book we included two of the worst affected countries by the financial and sovereign debt crisis in Europe (Greece and Spain) suffering from high levels of child poverty and youth unemployment. We also included a comparative analysis of EU countries that contrasts neoliberal austerity to redistributive welfare and highlights the significant role of universal welfare provision in some European countries in reducing child poverty and intergenerational poverty transmission.

In developing countries the global financial crisis slowed down economic growth and job creation, which has also been negatively affected by the increasing capital intensity of new investments (ILO, 2012: 37). This highly diminishes the employment prospects of young people and leads to lost potential for social and economic development that could accrue from the so-called "demographic dividend"[13] in the developing world. In many developing and developed countries, social and economic frustration among a significant number of youth who fail to make a successful transition to a decent work sparked protest movements amidst the global economic crisis: the Arab Spring of 2011, the "indignados" and "piazza movements" in Spain and Greece, the students mass protests in Chile against inequalities of access to education, but also the "Occupy Wall Street" movement in the US and similar movements in many other cities of the developed world where young people were prominent.

The magnitude and severity of child and youth poverty worldwide and failure to give to all youth a better start in the labor market necessitate the study of these phenomena across geographical regions. This can contribute to highlighting common challenges among countries at different levels of development and support the case for coordinated action at the global level along the lines of the SDGs, the ILO resolution of 2005 for "an

---

13   The temporary spike in the share of employment age individuals in the population that could lift per capita income (as a larger proportion of people work). However, if equity, productive, and macroeconomic policies do not result in well-paying jobs for the new entrants to the labor market, the demographic "dividend" may well become a "burden."

integrated and coherent approach that combines macroeconomic and microeconomic interventions and addresses both labor demand and supply and the quantity and quality of employment" (ILO, 2005: 4); as well as the UN Global Initiative on Decent Jobs for Youth launched in February 2016 at the ECOSOC Youth Forum.

The structure of the book

The book consists of two parts, covers various geographical regions (Europe, Latin America and the Caribbean, Africa, and Asia), and comprises comparative and single-country chapters. The first part includes three chapters that focus on child and youth poverty, rights and social protection, while the second part consists of six chapters dealing with various dimensions of the youth employment crisis around the world. Besides description and multidisciplinary analysis (ranging from multicountry regressions to ethnographic individual interviews), the authors also provide innovative methodological tools and policies to address these issues.

The first part starts with an examination of definitional and methodological issues with regard to data analysis and the measurement of child poverty. The chapter by Bastos reviews the methods used for measuring child poverty in European countries. As she argues, even though the reduction of poverty is high on the European Commission's agenda, poverty alleviation, with regard to children, remains seriously compromised, which puts into question the social dimension of the Europe 2020 Strategy (EU2020). Despite the importance of child poverty and the continuing concern about it, there is only partial acknowledgment of this problem. Bastos shows that the methods currently used do not permit a detailed and precise diagnosis of the problem in Europe and other developed countries. She critically examines the theoretical models and empirical studies already conducted in the European Union in order to highlight the advantages and disadvantages of the income-based approach to poverty (a unidimensional approach). Then she moves on to discuss the merits and problems associated with multidimensional frameworks embracing a set of indicators for child well-being (in a positive sense) or deprivation (in a negative sense), and thereby assessing several different dimensions of child lifestyles and living conditions. Finally, she explores the holistic and child rights approaches that attempt to evaluate children's livelihood in an overall sense through a combination of qualitative and quantitative panel data together with participatory poverty assessments. She concludes on a set of guidelines aiming at a better way of measuring child poverty, which reflects the reality of growing up in poverty.

Papanastassiou, Papatheodorou, and Petmesidou focus on child poverty and intergenerational poverty transmission in the European Union. On the basis of a comparative analysis, the authors trace the channels of the reproduction of poverty by examining some major socio-economic characteristics of the family of origin in relationship to the impact of the different social protection systems on child poverty and its intergenerational transmission. The authors utilize available comparable microdata for EU countries. The analysis embraces association statistics, correlation structures, and log-linear models in order to acquire empirical estimates on child monetary poverty and its intensity, examine poverty spell duration and the probability of exit from or reentry into poverty, and assess the magnitude of intergenerational mobility. Their main finding is that differences across Europe in child poverty and in intergenerational transmission of disadvantages are largely attributed to the impact of the social protection system that each country has developed. Even though parental background affects the offspring's poverty risk, different welfare state regimes can play an equally important role in the reproduction of poverty: in the countries of the social-democratic welfare state regime (i.e., the Nordic countries) a universal and (still) comparatively generous social protection system significantly minimizes the influence of a disadvantageous parental background on the offspring's poverty risk.

Henry-Lee examines child poverty in three Small Island Developing States (SIDS) in the Caribbean (Haiti, Jamaica, and Barbados). These islands have limited productive sectors, small labor markets, insufficient skilled labor, and high unemployment rates. Moreover, they are significantly susceptible to economic and environmental shocks. These vulnerabilities negatively affect Caribbean children, especially those living in poverty. What is striking about two of these small island states is that their high human development index (HDI) may not necessarily be associated with strong protection and respect for children's rights. Barbados's HDI value for 2012 is 0.825—in the very high human development category. Jamaica's HDI value is 0.730—in the high human development category. Haiti's HDI value is 0.456—in the low human development category. Nevertheless, children in these SIDS face similar challenges and threats.

Analysis of secondary data reveals that rights of children living in poverty in these SIDS are highly compromised. Weak institutional arrangements and poor access to good-quality basic social services undermine child rights. Some groups of children are even more susceptible to economic and environmental shocks: children with disabilities, those living and working on the streets, and children affected by and infected with HIV/AIDS. Unless, there is a special global policy focus and action on the vulnerabilities of SIDS, children in these islands will remain at-risk of having their rights violated. Unless social investment is increased and made more equitable, and there is commitment by both private and public institutions, the Convention on the Rights of the Child and the SDGs will remain "toothless" instruments, which have not advanced the rights of the children in poverty.

In the second part of the book, the chapter by Minujín, Born, Lombardía, and Delamónica analyzes the nexus (or lack thereof) between education and employment for adolescents and youngsters (A&Y) in Latin America and the Caribbean. The situation of those A&Y at risk in these areas and, consequently, vulnerable to social exclusion is quantified and described. The chapter begins by exploring the situation of A&Y who are not in education, employment, or training (NEETs). However, the authors find the NEET category wanting and propose an alternative. Many A&Y are clearly outside the education system as well as excluded from the labor market. This is the category known as NEETs. However, unlike the image commonly portrayed describing NEETs as dangerous young men, most of the NEETs are young women. They come mainly from the poorest families. They devote most of their time to raising children (their own or those of others) and to household chores. Nevertheless, there are differences within this group according to class.

Consequently, in order to understand more accurately the interface between education and work, a measure of Vulnerability in Education and Labor (VEL) is introduced. This measure goes beyond a simple classification based on whether or not A&Y participate in school and the labor market by capturing the highest level of formal education achieved and the type of labor market engagement (unemployed, informally employed, and formally employed). The percentage of A&Y with high vulnerability in education and labor is twice as high as the proportion of NEETs. Within countries there are variations based on wealth/income quintiles and the level of education of the parents.

Garrido, Gutiérrez, and Guillén examine the youth employment problem in Spain, which suffers from one of the most staggering unemployment rates among young people in Europe. The authors single out two outstanding traits of the Spanish labor market, namely: "the low quality of school to work transitions" and "the high intensity of the insider/outsider dualism in the labor market." Starting from this point, their analysis embraces three major issues: (1) The high incidence of long-term unemployment among the low-qualified youth, compared to young people with higher levels of educational attainment; (2) the pattern of temporary employment as the channel of incorporation of young people into the labor market, which has been prevalent for about three decades in Spain and has not been modified during the recession; and (3) the rapidly increasing poverty risk among young people over the last few years. The examination of these issues throws new light on the phenomenon of a dual labor market in Spain (where a group of "insiders" enjoy—more or less—secure jobs and sufficient social insurance coverage, while a number of "outsiders" work on temporary and precarious jobs and lack adequate social insurance coverage). The analysis brings to the fore a major trait, that of "biographical dualism," which links the temporary pattern of incorporation into the labor market with the age dimension.

After a brief examination of the Spanish case in a comparative context of youth employment regimes, the authors discuss the high and increasing gap of employment outcomes by educational level. Then the analysis moves on to the "temporary pattern" of incorporation into the labor market and the age distribution of the workforce. This is followed by a brief discussion of the increasing incidence of poverty among young people.

The following chapter focuses on the youth labor market in Greece. Dedoussopoulos and Papachristopoulou start their analysis with a brief review of the main theoretical currents guiding youth labor market studies. They also provide an account of significant macro-tendencies on the basis of a number of indices for Greek society over the period 1983–2013. The authors argue that the use of a single index, that is, unemployment rate, does not capture fully the social consequences of youth unemployment. Thus they opt for a range of indicators that can help us construct a composite index of the youth job crisis such as: the youth participation and employment rates; the unemployment rate; the ratio of youth unemployment rate to the unemployment rate of primary age workers; the share of youth unemployment to total unemployment; the rate of youth unemployment to youth population; the scholarization index, that is, the rate of youngsters in formal education to the youth population; and the rate of youngsters who are neither in education, employment, or training. The indicators are disaggregated by gender and a cohort analysis is carried out.

The chapter by Adam deals with social entrepreneurship and youth unemployment. The author attempts to assess the extent to which social economy activities and social entrepreneurship can be effective strategies against unemployment and social exclusion with particular reference to youngsters. This is a view promoted by various national and international organizations. Adam sets out to examine how and under what conditions these expectations can become reality by focusing on Greece, with some parallel reference to Latin American examples. After a brief review of the definitions of "social economy" and "social entrepreneurship," with an emphasis on the differences between the European and the Latin American traditions, the analysis focuses on Greece. The author traces the development of social enterprise on the basis of the available data from the social economy registry and critically examines recent legislation on promoting the social economy and the ensuing strategic plan formulated by the government. The author argues that a series of deficiencies/inconsistencies in policy implementation following the new legal framework have prevented social enterprises from delivering on their promises. By drawing upon the Latin American experience, the last part provides some insights on policies for the promotion of the so-called "solidarity economy" (i.e., cooperatives, mutual-benefit societies, social enterprises, and other similar economic efforts).

Schenk, Blaauw, and Viljoen focus on youth in the informal economy of South Africa. The country exhibits a record high youth unemployment rate. For many young unemployed persons with low education, waste picking on the streets and the landfill sites, and/or day laboring are the main options to earn a living. These are described by the authors as "survivalist" behaviors providing subsistence to disadvantaged youth. The analysis draws upon a case study conducted by the authors over a period of 10 years. The study combined a variety of quantitative (surveys) and qualitative data collection methods such as observations, ethnography, and individual interviews, with the aim to examine the socioeconomic profile of these two groups of young people in the informal economy (waste pickers and day laborers). Emphasis is given to the barriers of entry into the formal economy for these groups of youngsters, linked with the absence of a policy framework for dealing with such high youth unemployment in South Africa. The authors argue that a multidisciplinary and multisectoral approach is needed for tackling this complex issue of multiple disadvantages among unemployed youngsters, so as to improve skills and facilitate integration into the formal labor market, as well as to strengthen the psycho-social well-being of youth and, consequently, of society.

The issue of precarious, informal work among the young is examined also with regard to young Chinese migrant workers. Fang provides an ethnographic account of the life-course and work conditions of this group of Chinese youth, who, as she argues, epitomizes job precariousness and permanent mobility of youth. The author describes the changing life course of Chinese young migrant workers as a condition of becoming "independent, yet not grown up," and explains why these dual characteristics of adolescence are important for understanding young people's perceptions of social norms and of their own positioning in their social and work milieu. Leaving home in rural areas in order to become workers in the factory makes adolescents develop a sense of "becoming independent" from rural society, associated with backwardness and low quality of life. However, they soon realize that it is hard to "achieve adulthood" in the destination coastal cities due to the restraints imposed by the Chinese "hukou system" (household registry system), which does not allow them to settle permanently and get full membership in the urban Chinese context. This causes an incomplete transition to adulthood and urban life. The paradoxical characteristic is that labor demand by the party-state controlled factories triggers rural to urban migration by adolescents and, thus, an early transition to "adulthood," on the one hand; yet, on the other hand, they are barred from receiving citizens' rights and achieve full independence from the paternalistic authority pattern in their family of origin and the support of their family and rural community. The author concludes on the need to lift the barriers imposed by the hukou system on migrant workers and develop a social protection system that makes citizen rights fully accessible by them.

In the Conclusion the editors wrap up and reflect upon the major methodological innovations and empirical findings of the analysis undertaken in the two parts of the book. The emphasis is on how national and international anti-poverty agendas (e.g., the SDG agenda, the specific agendas of UN institutions like those of UNICEF and ILO, as well as the EU2020 Strategy and the ones of many national governments) can adequately (and, in a realistic policy-wise way) fit children's rights and child/youth poverty alleviation goals and youth labor market integration. They make a brief synthesis of the major findings regarding the structural causes of child poverty and its short- and long-term consequences within and across the countries examined in the chapters. This is followed by brief remarks on the interrelationships between cumulative disadvantage through childhood, adolescence, and early adulthood ages, on the one hand, and poor incorporation of youth into the labor market, as well as rapidly rising youth disengagement and exclusion, on the other. The rich and diverse set of policies to eliminate child poverty, youth unemployment, informality and labor precariousness, and social exclusion gathered throughout the book are briefly summed up.

The contributions to this volume bring evidence to bear upon a major paradox between the endeavors of the international development community to formulate a post-2015 global sustainable development agenda with an overarching poverty eradication goal, on the one hand, and a global consensus on austerity, on the other, that has hit hardest disadvantaged children and youth. In the light of this, the contributions highlight the challenges confronting a range of stakeholders in an international anti-poverty pact. Of utmost importance is the need for global development initiatives to tackle, in an integrated way, the major channels of intergenerational poverty transmission in both the developing and developed countries. This includes new proposals and ratification of old ones. Among the latter are improving access to and quality of education, addressing gender inequality, and promoting formal/decent work. From the former we can identify the issues related to encouraging equity across a vast array of dimensions, strengthening social protection for all families and children, and promoting child/adolescent participation in the decisions that affect their lives (including public policies and social entrepreneurship).

References

Ali, Mohamed 2014 "Youth unemployment: A global security challenge", *Harvard International Review*, Vol. 36, No.1. In <http://hir.harvard.edu/youth-unemployment-a-global-security-challenge/> accessed 2 October 2015.

Ayllón, Sara 2009 "Modelling state dependence and feedback effects between poverty, employment and parental home emancipation among European youth," *SOEP Paper* (Berlin: Deutsches Institut für Wirtschaftsforschung).

Bell, Daniel and Blanchflower, David 2009. "Young people and the Great Recession", *Discussion Paper No. 5674* (Bonn: Institute for the Study of Labour).

Brooks-Gunn, Jeanne and Dunkan, Greg J. 1997 "The effects of poverty on children" *Future Child* (Princeton, NJ), Vol. 7, No. 2, 55–71.

Chenery, Hollis, Ahluwalia, Montek, Duloy, John, Bell, C.L.G. and Jolly, Richard 1974 *Redistribution with growth* (Oxford: Oxford University Press).

Christian Children's Fund 2005 "Understanding children's experience of poverty: An introduction to the DEV framework," *Children & Poverty Working Paper 1* (Richmond, Virginia).

Cunningham, Hugh 1996 "Combating child labour: The British experience" in Cunningham Hugh and Viazzo Peier Paolo (eds.) in *Child labour in historical perspective* (Florence: UNICEF, Istituto degli Innocenti di Firenze).

ECLAC and UNICEF 2010 *La pobreza infantil en América Latina y el Caribe* (Santiago de Chile: ECLAC and UNICEF).

Eichhorst, Werner and Neder, Franzisca 2014 "Youth unemployment in Mediterranean countries," *IZA Policy Paper No 80*, in <http://www.iza.org/en/webcontent/publications/policypapers> accessed 5 September 2015.

Eurofound 2013 "Youth Guarantee: EU leaders intensify efforts to tackle youth unemployment" in <http://www.eurofound.europa.eu/el/node/4294> accessed 10 October 2014.

Gibbons, Elisabeth, Huebler, Friedrich and Loaiza, Edilberto 2005 "Child labour, education and the principle of non-discrimination" in Alston, Philip and Robinson, Mary (eds.) 2005 *Human rights and development: Towards mutual reinforcement* (Oxford: Oxford University Press).

Gordon, David, Nandy, Shailen, Pantazis, Christina, Pemberton, Simon and Townsend, Peter 2003. *Child poverty in the developing world* (Bristol: Policy Press).

Helgesson, Magnus, Johansson, Bo, Nordqvist, Tobias, Lundberg, Ingvar and Vingård, Eva 2013 "Unemployment at a young age and later unemployment in native Swedish and immigrant young adults" in *Modern Economy* Vol. 5, No. 1. in <http://file.scirp.org/Html/4-7200658_42083.htm> accessed 20 January 2014.

Iacovou, Maria and Aassve, Arnstein 2007. *Youth poverty* (York: JRF).

ILO 1999 "Decent Work." *Report of the Director-General to the 87th Session of the International Labour Conference* (Geneva: ILO).

ILO 2005 *Resolutions adopted by the International Labour Conference at its 93rd Session* (Geneva: ILO).

ILO 2012 *The youth employment crisis: Time for action, Report V, International Labour Conference* (Geneva: ILO).

ILO 2013 *Making progress against child labour* (Geneva: ILO).

ILO 2014 *World of work report. Developing with jobs* (Geneva: ILO).

ILO 2015a *Global employment trends for youth* (Geneva: ILO).

ILO 2015b. *World employment social outlook* (Geneva: ILO).

McNamara, Robert 1974 *Address to the Board of Governors of the World Bank* (Nairobi).

Minujin, Alberto and Nandy, Shailen (eds.) 2012 *Global child poverty and well-being: Measurement, concepts, policy and action* (Bristol: Policy Press).

Minujin, Alberto, McCaffrey, Carolyn, Patel, Mahesh and Paienjton, Qimti 2014 "Redefining poverty: Deprivation among children in East Asia and the Pacific" in *Global Social Policy*, Vol. 14, No. 1.

Ortiz, Isabel and Cummins, Matthew 2012 "When the global crisis and the youth bulge collide," *UNICEF Social and Economic Policy Paper* (New York: UNICEF).

Petmesidou, Maria and González-Menéndez, Maria (eds.) 2015. "Barriers to and triggers of policy innovation and knowledge transfer," *STYLE Project Working Paper WP4.1* in <http://www.style-research.eu/publications/working-papers/> accessed 10 September 2015.

Sullivan, Daniel and von Wachter, Till von 2009 "Job displacement and mortality: an analysis of using administrative data", *The Quarterly Journal of Economics*, Vol. 124, No. 3, 1265–1306.

UNICEF 2014 *Africa generation 2030* (New York: UNICEF).

UNICEF 2000 *Poverty reduction begins with children* (New York: UNICEF).

UNICEF 2007 *Global study on child poverty and disparities* (New York: UNICEF Global Policy Section, Division of Policy and Planning).

Walther, Andreas and Pohl, Axel 2005 "Thematic study of policy measures concerning disadvantaged youth," *Study Report* (Tübingen: Institute for Regional Innovation and Social Research – IRIS).

PART I:
CHILD AND YOUTH POVERTY, RIGHTS AND SOCIAL PROTECTION

PART I

THE RIGHT TO SEEK RIGHTS AND SOCIAL PROTECTION

A REVIEW OF CHILD POVERTY APPROACHES:
The European Union Experience

Amélia Bastos

Poverty causes lifelong damage to children's minds and bodies, turning them into adults who perpetuate the cycle of poverty by transmitting it to their children. This is why poverty reduction must begin with the protection and the realization of the human rights of children. Investments in children are the best guarantee for achieving equitable and sustainable human development. (UNICEF, 2000 : V)

Child poverty is still a major issue within the European Union, despite the efforts that have been made to tackle it. The statistics of EUROSTAT show that in the European Union around one in every four children is poor (according to the measurement whose methodology is described later in the chapter). This highlights the scale of child poverty within the European Union and suggests that there is an obvious reason for social concern about the future of these children. Moreover, it is broadly acknowledged that the experience of poverty is long-lasting, leading to consequences that may last until adulthood (Duncan and Brooks-Gunn, 1997; Ridge, 2004, 2011; Fernandes et al., 2012).

Populations also pay a significant price for child poverty in terms of reduced productivity, lower levels of health as well as of education achievement, increased welfare costs and unemployment, higher costs of social protection and justice, and threats to social cohesion (UNICEF, 2012).[1] Moreover, as children depend on adults, they are not responsible for their living conditions. Therefore, child poverty is also a question of social justice. Finally, eliminating child poverty is an important step in the process of tackling the problem of poverty more generally (Minujín *et al.*, 2006). It should also be mentioned that despite the relation between children and adults child poverty differs from adult poverty in its specificities,

---

[1] For a detailed analysis of these costs, see Griggs and Walker (2008).

manifestations, causes, and consequences (Minujín *et al.*, 2006; Delamónica, 2014). The lack of visibility of children within the poverty debate has negative consequences on polices designed to eradicate the problem and also on the development of a holistic approach to tackle it that includes children and their families (Minujín *et al.*, 2006).

To get beyond a static picture of poverty, it is important to investigate poverty spell duration for children as well as patterns of exit from and entry into poverty, and poverty intensity. These elements may produce different short-term and long-term impacts. Children who spend a long time in poverty are currently worse off than those who have just experienced short spells. Transitory routes in and out of poverty are considered to have fewer consequences than long-term spells. The intensity of poverty also matters, as long-term spells of moderate poverty are considered to have a less adverse impact than short-term spells of severe poverty. Finally, it is worth mentioning that the nature of the routes to poverty is also important for policy design purposes. With low turnover rates (i.e., entries and exits from poverty), there is a relatively stable group of poor children, whereas in the case of high turnover rates, the changes in the composition of the poor call for the continuous adjustment of policies.

The use of panel data has broadened the study of the poverty causality process. Cappellari and Jenkins (2002) refer to the dynamic approach to poverty: "If one takes the dynamic perspective, then the salient research questions change from 'who is most likely to be poor at the moment?' to 'who is most likely to remain poor and who is most at risk of becoming poor?' The dynamic approach complements the conventional perspective that is provided by cross-sectional analysis and attempts to provide a basis for assessing what triggers child poverty movements into, and out of poverty"(2002: C60). Although it is widely accepted that it is important to develop strategies against child poverty, our knowledge about it is not very advanced. Indeed, the statistics on the subject are currently aimed at quantifying child poverty rates for all children and, appropriately, disaggregating according to specific criteria, such as family structure, parents' employment, and location, among others. Moreover, while the situation of persistently poor children is fairly well acknowledged, information about the processes that underlie the routes into and out of poverty is far from known.

There is a need to design effective social policies to alleviate child poverty. However, in order to ensure the efficiency of such policies, to accurately diagnose the problem, and to be able to understand the process that underlies it, it is important to possess knowledge of child poverty and its features. The methodological framework used to define child poverty is a key factor in this context. It is widely accepted that the concepts and measurements used play a crucial role in the process of analysis (Ben-Arieh, 2000). Moreover, a workable methodological framework is also an important tool for policy purposes, as it facilitates a rigorous and detailed identification of the problem. However, there is a lack of consensus within the academic community about methodological aspects, such as:

(1) The definition of poverty—unidimensional or multidimensional
(2) The unit of measurement—the household or the child
(3) The dimensions and indicators to be considered—selection criteria, quantitative or qualitative, age-specific ones or the same for all children
(4) The methods used to construct aggregate measurements to assess how children are faring—simple counting measurements or complex indices, weighted or not
(5) Data requirements

The aim of this chapter is to contribute to the analysis of the methods used to analyze child poverty and extract lessons learned from it to improve and adapt the currently applied approaches for the context of the European Union. The text is organized as follows: After this introductory section, the second section presents the different methodological approaches currently used to analyze child poverty in Europe. In the third section an appraisal of their advantages and disadvantages is carried out. The conclusions are to be found in the last section, along with their implications for future design methods.

Methodological frameworks

Empirical studies about the association between household income and children's well-being have been producing results with very varied outcomes. Duncan and Brooks-Gunn (1997) conducted their research with American children. They found that family income primarily affects children's development and achievements but not their mental and physical health. Mayer (1997) found that family income influences most of children's outcomes to some extent, due to the fact that social policies guarantee the satisfaction of core basic necessities. Recent studies of European children, such as those of the European Commission (2012), Ajzenstadt and Gal (2010), or the Tarki Social Research Institute and Applica consortium (2010), have analyzed the effect of family income on children's well-being, and also on their economic and social success as adults. Despite the fact that the importance of family income on children's well-being was pointed out in these studies, they also denote that income is not the sole determinant.

Despite its limitations, income (or consumption) has been commonly used for the analysis of poverty, especially in the case of poverty dynamics. With regard to child poverty, there are basically two theories that explain the relationship between household resources and children's well-being.[2]

The economic or investment theory considers that income directly affects a child's well-being. Despite the importance of parents' economic resources, the models constructed upon this theory predict that children's outcomes also depend on other factors, rather than only parents' investment, some of these being genetic characteristics, educational achievements, and particular abilities. In poor families, family income is found to play an important role in children's outcomes, as endowments passed on to children by better-off families depend more on parents' decisions about how to invest in their children, rather than on disposable income. In theory, social transfers could equalize opportunities for all children, but in practice, parents' choice regarding their expenses is the key determinant. Therefore, social transfers may be needed but may not be sufficient in promoting opportunity standardization for children.

The literature on poverty commonly assumes that all household members share equally the family resources. However, intra-household allocations may ameliorate or sacrifice children's living conditions. Some adults may choose to invest their scarce resources in their children's future. Also, a gender bias in favor of male children may occur (Cockburn *et al.*, 2009). Neglecting the distributional resource model within the house-

---

[2] For a detailed analysis of these theories, see Mayer (1997).

hold leads to measurement and identification errors. Cockburn *et al.* (2009) conclude that nearly one-third of children are wrongly classified in terms of poverty, when the equal share hypothesis is assumed.

The non-economic theory, or "good-parent theory," states that children's outcomes depend firstly on parents' profile characteristics, namely their personality and parenting style. Therefore, income constraints only indirectly reduce children's outcomes because they decrease the level of interactions between parents and their children. Moreover, low income is commonly associated with values and behaviors that encompass a type of *culture of poverty* that does not lead to economic and social success. In this context, increasing family income is not a route for escaping poverty, as poverty is more a consequence of life style and attitudes, than an outcome of income scarcity. Changing this culture and its inherent attitudes and values is the most effective way to reduce poverty and income transfers are not needed at all.

Thus, the definition of poverty is crucial to the research on this issue. The multidimensional nature of the problem introduces a complexity to its definition, which has been widely discussed within the academic literature.[3] With specific regard to child poverty, different analytical approaches have been applied in an effort to capture those child-specific characteristics that contribute to conceptualizing child well-being, with identification and aggregation choices proving to be key issues that constrain their effectiveness (Pollard and Lee, 2003; Minujin et al. 2006), issues that are detailed further in this section. Despite their content, these approaches are driven by a trade-off between the simple and the practical, and the complex and the informative. Moreover, all such approaches involve value judgment, whether theoretically and/or empirically justified. In developing such approaches, one has to take into account the constraints posed by the scope of availability of statistical data on children in order to guarantee feasibility and reliability.

A range of approaches have been designed and developed to capture the complexity of child poverty-related phenomena. The main approaches are analyzed by considering the monetary-based measurement,

---

[3] For a comprehensive discussion on this issue see, for example, Neubourg et al. (2014); UNICEF (2013); Alkire and Roche (2012); Notten and Roelen (2011); and Bradshaw et al. (2007).

multidimensional methods, the holistic perspective, the child rights framework, and the combined one applied by the European Union.

The Monetary-based approach

The income issue firstly brings to attention the need to define the concept of poverty to be used. Beyond this definition, the analysis of the problem of poverty needs to identify which factors are associated with it—preferably the ones that have a causal relation with monetary poverty. In the early 2000s, studies such as that of Bradbury et al. (2001) provided some information about the association between monetary poverty and factors such as age, employment status, family composition and education level, at the individual level. Cappellari and Jenkins (2002) continued this analysis by modeling poverty transitions, noting/emphasizing the importance of dealing with problems such as heterogeneity, state dependence, initial conditions and attrition. More recently, authors such as Callens et al. (2005) and Brady et al. (2009) have showed that macro factors such as family benefits having an important effect on monetary poverty odds (that is, the probabilities of being poor /non poor). There is an increasing interest in developing an aggregate measurement of poverty which encompasses individual income profile along time (Gradín and Cantó, 2012). These are some of the causes and/or consequences of child poverty.

Based upon the observation of family income, this method applies the hypothesis that household material resources have a strong influence on present and future child well-being (Bradbury and Jantti, 2001; Oxley et al., 2001 and UNICEF, 2005 apply this method). This is the approach to child poverty which was applied in the majority of the studies carried out in the 1990s.

The identification mechanism is focused on household income (or consumption) and is constructed upon the definition of a cut-off point—the poverty line. This procedure identifies children living in poor households and considers that, given the importance of family resources on children's living standards, these children are also poor. The poverty line threshold may be absolute, or relative. In the first case, its value should guarantee that the household has the ability to purchase a basket of goods and services that are considered to be essential (Corak, 2006). In the second case, the relative character of the poverty line is derived from the fact that the cut-off point is calculated based on the national standard of living. Its value could be set at, for instance, 50% or 60% of the median income per equivalent adult, which implies the use of equivalence scales. This is in fact a questionable method (Minujin et al., 2006) as it does not take into account children's specific needs.[4]

Data requirements for this framework involve using microdata on income or consumption. At the EU level, the Statistics on Income and Living Conditions (EU-SILC) is the main data set used. This is an annual survey that includes information about the income and living conditions of households and individuals. However, the information included is not child specific, which constitutes a limitation with regard to the context of child poverty analysis.

Despite the fact that the child is the unit of investigation, and therefore that the child should be the unit of analysis, the household is adopted as the unit of measurement, in keeping with data availability[5]. Building on the work of Foster et al. (1984), within this approach the incidence, intensity, and severity of child poverty can be estimated. In addition, a dynamic perspective, using indicators such as turnover statistics, the longitudinal classification of the poor, and the analysis of the duration of poverty spells, can be applied (Arranz and Cantó, 2010; Bane and Ellwood, 1986). These are important indicators for monitoring the percentage of children in monetary poor households. Furthermore, they are amenable to international comparisons, which is one of the main advantages of this approach.

The monetary-based approach is a one-dimensional method, and therefore it relies only on the information of a single variable to analyze poverty. In the context of child poverty, this fact has important implications, which are related to (1) the information derived from household income or consumption about child well-being, (2) the hypothesis of equal-

---

4 According to EUROSTAT (2015b): "This indicator does not measure wealth or poverty, but low income in comparison to other residents in that country, which does not necessarily imply a low standard of living" (http://ec.europa.eu/eurostat/statisticsexplained/index.php/Glossary:Atriskofpoverty_rate).

5 Despite the importance of a genuinely child-focused analysis, some authors consider that the household should be the unit of analysis, as basic children's needs are provided by the family. In addition, for these authors, the intra-household distribution of resources is adequately represented by equivalence scales (Corak, 2005), a questionable proposition (see also the section on the EU approach).

ly shared resources within the household, (3) the parental living project, (4) the unit of analysis/measurement considered, and (5) reference to nonmarket-based goods. Next, these implications are examined in detail:

1. With regard to income/consumption, it is worth analyzing the limitations associated with its use as a resource variable. The first problem arises with the reliability of data on income, as commonly these data underreport earnings. Moreover, households' resources are determined not only by current income but also by home ownership and house values, family solidarity, and savings are not captured by income at a point in time. In the context of child poverty, despite the importance of family monetary availability, which has already been analyzed, children's well-being is also conditioned by other factors related to housing, leisure, and emotional support, which are neglected by this methodology.

2. The hypothesis of equally shared resources within the household is not a consensual issue among academics (Jenkins, 2000). It assumes that all members of the family share fortunes and misfortunes equally (Alkire and Roche, 2012). This approach assumes the household to be a *black box*, within which incoming resources are equally shared among household members (Pahl, 1983). This is in fact a strong hypothesis, as children do not participate in resource allocation and are therefore dependent on their parents' management of resources. An in-depth analysis of household resources would require complementary micro-level data, in order to disclose the complexity within the *black box*.

3. Parental project[6] and capacity are important conditioners of children's well-being, which cannot be evaluated through income. The current living conditions of children will play an important role in the future, as they include options about such aspects as school attainment, leisure activities, and health care, for example. Beyond the material conditions, these aspects are also derived from parents' choices in allocating their disposable resources. Moreover, they are also conditioned by parents'

---

6 That is, family organization and functioning, and parental plans with regard to children.

parental capacity to contribute to the positive development of their children (Cockburn et al., 2009).

4. To analyze child poverty the *natural* unit of analysis is the child. This calls for the investigation of children-related well-being issues, which are in nature different from those of adults. However, the monetary-based approach considers the household as the unit of measurement. The results obtained in terms of child poverty came directly from household disaggregation. Therefore, these results do not differentiate the factors that condition children's well-being from the other members of the family.

5. Moreover, income is assumed as the sole determinant of children's well-being. This is a strong hypothesis as in fact, their well-being is also determined by nonmarket-based goods, such as health and education services, leisure equipment, safety environment, and others that are commanded by the public sector in accordance with the infant and youth policy pursued.[7]

For these reasons, a methodology that goes beyond income/consumption is needed. Several methods doing this are discussed in the next subsection.

Multidimensional methods

Academics have long stressed that as poverty is a multifaceted problem, it needs to be analyzed through a multidimensional approach (Gordon and Townsend, 2000; Nolan, 2001; Corak, 2005; Gordon et al., 2006a, 2006b; and Bradshaw et al., 2007 are among those advocating this approach). This is particularly true for children, as a child-focused approach seeks to capture the specific features of child poverty. Furthermore, the concept of children's well-being implicitly involves respect for the Convention on the Rights of the Child (CRC, see next subsection), which thus effectively calls for a multidimensional approach to analyzing child poverty.

From a macro perspective, child poverty index measurements are aggregate statistics that combine multiple information, and they can there-

---

7   For a more detailed analysis of these limitations, see for example, Minujin and Nandy (2012) and Minujin et al. (2006).

fore be considered a multidimensional method. However, it should be noted that these measurements are not derived from micro-data sets. Consequently, they do not allow the identification of poor children. The Human Poverty Index (UNDP, 2007) is an example of such measurement. For a selected group of high-income OECD countries, which covers the European Union, it includes information on four domains, considered as essential elements of human life: health, education, standard of living, and social exclusion.

The Multidimensional Poverty Index (UNDP, 2010)[8] is also a macro index. It follows the Human Poverty Index but it measures deprivation trough household surveys. Therefore, it includes an identification procedure, given by the number of deprivations experienced. It includes the same domains as the Human Poverty Index and is constructed upon the observation of 10 indicators.[9]

In order to identify individual poor children, Corak (2005, 2006) put forward some guidelines for contextualizing child poverty analysis. After consideration that these approaches have to be multidimensional, this author suggested a headcount poverty rate similar to the corresponding indicator in the monetary-based method. However, he goes further by complementing this indicator with other measurements as a means of internalizing other dimensions of child poverty.

Bradshaw et al. (2007) suggested a child well-being index to comparatively evaluate the situation of children across the EU member states. It consists of eight clusters of well-being: material situation, housing, health, subjective well-being, education, children's relationships, and risk and safety. The statistical techniques involved are quite sophisticated and this method requires micro-data that consider the child as the unit of observation and measurement.

The framework adopted by the multidimensional methods incorporates definitions of indicators for well-being (in a positive sense) or deprivation (in a negative sense), and thereby evaluates several different dimensions of child lifestyles and living conditions. However, there is no

---

8   For a detailed description, see Alkire and Santos (2010).
9   The Multidimensional Poverty Index is the product of two numbers: the percentage of income poor individuals and the average intensity of deprivation captured by the areas in which individuals are deprived.

actual consensus about the best set of indicators. In fact, measuring all the dimensions for well-being proves to be very difficult, if not impossible. However, it is worth noting that for poverty analysis, there has to be a selection of the dimensions associated with material deprivations that constitute rights violations.

Within the multidimensional approach, measurements vary from simple count measures (Nolan, 2001), to more complex formulae (Bradshaw et al., 2007). Various methods have been tested to setting weights in multidimensional indices. These methods include data-driven weights (e.g., frequency-based and regression-based weights) and normative-based weights. For instance, using Fuzzy Set Theory, Bastos and Machado (2009) propose an index that aggregates micro-data information on income and living conditions through the use of unequal weights. The weighting procedure employed gives more importance to the indicators in which deprivation is not widespread, pointing out items for which nonpossession means a strong feeling of deprivation.[10]

However, given that the more complex the measurements, the less useful the outputs (UNICEF, 2005), this results in a trade-off between the information gathered and the interpretation provided. Accurate and reliable data at the individual child level is an important constraint for these methods. Moreover, as children's well-being depends on different factors in accordance with their changing ages, gauging the most appropriate range of indicators proves to be difficult. However, combining deprivations for different age groups is simple and straightforward (Delamónica, 2014). Clearly, the indicators used in developing countries should be adapted for the European context (while the dimensions should be the same). One such set of indicators has been offered by UNICEF (2012), which among its 14 indicators includes: at least one meal a day with meat, chicken, or fish (or a vegetarian equivalent); books suitable for the child's age and knowledge level (not including school books); outdoor leisure equipment (bicycle, roller-skates, etc.); a quiet place with enough room and light to do homework; and some new clothes (i.e., not all second-hand). All of them have equal weight. However, if they were clustered in dimensions related to rights (see next section; e.g., those related to food and nutrition, education

---

10   For a discussion on the various methods of setting weights, see for example, DeCanq and Lugo (2008).

and learning, leisure and recreation, etc.), the dimensions would have equal weight but indicators *within* each dimension could be weighted in order to give more salience to the indicators in which deprivation is not widespread, which would highlight items for which insufficiency of access/enjoyment (or complete lack of it) denotes more deprivation.

The holistic framework and the child's rights approach

Holistic framework

This approach comprises methodologies that inclusively evaluate children's livelihood in an overall sense, through a combination of qualitative and quantitative data, together with participatory poverty assessments (e.g., Christian Children's Fund, 2005). The application of longitudinal data enables the calculation of poverty trajectories and therefore sheds light on the causes and consequences of child poverty.

Among these causes/consequences, the holistic framework identifies the importance of the effects of parents' socioeconomic status, occupation, and resources on young adult outcomes. The holistic approach provides a wide range of information that directly or indirectly affects child poverty.

A particular application of this method[11] uses an identification process that is based on six child-specific outcomes: nutritional status, physical morbidity, mental morbidity, life skills (literacy, work, etc.), development level for age, and subjective perception of well-being and future life opportunities.

The participatory component is very important for this approach. In fact, data on issues such as subjective perception of well-being and future life opportunities are driven from children's answers to the questions asked by the interviewers who routinely collect this information. Children's voices are an important source of information within this approach, pointing the focus on the child rather than on the family. Despite the potential problems with the accuracy of this type of subjective data, their content is important to understanding the actual feelings of children of their present living conditions and their expectations on the future.

---

11 The Young Lives project (2015), www.younglives.org.uk

In fact, the principal advantage of this approach lies with the type of information that is collected to enable a diagnosis of child poverty. This information includes outcomes, inputs, social policy issues, and facts that are related to child poverty as a means of dismembering the process that governs children's impoverishment. It uses factual and subjective data that originate from a variety of sources.

A major disadvantage of this methodology is the large amount of data that is required. By the same token, the analytical complexity of incorporating different sources of information, compounded by the lack of synthetic indicators, makes this methodology difficult to apply and disseminate. However, it has the merit of pointing out the importance of longitudinal data in the analysis of child poverty, as well as the use of a wide set of information for capturing how children live and their experience of being in poverty. In addition, this information may be complemented by the micro-data from household surveys.

The child's rights approach

The United Nation's CRC, which was established in 1989, is the most widely ratified human rights convention (only two countries have not ratified it). It is a normative framework that advocates a set of human rights for children in a wide range of domains, which are intended to cover all the relevant areas of their lives. This approach is child-centered and can thus be considered to be holistic, as it takes into consideration the child as a whole, giving attention to all aspects of children's lives.

The rights included in the CRC are guided by four general principles: the first concerns nondiscrimination, irrespective of race, color, gender, language, religion, political, ethnic, social origin, disability, or other status; the second considers that all actions developed for children should be guided by a child's best interest; the third establishes the obligation to ensure a child's survival and development; and finally, the fourth principle is to protect children's views and opinion in all issues that are related to them.

Countries that ratify the convention (State Parties) should periodically report to the Committee of the Rights of the Child on their progress toward fulfilling child's rights. Data requirements for these reports cover a wide range of aspects, in order to assure the complete verification of all rights contemplated in CRC. However, it is worth noting that within poverty analysis, it is important to select the rights associated with *poverty*, not all possible rights violations. For instance, in spite of the importance of rights such as religion expression or nongender discrimination for example, their fulfillment does not guarantee nonpoverty situations nor does their violation entail poverty.

A measure based on the CRC would define child poverty as multidimensional.

Following the UN Office of the High Commissioner of Human Rights (OHCHR, 2004), two types of rights can be differentiated: those that *constitute* poverty, that is, those which make a person poor just because these rights are not fulfilled (e.g., health, education, housing, etc.) and instrumental rights, that is, those that can help to reduce poverty but which do not define who is poor when the rights are unfulfilled, such as voting or the right to express opinions freely.

In addition, the CRC aims to guarantee the empowerment of children to face their challenges and to have the healthy development to which they have the right. It involves the examination of living standards, as the multidimensional methods, but it goes beyond it. The emphasis on the empowerment of the poor claims for the introduction of instrumental rights (e.g., civil and political rights) in the poverty analysis, complementing aspects that are out of the scope of living conditions. Furthermore, these rights ensure that the social participation of individuals is considered in all aspects of their lives.

The recent European Commission recommendations on investment in children (European Commission, 2013) highlight the importance of tackling child poverty and explicitly suggest that the problem of child poverty be addressed from a children's rights approach, which emphasizes the social character of combating child poverty. Moreover, the European Union considers that poverty reduction and human rights are two integrated parts of the same project. Thus, the EU approach is explored in the following subsection.

The EU approach

The Recommendation of the European Union launched on February 2013 (European Commission, 2013) points out the importance of tackling child poverty not only because of its scale and immediate consequences but also as a means of reducing the more general problem of poverty. It suggests a strategy to empower children and to alleviate them from the effects of the economic crisis. This recommendation is in line with the Europe 2020 strategic social plan and more specifically with one of its integrated objectives—to lift 20 million persons out of poverty and/or social exclusion.

Recognizing the importance of adopting a multidimensional approach to poverty, the concept of poverty or social exclusion is central in the monitoring process of the Europe 2020 Strategy. EU-SILC constitutes the dataset used to collect the statistical information for monitoring and comparative analysis.

According to the definition of EUROSTAT, the population living at-risk-of-poverty-or-social-exclusion (AROPE) is identified as being included in at least one of the following categories[12]:

1. People at-risk-of-poverty after social transfers—people living in a household with an equivalized disposable income[13] below the poverty line, set at 60% of the national median equivalized disposable income (after social transfers). This is an application of the standard monetary poverty definition.
2. Severely materially deprived people—people who are strongly constrained in their living conditions, experiencing at least 4 out of 9 aspects of deprivation.[14] The analysis of material deprivation conducted combines the methods discussed within the multidimensional approach to poverty presented in the previous point.
3. People living in households with very low work intensity—people aged 0–59 (excluding students) living in a

---

12 For a detailed presentation of this indicator, see EUROSTAT (2015).
13 The OECD-modified scale is used to take into account differences in household size and composition. This scale considers a weight of 1.0 for the first adult in the household, 0.5 for the sequent members aged 14 and over and 0.3 for those aged less than 14.
14 To analyze material deprivation EUROSTAT considers the following 9 indicators of deprivation: people cannot afford to pay their rent, mortgage or utility bills; to keep their home adequately warm; to face unexpected expenses; to eat meat or proteins every second day; to go on weekly holiday away from home; to buy a color television set; to buy a washing machine; to buy a car; and to buy a telephone.

household where the adults worked less than 20% of their work potential time during the past year. This class intends to take into account the effects of one of the most important determinant of poverty, employment.

In the context of child poverty, the direct application of this framework may bias the results we discussed earlier. In fact, the child is the statistical unit of analysis but the household is the unit of measurement. In order to avoid this potential bias EUROSTAT suggested a set of indicators to review the material deprivation component of AROPE among children in 2015 (European Commission, 2012).[15]

The indicators suggested include information about the household where the child lives and specific children items. The proposal is to include:

1. Household: Replace worn-out furniture (enforced lack)
2. Household: Arrears
3. Household: Computer and internet (enforced lack)
4. Household: Home adequately warm (enforced lack)
5. Household: Car (enforced lack)
6. Child: Some new clothes (enforced lack)
7. Child: Two pairs of shoes (enforced lack)
8. Child: Fresh fruits and vegetables daily (enforced lack)
9. Child: Meat, chicken, or fish daily (enforced lack)
10. Child: Suitable books (enforced lack)
11. Child: Outdoor leisure equipment (enforced lack)
12. Child: Indoor games (enforced lack)
13. Child: Place to do homework
14. Child: Leisure activities (enforced lack)
15. Child: Celebrations (enforced lack)
16. Child: Invite friends (enforced lack)
17. Child: School trips (enforced lack)
18. Child: Holiday (enforced lack)

---

15 The ad-hoc module of EU-SILC 2009 wave intended to complete the information about material deprivation and already included some children-specific indicators.

The detailed discussion of this methodology is out of the scope of this chapter. However, we would like to give note for the following issues that may potentially compromise its effectiveness in the analysis of child poverty: the information is gathered from the adult respondent, and therefore children's voices are out of this framework; it is assumed that if at least one child in the household lacks one of the items considered this also applies to the other children in that household; these indicators apply indifferently to children aged 1–15; and finally, the aggregation method suggested is a simple counting scheme, which does not take into account the relative character of deprivation. However, it should be mentioned that these are robust and statistically validated indicators, specifically designed for children. Their systematic application will certainly contribute to better monitoring child poverty in the European Union.

Besides this framework and in order to help member states to implement the 2013 European Recommendation, the European Commission launched the European Platform for Investing in Children (EPIC).[16] This is an online platform that provides information about policymaking for children and their families aimed at strengthening their capacities to face the consequences of the current economic crisis in Europe and, in particular, to tackle child poverty. The platform includes a list of indicators developed around the three key pillars included in the 2013 European Recommendation: access to adequate resources, access to affordable quality services and children's right to participate.

Discussion of the principal findings: Contrasting the approaches

Child poverty approaches assume different forms in their efforts to capture exactly how children live and what poverty means to them. These approaches differ in terms of scope and in their units of analysis. The identification and aggregation framework produce different measurements.

Five issues summarize the most important content of child poverty approaches:
1. The definition of child poverty and identification of poor children: Defining well-being or poverty is one of the first points of divergence

---

16 For a detailed presentation of EPIC, see http://europa.eu/epic/.

among the approaches currently used to analyze and evaluate child poverty. The use of a single indicator, such as income (or consumption), may bias the identification process. Besides its own limitation as a resource variable, it is not child centered. The identification process is crucial in mapping child poverty, and this process should therefore be able to capture child specificities in terms of current living conditions.

Despite the simplicity of the identification procedure used in the monetary-based approach, this method does not capture all relevant inter-country differences, an example being those that are related to the community and social provision of goods related to school, health, and leisure. In rich countries, families are the main provider for children, and therefore income may be a good resource variable. However, even in these countries, the social system features the services offered, as well as their quality, are potential sources of misidentification of poor (and nonpoor) children. Thus, simultaneously analyzing various dimensions provides a more realistic and complete analysis of child deprivation and poverty.

2. The unit of analysis: It does not make sense to try to estimate child poverty without understanding what happens specifically to children. Thus, the unit of analysis should be the child. However, this does not imply that children live in a vacuum. While the unit of analysis is definitely the child, and child-specific indicators should be used (see the next point), household indicators could and should also be used (e.g., housing indicators representing the living conditions of children).

3. The dimensions and indicators to be used: The choice of indicators is a crucial element for multidimensional methods. Obviously, the identification methods employed by multidimensional approaches depend on the selected dimensions and indicators. In spite of differences in the choice of indicators (and the rationale behind the choices) among the approaches, there is quite a good deal of convergence on the dimensions and the main indicators to be used.

Caution should be taken when using subjective information, as this type of data may not be reliable. In order to avoid these problems, it is very important to pay attention to the interview techniques employed. When considered alongside confirmatory analysis tools, these informal conversations may be an interesting option, despite the fact that they are time consuming.

A more reliable guide for choosing dimensions is provided by the child rights approach and the concomitant concept of constitutive rights (i.e., those that are related to material deprivation[17]). Although the dimensions are the same for all children, the way their rights are satisfied is different at different life stages. For example, the periodicity and type of health services required by babies and teenagers to fulfill their right to health is very different. The same is true in terms of the right to education or nutrition.

4. The methods used: The aggregation method used in the construction of multidimensional child poverty measurements or indicators also varies across approaches. After the identification of children with a deficit in one or more dimensions, the next step is to aggregate this information into a poverty measurement. A summary statistic is a very important tool for comparative purposes in terms of time and place, as well as being a valuable input for policy designs.

The measurements designed by Foster et al. (1984) within the monetary-based approach to provide information about the incidence, intensity, and severity of monetary poverty can be adapted to measure the incidence, depth, and severity of child poverty within the multidimensional approaches (see e.g., Minujin and Delamónica, 2007; Bastos and Machado, 2009).

Normalization, aggregation and weighting techniques are important issues for multidimensional measurements. Most of the approaches mentioned previously use equal weights for domains/dimensions. This is appropriate due to the fact that, according to the CRC, all rights are equally important.[18] As each dimension corresponds to a particular right constitutive of poverty, they should not be weighted. This is, for instance, the approach taken by Alkire and Roche (2012).

The holistic child poverty assessment often uses more than one measurement, as well as qualitative data, as a means of capturing the

---

17 As opposed to other rights which, although not less important, are not associated to lack of resources such as the right to free expression, avoiding violence, birth registration or freedom of religion.
18 As mentioned above, indicators *within* each dimension could be weighted.

various dimensions of child poverty, namely its causes, consequences, and perceptions. Despite the potential difficulty in dealing with qualitative data (in terms of adding to/incorporating with quantitative data), their informative content is an important input to the diagnosis of the problem and also for policy design purposes.

5. Data requirements: Data requirements are an important constraint for child poverty approaches. The monetary-based approach assumes that the income or consumption pattern of individuals and households is known, information that is generally gathered at a national level. The EU-SILC is the main source of information in the European Union, which was launched by EUROSTAT in 2004. It is published annually, and is also an important tool for multidimensional assessments. Its 2009 ad-hoc module details information about children's living conditions, which is then used to formulate a child-centered analysis for that specific year.

In the case of the multidimensional methods, the range of domains determines the information that needs to be collected. Moreover, the collection of data for areas such as social interaction or poverty perception may be difficult, as well as costly.

The holistic methods have strong data requirements at a national and local level. The use of qualitative data may be a difficult exercise. The Young Lives Project integrates the information given by quantitative and qualitative variables. The first ones are intended to assess living standards in the domains of education, health, childcare, and child work. The qualitative information aims to capture the perception of well-being and life opportunities directly from children, emphasizing the importance of participatory methods. The dynamic character of the information used to identify the casual process that is behind impoverishment is one of the strengths of this method. This is also one of its disadvantages as it is based upon longitudinal data gathered within a time window of 15 years and, thus, is only available for a handful of countries.

For a dynamic analysis of poverty, the commonly used statistics that are often calculated in terms of monetary poverty are turnover rate, poverty spells' duration analysis, and the longitudinal classification of poverty trajectories (namely entries into and exit from poverty). EUROSTAT has available data for these estimates for adults. Similar analysis can give important information about child poverty. Moreover, the EU-SILC could provide data for dynamic analysis of multidimensional poverty.

Concluding remarks

The analysis undertaken in this chapter aims to highlight the principal characteristics of the currently used child poverty approaches. The identification of the problems and limitations listed above may constitute an important step to improving such approaches and applying them in the context of European countries.

As expansive and comprehensive as the EUROSTAT estimation of child poverty is, and in spite of the presence of the term "Social Exclusion," the measurement is focused on resources and material deprivation, not other problems like violence, abuse, unhappiness, voting rights, or racial discrimination. In other words, it is not an overall measure of well-being or all bad things that can happen to children. It deals, as it should, specifically with "lacks," that is, deprivations and poverty. In order to improve on current efforts to measure child poverty in the European Union, five guidelines are suggested:

- Multidimensional definition of child poverty: Estimations and analyses should integrate the range of dimensions/domains/rights that constitute child poverty. Appropriately, this is the approach used by EUROSTAT.

- Unit of analysis: As the child is the central unit of observation in child poverty analyses, the assessments should be child focused. Despite the importance of the family and household in the child's everyday life, even the integration of the family's conditions in the analysis should be carried out through indicators that could measure the impact of these conditions on children and therefore, child poverty assessments should avoid the inclusion of data that are not related to children's well-being. Again, combining child-specific and household data is the appropriate approach and it is the one used by EUROSTAT.

- The dimensions and type of indicators: child poverty measurement should preferably be based on quantifiable variables, in order to guarantee objectivity and precision, which is the approach taken by EUROSTAT. In addition, quantifiable variables facilitate comparisons and also the monitoring of problems, in terms of time and space. The dimensions should be selected to represent the constitutive rights of poverty (the dimensions of child poverty). Moreover, the dimensions should be clearly specified in terms of rights and indicators should be grouped in clusters. Furthermore, EUROSTAT could make further efforts to differentiate indicators for different age groups (e.g. early childhood, middle childhood, and adolescents). As mentioned earlier, child-specific and household indicators should both be included to estimate child poverty. Concerning the indicators related to the family, it is proposed to collect information about family composition, parents' education level, parents' professional occupation, and also their type of participation in the labor market as these elements are crucial determinants of children's lives in the short and long run. In terms of the indicators that evaluate children's living standards and perspectives, it is suggested that these indicators should be added to the current EUROSTAT list: children's health (level of development, medical attainment, lifestyle, and access to appropriate services) and children's education attendance (grade repetition and school failure).

- Methods: Currently, EUROSTAT considers three elements in the measurement of poverty, one of which consists of a multidimensional analysis of deprivations. In both cases (i.e., when combining the three elements and when combining the dimensions) no weights are given. Following a human rights approach and the CRC, this would be the most advisable way to proceed for the estimation of child poverty because all child rights are equally valuable. However, if various indicators were clustered together, weights could be used for indicators within each domain/dimension.

- Data employed: Child poverty measurements should be based on data comparable across countries and time. The accuracy of the methods used to collect information, the comparative character of the data in terms of time and space, the precise definition and characteristics of the variables included in the data set are crucial issues, thus the importance of the work by the European Commission (2012) to establish the suitability, validity, reliability and additivity of indicators. Taking into account the nature of child poverty and its long-lasting consequences, it is important to consider longitudinal information alongside cross-section data. The dynamic perspective is important for gaining knowledge about the impoverishment process that is crucial for the analysis of multi-dimensional child poverty.

We recognize that there are no perfect methods to analyze socio-economic problems and in particular, child poverty. Choices stem from weighing the advantages and disadvantages of each specific framework, subject to the availability of data, and taking into account the main analytical goals. However, the importance of children in our lives and societies calls for the construction and improvement of the methods of analysis, in order to ensure the provision of rigorous, actual, and pertinent information about children's living conditions and, consequently, about child poverty.

The collection of the information referred is difficult and costly. Moreover, for the analysis (not for the measurement) of child poverty, it is important to obtain the full picture in terms of the experience and feelings as well as the perception of causes, constraints, characteristics, and consequences of child poverty. Consequently, the quantitative measurement would be well-served by a qualitative analysis complementing the diagnosis of child poverty and informing the design of effective social policies to tackle and eliminate it.

References

Alkire, Sabina and Roche, José 2012 "Beyond Headcount: Measures that Reflect the Breath and Components of Child Poverty" in Minujin, Alberto and Nandy, Shailen (eds.) *Global child poverty and well-being. Measurement, concepts, policy and action* (Bristol: The Policy Press).

Alkire, Sabina and Santos, Maria Emma 2010 "Acute multidimensional poverty: a new index for developing countries", *Working Paper 38, Oxford Poverty and Human Development Initiative* (Oxford: University of Oxford).

Ajzenstadt, Mimi and Gal, John (eds.) 2010 *Children, Gender and Families in Mediterranean Welfare States* (Springer: London, New York).

Arranz, Jose and Cantó, Olga 2010 "Measuring the effect of spell recurrence on poverty dynamics,", United Nationa University - *WIDER Working Paper, no 2010/72* (Helsinki: UNU-WIDER).

Bane, Jo and Ellwood, David 1986 "Slipping into and out of poverty: the dynamics of spells," *Journal of Human Resources*, Vol. 21, No. 1, 1–23.

Bastos, Amélia and Machado, Carla 2009 "Child poverty: a multidimensional measurement," *International Journal of Social Economics*, Vol. 36, No. 3, 237–251.

Ben-Arieh, Asher 2000 "Beyond welfare: measuring and monitoring the state of children—new trends and domains," *Social Indicators Research*, Vol. 52, No. 3, 235–257.

Bradbury, Bruce and Jantti, Markus 2001 "Child poverty across industrialised world: evidence from the Luxembourg income study" in Velminckx, Koen and Smeeding, Timothy (eds.) *Child well-being, child poverty and child policy in modern nations. What do we know?* (Bristol: The Policy Press).

Bradbury, Bruce; Jenkins, Stephens and Micklewright, John 2001 "Conceptual and Measurement Issues" in: Bradbury, Jenkins and Micklewright (ed.) *The Dynamics of Child Poverty in Industrialized Countries*, (Cambridge: Cambridge University Press), pp. 27–62.

Bradshaw, Johnathan, Hoelscher, Peter and Richardson, Dominic 2007 "An Index of Child Well-Being in the European Union," *Journal of Social Indicators*, Vol. 80, No. 1, 133–177.

Brady, David, Fullerton, Andrew and Moren-Cross, Jennifer 2009 "Putting poverty in political context: A multi-level analysis of adult poverty across 18 affluent Western democracies," *Social Forces*, Vol. 88, No. 1, 271–300.

Callens, Marc, Croux, Cristophe and Avramov, Dragana 2005 *Poverty dynamics in Europe: A Multi-level discrete-time Recurrent Hazard Analysis*, mimeo presented at EPUNet (EuroPanel users Network) conference.

Cappellari, Lorenzo and Jenkins, Stephen 2002 "Who Stays Poor? Who Becomes Poor? Evidence from the British Household Panel Survey," *Economic Journal*, Vol. 112, No. XX, C60–C67.

Christian Children's Fund 2005 "Understanding Children's Experience of Poverty: An Introduction to the DEV Framework", *Children & Poverty Working Paper 1* (Richmond: Christian Children's Fund).

Cockburn, John, Dauphin, Anyck and Razzaque, Mohammad 2009 "Child poverty and intra-household allocation," *Children, Youth and Environments*, Vol. 19, No. 2, 36–53.

Corak, Miles 2005 "Principles and practicalities of measuring child poverty in the rich countries", *Institute for the Study of Labor—IZA, Discussion Paper no 1579* (Bonn: Institute for the Study of Labor).

Corak, Miles 2006 "Principles and practicalities for measuring child poverty," *International Social Security Review*, Vol. 59, No. 2, 3–36.

Delamónica, Enrique (2014) "Separating and combining child and adult poverty: Why? How?", in Etienne Nel (ed.) CROP *Poverty Brief* (Bergen: CROP)

DeCanq, Koen and Lugo, Maria 2008 "Setting weights in multidimensional indices of well-being" *OPHI Working Paper no 18* (Oxford: University of Oxford).

Duncan, Greg and Brooks-Gunn, Jeanne (eds.) 1997 *Consequences of Growing Up Poor* (New York: Russel Sage Foundation).

European Commission 2012 "Measuring material deprivation in the EU. Indicators for the whole population and child-specific indicators" in *EUROSTAT Task-Force on Material Deprivation*, (Brussels: European Commission).

European Commission 2013 "Investing in children: breaking the cycle of disadvantage" in Commission Recommendation of 20.2.2013 (Brussels: European Commission).

Eurostat 2015 "People at risk of poverty or social exclusion" in <http://ec.europa.eu/eu rostat/statisticsexplained/index.php/People_at_risk_of_poverty_or_social_excl usion> accessed 25 March 2016.

Fernandes, Liliana, Mendes, Américo and Teixeira, Aurora 2012 "A review essay on the measurement of child well-being," *Social Indicators Research*, Vol. 106, No. 2, 239–257.

Foster, James, Greer, Joel and Thorbecke, Eric 1984 "A Class of Decomposable Poverty Measures," *Econometrica*, Vol. 52, No. 3, 761–766.

Gordon, David, Townsend, Peter and Pantazis, Christina 2006a "The International measurement of 'absolute' and 'overall' poverty: applying the 1995 Copenhagen definitions to Britain" in D Gordon, David, Levitas, Ruth and Pantazis, Christina (eds.) *Poverty and Social Exclusion in Britain: The Millennium Survey* (Bristol: The Policy Press).

Gordon, David, Halleröd, Björn, Larsson, Daniel and Ritakallio, Veli-Matti 2006b "Relative deprivation: a comparative analysis of Britain, Finland and Sweden," *Journal of European Social Policy*, Vol. 16, No. 4, 328–345.

Gordon, David and Townsend, Peter 2000 *Breadline Europe: The Measurement of Poverty* (Bristol: The Policy Press).

Gradín, Carlos and Cantó, Olga 2012 "Why are child poverty rates so persistently high in Spain?" *The Manchester School*, Vol. 80, No. 1, 117–143.

Griggs, Julia and Walker, Robert 2008 *The costs of child poverty for individuals and society. A literature review* (York: Joseph Rowntree Foundation).

Jenkins, Stephen 2000 "Modelling household income dynamics," *Journal of Population Economics*, Vol. 13, No. 4, 529–567.

Mayer, Susan 1997 *What Money Can't Buy: Family Income and Children's Life Chances* (Cambridge, MA: Harvard University Press).

Minujin, Alberto and Delamónica, Enrique 2007 "Incidence, depth and severity of children in poverty," *Social Indicators Research*, Vol. 82, No. 2, 361–374.

Minujin, Alberto, Delamónica, Enrique, Davidziuk, Alejandra and Gonzalez, Edward 2006 "The definition of child poverty: a discussion of concepts and measurements," *Environment and Urbanization*, Vol. 18, No. 2, 481–500.

Minujin, Alberto and Nandy, Shailen (eds.) 2012 *Global Child Poverty and Well-being: Measurement, concepts, policy and action* (Bristol: Policy Press).

Neubourg, Chris, Milliano, Marlous and Plavgo, Ilze 2014 "Lost (in) dimensions. Consolidating progress in multidimensional poverty research," IWP-2014-04 (Florence: UNICEF Office of Research Innocenti Research Centre).

Nolan, Brian 2001 "The evolution of child poverty in Ireland" in Velminckx, Koen and Smeeding, Timothy (eds.) *Child Well-being: Child Poverty and Child Policy in Modern Nations. What Do We Know?* (Bristol: The Policy Press).

Notten, Geranda and Roelen, Keetie 2011 "Monitoring child well-being in the European Union: measuring cumulative deprivation," IWP-2011-03 (Florence: UNICEF Office of Research Innocenti Research Centre).

OHCHR 2004 *Human Rights and Poverty Reduction* (Geneva: UNOHCHR).

Oxley, Howard, Dang, Thai-Thanh, Forster, Michael and Pellizzari, Michele 2001 "Income inequalities and poverty among children and households with children in selected OECD countries: Trends and determinants" in Velminckx, Koen and Smeeding, Timothy (eds.) *Child well-being, child poverty and child policy in modern nations. What do we know?* (Bristol: The Policy Press).

Pahl, Jan 1983 "The allocation of money and the structuring of inequality within marriage," *Sociological Review,* Vol. 31, No. 2, 237–262.

Pollard, Elizabeth and Lee, Patrice 2003 "Child well-being: a systematic review of the literature," *Social Indicators Research,* Vol. 61, No. 1, 59–78.

Ridge, Tess 2004 *Childhood poverty and social exclusion* (Bristol: The Policy Press).

Ridge, Tess 2011 "The everyday costs of poverty in childhood: a review of qualitative research exploring the lives and experiences of low-income children in the UK," *Children & Society,* Vol. 25, No. 1, 73–84.

Tarki Social Research Institute and Applica consortium 2010 "Child poverty and child well-being in the European Union," Report prepared for the DG Employment, Social Affairs and Equal Opportunities (Budapest: Unite E.2 of the European Commission).

UNDP 2007 *Human Development Report,* United Nations Development Programme (New York: UNDP).

UNDP 2010 *Human Development Report,* United Nations Development Programme (New York: UNDP).

UNICEF 2000 Poverty *Reduction Begins with Children* (New York: UNICEF).

UNICEF 2005 "Child poverty in rich countries 2005," *Innocenti Report Card* No.6 (Florence: UNICEF Office of Research Innocenti Research Centre).

UNICEF 2012 "Measuring child poverty. New league tables of child poverty in the world's rich countries," *Innocenti Report Card* No.10 (Florence: UNICEF Office of Research Innocenti Research Centre).

UNICEF 2013 "Child well-being in rich countries. A comparative overview," *Innocenti Report Card* No. 11 (Florence: UNICEF Office of Research Innocenti Research Centre).

CHILD POVERTY AND INTERGENERATIONAL POVERTY TRANSMISSION IN THE EU: What is the impact of social protection policies and institutions?

Stefanos Papanastasiou, Christos Papatheodorou, and Maria Petmesidou

In March 2006, the European Council asked member states to take measures to rapidly and significantly reduce child poverty, giving all children equal opportunities, regardless of their social background. Since then, child poverty reduction has been placed high on the EU policy agenda and rhetoric, but no significant progress has been made on this policy priority yet. Moreover, the Great Recession and the way the majority of the EU countries have responded to it, mainly through fiscal discipline and labor market deregulation, have further exacerbated poverty that greatly affected families with children (Petmesidou, 2013; Papatheodorou, 2014). Consequently, children are up against a significantly higher poverty risk than the average figure for the total population (Papatheodorou and Dafermos, 2010; Vilaplana-Lopez, 2013).

What are the repercussions of growing up poor? Poverty that is lived in childhood can seriously undermine an individual's well-being and socioeconomic status. Poor children are less likely to have good health, fare well in school, find a decent job, and achieve their full potential later in life, while they are more likely to become boxed in a poverty trap lasting many years or even throughout their life course (Duncan and Brooks-Gunn, 1997; Corcoran, 2001). As the 2008 economic crisis and the subsequent weak recovery are pushing more families with children into socioeconomically vulnerable and precarious positions, dealing with the causes and effects of child poverty becomes highly critical. The latter is crucial because it is seen as the basic means to intercept the intergenerational poverty transmission. This concept is meant to convey that the parental disadvantage is passed on to children and the relative intractability of poverty accounts for the reproduction of a vicious cycle of poverty across generations (Papatheodorou and Papanastasiou, 2010b).

Child poverty and adult poverty are two sides of the same coin. Still, the differentiation of child poverty from adult poverty in terms of EU policy priorities leads to an implicit distinction between voluntary and involuntary poverty. In that sense, children are generally considered to be the involuntary poor, while adults and consequently parents *acquire* the status of the voluntary poor. This is leading to the reemergence of the old, but precarious, idea of the *undeserving* versus the *deserving* poor (Papatheodorou and Dafermos, 2010). Such an idea affects the public and political discussion over the appropriate policy responses to combating poverty, thereby prioritizing *enabling* policies (i.e., education, training, and lifelong learning) instead of *decommodifying* ones (i.e., social transfers). Yet, empirical research has shown that the social protection system and the corresponding transfers are basic determinants of poverty and of the impact of the family of origin on the reproduction of poverty (Papatheodorou and Papanastasiou, 2010a; Papatheodorou and Papanastasiou, 2010b; Dafermos and Papatheodorou, 2013). Thus, this chapter provides a comparative analysis of various aspects (i.e., incidence, determinants, transmission) of child poverty in the EU-15 countries (or simple, "the EU-15") from a social policy perspective.

The chapter is structured as follows: In the next two sections, we discuss critical conceptual, operational, causal, and political dimensions of child poverty and briefly present the data and the methodology of the analysis. Main empirical findings and descriptive statistics on child poverty in the EU countries are discussed in the following section. Then we present an empirical analysis on the intergenerational poverty transmission and the impact of the social protection system in mitigating the influence of the family of origin on children's future outcomes and attainments. In the conclusion we summarize our main findings and make some policy recommendations.

Conceptual and theoretical aspects of child poverty

A number of alternative definitions have been put forward for assessing and measuring child poverty. For instance, the UNICEF's (2005) definition conceptualizes child poverty as a multifaceted capability deprivation—in Amartya Sen's tradition—in which there is a dearth of fundamental human freedom and/or of fulfillment of basic needs (Sen, 1992). Most often, operationalizing child poverty goes beyond income and consumption measures—like the AROPE[1] indicator in Eurostat (2012), which is defined as the share of children in at least one of the following three conditions: a) at risk of poverty, b) in a situation of severe material deprivation, or c) living in a household with a very low work intensity.[2] However in practice, EU countries have opted for a relative child poverty threshold based on a certain percentage of the median income in each country.

Lately, the popularity and the prevalence of the term "social exclusion" has been diminishing as a conceptual tool to comprehend poverty-related issues,[3] whereas it is acknowledged that poverty should be viewed with reference to the power structure under capitalism (Bracking, 2003). In this context, Murray (2002) argues that a *structural* or *relational* view of poverty leads to an understanding of the production and reproduction of poverty that is driven by inequalities of power. Therefore, Murray (2002) puts forward the notion of *adverse* or *differential incorporation* into the state, the market, and society in general—a term that he deems more appropriate than the conventionally prevalent one of social exclusion. *Adverse* or *differential incorporation* conceptualizes poverty as a dynamic, diversified, and stratified category of individuals and groups that are adversely and differentially incorporated into processes of neoliberal globalization.

On the same critical line of thinking, Hariss-White (2005) argues that although it is possible to mitigate poverty through social transfers, it is rather impossible to eradicate the root causes of poverty that are endemic to capitalism. On the contrary, poverty is continually being created and recreated under the structures and institutions of capitalism. The viewpoint of child poverty that centers on a structural or relational dimension is

---

[1] The *At Risk of Poverty or Social Exclusion* indicator has been proclaimed as the leading indicator for monitoring the EU strategy on child poverty, deprivation and social exclusion up to the hallmark year of 2020.

[2] Children at risk of poverty who live in households with an equivalized disposable income below 60% of the corresponding national median income. Severe material deprivation refers to someone's inability to afford at least four out of nine main goods and services related to economic strain and durables. Persons are considered living in households with very low work intensity if they are aged 0–59 and the working age members in the household worked less than 20% of their potential during the past year.

[3] According to Kahn and Kamerman (2002: 27), the term "social exclusion" captures "the inequalities in basic living; family economic participation; housing; education; public space; social participation; as well as the subjective experience of social exclusion."

embraced in this chapter, as it is acknowledged that the power relationships that are embedded in institutions within capitalism (e.g., family, school, workplace, church, community, etc.) perpetuate poverty.[4] What is important is that viewing child poverty from a structural or relational standpoint can help understand the primacy of socioeconomic and political factors in perpetuating poverty, which are often neglected by mainstream social research, such as the welfare state, the labor market, the political decision-making, the social stratification patterns, to name but a few.

The main theoretical explanations about the causes of child poverty can be classified into two broad categories: *social causation* and *social selection* (Conger & Donnellan, 2007). The social causation theories ascribe poverty to the socioeconomic and political institutions and structures of capitalism.[5] More specifically, the primary causes of poverty lie in the scarcity of institutional opportunities, the retrenchment of the welfare state, the expansion of particularly low-paying jobs in capitalist societies, etc. According to this view, there is no window of opportunity for the poor segments of the world population within neoliberal globalization whatsoever, insofar as *adverse* or *differential incorporation* is steadily becoming the norm for the less well-off and less privileged.

On the other hand, the social selection theories ascribe poverty to individual characteristics, such as health, skillfulness, cleverness, motivation, etc. The main argument is that children born in poor families will lag behind in terms of skills and achieve fewer things in life, largely because of poor genetic and environmental endowments from the family and the broader community they live in. Nevertheless, the evidence supporting this argument is inconclusive and imprecise as there is a large amount of *confounding factors* in the association between poverty and individual traits. More importantly though, it cultivates the conviction that the individual is responsible for its poverty, by not being activated enough to acquire the necessary means of living in the knowledge economy of the 21st century. In

---

4   As Foucault (1991; emphasis added) puts it, *"power is everywhere,* that is, power is diffused rather than concentrated and embodied in discursive rather than coercive practices, creating, thus, layers of hierarchies in every aspect of human life."
5   For instance, Myrdal (1962) had been an influential author who theorized about the accumulated disadvantage of the poor, as a result of structural causes, such as the lack of redistributive policies, structural unemployment, and social discrimination.

other terms, social selection theories have been labeled as blame-the-victim theories due to the scapegoating of the poor.

From a policy perspective, the prevalent socioeconomic paradigm that entails economic liberalization, labor market deregulation, and activation measures fails to recognize the policies of global regulation and redistribution, which are needed to tackle the processes within capitalism that create and sustain poverty (Bracking, 2003). In contrast, there is a widespread belief that the old welfare state provisions are incapable of dealing with the new social risks (hence their labeling as passive policies, which has a negative connotation), while the new workfare and activation policies—or *social investment*—that have increasingly gained ground in welfare reform are viewed as the most adequate policy responses (Petmesidou, 2014).

The concept of social investment has been salient over recent years in the EU and its member states' rhetoric. However, in practice, social investment has taken diversified forms in the different welfare state regimes in the European Union. Drawing upon the welfare state typology adjusted for families, women, and children, which was put forward by Esping-Andersen (2002), we can distinguish between: a) familialistic policies in the countries of the conservative welfare state regime (i.e., traditional family, low female employment, and less public investment in children); b) state interventions in the countries of the social-democratic welfare state regime (promoting gender equality, child well-being, female employment and the harmonization of work and family life), and c) market solutions in the countries of the liberal welfare state regime (leading to high female employment but also work/family tensions). As in the countries of a liberal welfare regime, low family support by the welfare state also characterizes South European societies. However, contrary to the former regime, there is a prevalent gender division of paid and unpaid work in South Europe and care for children largely depends upon extended family and kin networks (Engster and Stensöta, 2011).[6]

---

6   There is an extensive literature on the gender dimension of welfare state regimes and how different family policy arrangement among them significantly affects children's well-being. Three dimensions of family policy are important in this respect, namely services, benefits, and time (i.e., duration and generosity of parental leave); see, among others, Kahn and Kamerman, 1994; Korpi, 2000; Pfenning and Bahle, 2000; Venturini, 2008; Thévenon and Neyer, 2014.

On a broader scale, social investment becomes the vehicle of a wide restructuring of the welfare state in order to meet the new challenges and risks of modern capitalist societies. The restructuring trajectory is closely associated with the dispensation of *decommodifying* policies that are substituted by *enabling* policies, at the heart of which lie the cognitive and human capital development, so that the individuals can cope with the individualized social risks in a proactive manner (Petmesidou, 2014). Nonetheless, social investment signifies a turning point in the welfare function of modern societies, insofar as there is a shift from the collective to the individual responsibility in sustaining basic living standards. This is a direct outcome of the predominance of neoliberalism across the globe, which favors the minimal state, the minimum social safety nets, and the human capital perspective, despite the augmenting social risks arising from the liberalization and deregulation of socioeconomic processes.

Data and methodology

The analysis utilizes micro-data from the EU Survey on Income and Living Conditions (EU-SILC).[7] Under the recognition that the parental socioeconomic status has many influences on the poverty risk of individuals from childhood to adulthood, Eurostat carried out the EU-SILC module on the intergenerational transmission of poverty in 2005, and in 2011 this module was repeated to allow an analysis of the evolution of the results. The 2011 module includes 21 variables; all of them refer to the period when the respondents were around 14 years of age and the information is provided for respondents aged 25–59, that is, those with a year of birth between 1951 and 1985 (Eurostat, 2012).

This chapter employs child poverty as a response variable, that is, children living in households with an equivalized disposable income below 60% of the corresponding national median income. The total disposable income of a household is calculated by adding the income received by all household members plus the income received at household level. The total disposable household income is equivalized in order to take into account differences in household size and composition. The equivalized income ascribed to each household member is computed by dividing the total dis-

---

[7] Access to EU-SILC UDB is provided according to contracts EU-SILC/2011/27 with Democritus University of Thrace.

posable income of the household by the equivalization factor. We employ the OECD-modified equivalence scale, which is broadly used by Eurostat in relevant studies. This scale assigns a weight of 1.0 to the first adult of the household, 0.5 to each additional adult and 0.3 to each child (Hagenaars et al., 1994).

In investigating child poverty and its intergenerational transmission, we employ plots, association tests, correlation structures, and log-linear analysis. The aim is to paint a more complete picture of child poverty by investigating important aspects such as incidence, determinants, transmission, etc. The comparative orientation of the text is satisfied by incorporating into the analysis the EU-15 countries. What is more, these EU countries are classified into four welfare clusters following Esping-Andersen's (1992) typology and the relevant academic debate on the welfare state of the South European countries (Leibfried, 1992; Ferrera, 1996; Bonoli, 1997; Papatheodorou and Petmesidou, 2004, 2005).

The primary focus on the welfare state as a socioeconomic determinant of child poverty runs through the empirical analysis. In this respect, it is acknowledged that the social protection system plays a pivotal role in social welfare as well as in shaping social stratification patterns. These, in turn, are responsible for the poverty trajectories that are created largely by inequalities in the distribution of power and resources among social strata in capitalism. Therefore, the welfare state is viewed as a central explanatory variable of the cross-country variability in the figures of poverty and inequality (Dafermos and Papatheodorou, 2013; Papatheodorou, 2014). In effect, the main objective of this chapter is to assess the cross-country variability in child poverty that in the main is accounted for by differences in the welfare state institutions and policies throughout the EU-15.

The main working hypothesis underlying our analysis can be delineated as follows: The welfare state institutions and policies are basic determinants of child poverty, inasmuch as they affect the welfare status of families both directly and indirectly (see Figure 1). These policies either affect the family's financial situation and, in turn, the children's well-being through transfers, wages, services, etc. or affect the children's well-being through services (i.e., healthcare, childcare, welfare, etc.). Moreover, they may act as moderators on the association between the family's financial situation and the offspring's well-being, for instance, by altering the strength of this association.

Figure 1: The causal model of the welfare state effect on an offspring's well-being

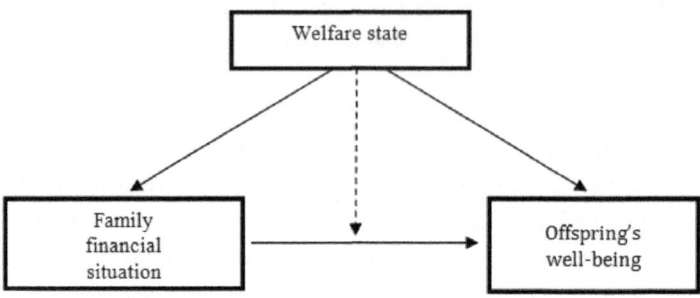

Empirical findings on child poverty

We begin our analysis by depicting in Figure 2 the overall poverty and child poverty rates across the EU-15. In most countries, it is evident that children face a significantly higher poverty risk than the average figure for the total population. Notable exceptions are Denmark, Finland, and Sweden—the most representative countries of the social-democratic welfare regime. Hence, the numbers in Figure 2 have sparked off a lively debate on the social situation of children in the European Union as well as on the appropriate policy responses to mitigate child poverty. Child poverty rates are particularly high in the countries South European and the liberal welfare state regimes and particularly low in the countries of the social-democratic welfare regime. This finding provides a rough indication that the countries of the social-democratic welfare state regime, are more efficient in reducing poverty among families with children.

Figure 2: Overall poverty and child poverty rates, EU-15 (1995-2013 average values)

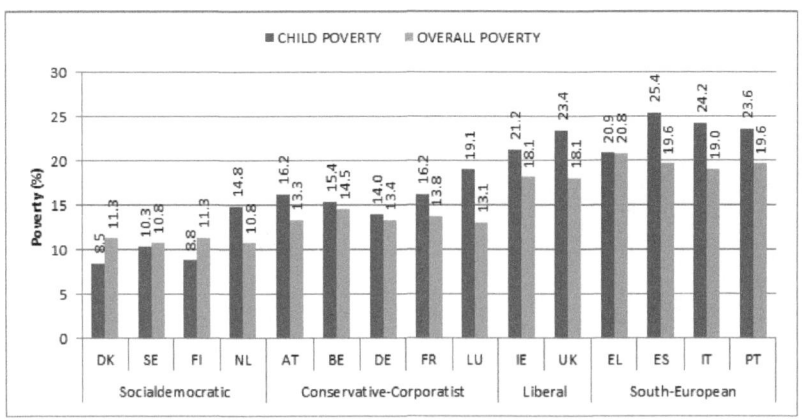

Source: Eurostat (http://ec.europa.eu/eurostat/data/database)
Note: Denmark (DK), Sweden (SE), Finland (FI), the Netherlands (NL), Austria (AT), Belgium (BE), Germany (DE), France (FR), Luxembourg (LU), Ireland (IE), United Kingdom (UK), Greece (EL), Spain (ES), Italy (IT), Portugal (PT)

In order to investigate the impact of the social protection systems on child poverty in more detail, Figure 3 depicts the child poverty rates for incomes before and after social transfers. The rationale behind this analysis is that the structure of social transfers may account for the variability in child poverty rates among the welfare clusters in the EU-15.[8] After pensions, child poverty is significantly reduced in South European countries. By contrast, after total social transfers, there appears to be a sizable reduction in child poverty in the remaining EU-15 countries. Thus, child poverty is mainly reduced through pension receipts of the adult members of the household in the countries of the South European welfare model,[9] while it is vastly reduced through other social transfers in countries of the social-democratic, the conservative, and the liberal welfare model.

---

[8] For instance, a number of studies have shown that the variability of poverty rates among the EU countries is mainly accounted for by the level and structure of social transfers (i.e., pensions and other social transfers) (Papatheodorou and Petmesidou, 2004, 2005; Papatheodorou and Dafermos, 2010).

[9] A finding indicating the significance of family and kin in welfare provision in South European countries.

Figure 3: Child poverty before and after social transfers, EU-15 (1995–2013 average values)

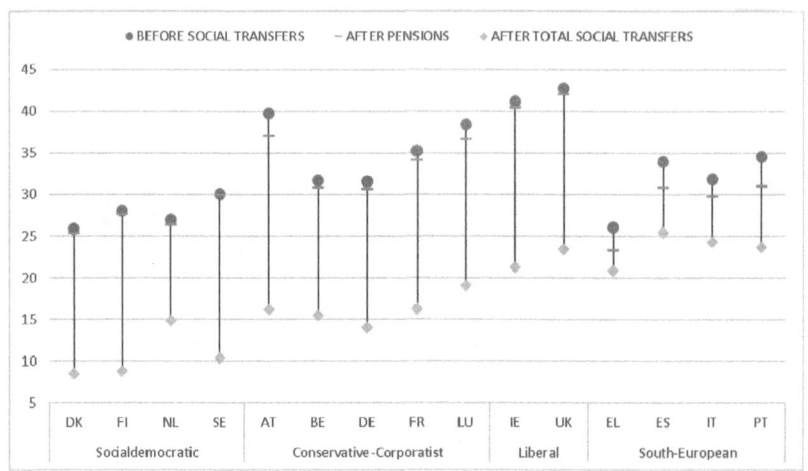

Source: Eurostat (http://ec.europa.eu/eurostat/data/database)

We delve into the welfare state effect on child poverty, as presented in Figure 4, which provides a fairly tight correlation structure of child poverty (as % of total population) and total social expenditure (as % of GDP). In fact, there appears to be a pattern in the clustering of countries in terms of total social spending and child poverty rates. Therefore, the overall picture justifies the choice of examining child poverty with reference to the EU-15 social protection systems, as social expenditures appear to be a consistent predictor of the variability in child poverty rates across the EU-15.

Figure 4: Child poverty and total social expenditure (% of GDP), EU-15 (1995-2013 average values)

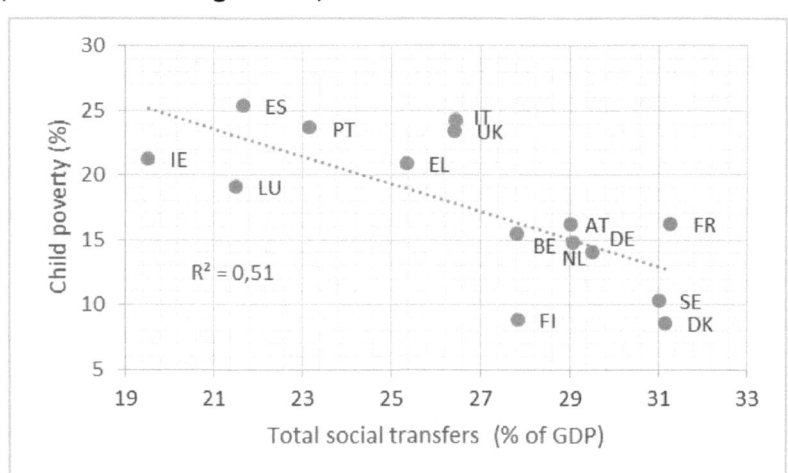

Source: Eurostat (http://ec.europa.eu/eurostat/data/database)

The degree of variability of child poverty across the EU-15 that is explained by the welfare state institutions and policies becomes even more noticeable and large, if we plot child poverty against social expenditure after having subtracted the old age and survivor pensions (Figure 5). The coefficient of determination (R^2) reads 0.82, a figure that denotes a great interpretability of the variability of child poverty rates across the EU-15 by social expenditure, except pensions (i.e., various social benefits and provisions). In other words, social expenditure in cash and in kind (except pensions) could alone explain almost 88% of the variability of child poverty across the EU countries. To a large extent, this reflects the variability of benefits and service provisions to families among the EU-15 countries.

The Nordic countries stand out as having the lowest child poverty rates and the highest rate of social spending on benefits (other than pensions) and service provision. As other studies have shown (Korpi, 2000; Kangas and Palme 2000; Ferrarini, 2006; Venturini, 2008; Bäckman and Ferrarini, 2010; Engster and Stensöta, 2011), the Nordic countries illustrate a pattern of institutional arrangements exhibiting the lowest inequality in care use among income groups (a childcare place is guaranteed as a social right) in the European Union. Comprehensive services are complemented by generous parental leaves and direct transfers to the family. Thus, a family/work balance is achieved that is highly supportive to working parents. Women-friendly policies account for the comparatively high rate of working mothers and the condition of dual earners in the family is one more factor that positively impacts children's well-being.

Figure 5: Child poverty and social expenditure excluding pensions, EU-15 (1995–2013 average values)

Source: Eurostat (http://ec.europa.eu/eurostat/data/database)

In some of the countries of the conservative welfare state regime (e.g., Germany and Austria), family policies tend to support a gendered division of paid and unpaid labor (family benefits are of medium generosity, and there is low availability of care services and tax deductions for a dependent spouse to support traditional family structures).[10] The countries with a liberal welfare state regime (United Kingdom and Ireland) are characterized by a residual support to families provided through means-testing. Meager support characterizes the South European countries and this has further been reduced during the economic crisis.[11] Overall, the best per-

---

10   France and Belgium come closer to the Nordic countries in terms of the generosity of family allowances and a developed network of social services. However, compared to the latter countries, incomes fall significantly during parental leave and there are also notable inequalities of access to care services (Richardson and Bradshaw, 2014).

11   In Portugal, family and children support was reduced by about 30% in 2010 and 2011 and eligibility criteria were tightened. In Spain, a baby cheque provision for new born children—that was the only universal benefit for families with children—

forming countries in terms of child poverty rates are those with universal child benefits, care services, and tax concessions that are not strictly targeted to low-income families.

By contrast, the prevalent rhetoric over the beneficial effect of economic growth on overall poverty and, as a consequence, on child poverty is not corroborated by the data when we plot child poverty against GDP based on PPS per capita (see Figure 6; Luxembourg was left out of the analysis as an outlier). The coefficient of determination (R^2) reads 0.34 which is a rather moderate predictive capacity of GDP concerning child poverty rates. This finding puts into doubt the argument of pro-poor growth that drives EU societies toward a neoliberal pathway. In contrast, a strategy to reinforce the mechanisms by which the welfare state impacts upon people's lives seems to be *desideratum* in the age of the Great Recession.

Figure 6: Child poverty and GDP per capita (in PPS), EU-14 (1995–2013 average values)

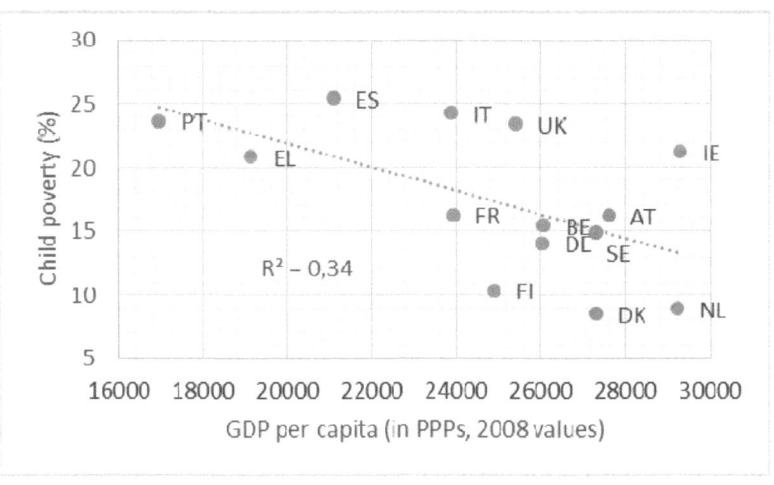

Source: Eurostat (http://ec.europa.eu/eurostat/data/database)

---

as abolished in 2010 and this was accompanied by a significant reduction in child benefits (Janta and Henham 2014). In Greece, in 2012, provisions to families with three or more children were significantly curtailed and replaced by a strongly means-tested meager child benefit.

Intergenerational poverty transmission and social protection systems

We expand our analysis on child poverty by investigating the intergenerational poverty transmission and the impact of the welfare state on the influence of the family of origin on an offspring's outcomes and attainments in the EU-15. First, in Table 1 we present the cross-tabulation of the people's poverty rates according to their father's occupation in the EU-15 welfare clusters. We have run likelihood ratio tests of the association between the father's occupation and the offspring's poverty risk in all welfare regimes respectively. The results indicate that there is a statistically significant association in all welfare clusters except for the social-democratic one. The analysis shows that offspring with a father on low levels of the socio-occupational hierarchy appear to be more susceptible to the poverty risk. Nevertheless, there is a huge difference in poverty rates at the low levels of social stratification between the social-democratic and the South European welfare regime, while the conservative and the liberal welfare regime lie somewhere in between based on that criterion.

Table 1: Father's occupation and offspring's poverty risk by welfare regimes

(POVERTY RISK)	Manual (%)	Lower skilled nonmanual (%)	Higher skilled nonmanual (%)
SOCIAL-DEMOCRATIC	7	5	6
LIBERAL	14	12	10
CONSERVATIVE-CORPORATIST	13	9	8

Source: Authors' estimates based on EU-SILC 2011 UDB

We also employ the odds ratio as a measure of the strength of the association between the categorical variables of interest. The analysis is conducted on the basis of the four welfare clusters in the EU-15. Table 2 provides estimates of the odds of children, whose father has manual work, facing poverty risk against the odds of children whose fathers have a higher skilled nonmanual work. The odds ratio hovers between 1.06 in the social-democratic welfare state–type and 1.93 in the welfare state–type of the South European countries. In other words, in South-European countries those children with a father in manual work are 93% more likely to fall below the poverty line compared with those with a father in higher skilled nonmanual work. On the contrary, in the social democratic regime, this figure is only 6%. The average figures in countries with a liberal and a conservative welfare regime are 42% and 51%, respectively. Undoubtedly, the countries of the social-democratic welfare state type present a remarkably low odds ratio, implying that the effect of the father's occupation (x) on the adults' poverty risk (y) is virtually marginal (assuming plausible causality of x on y).

Table 2: Odds ratio of poverty risk for offspring with a father in manual work against those with a father in higher skilled nonmanual work

WELFARE REGIME	ODDS RATIO
SOCIAL-DEMOCRATIC	1.06
LIBERAL	1.42
CORSERVATIVE-CORPORATIST	1.51
SOUTH-EUROPEAN	1.93

Source: Authors' estimates based on EU-SILC 2011 UDB

Furthering the analysis, we consider the associations and interactions between the welfare state, the family background (proxied by the father's occupation and education), and the offspring's education and poverty risk. In preliminary analyses, we considered the aforementioned associations, including the mother's occupation and education, as factors of child poverty. However, both variables were dropped out from the statistical model due to the *accumulated effect* with other parental traits (Papatheodorou, 1997). The statistical model that is used to investigate the aforementioned associations and interactions is a general log-linear model, which is a specialized case of Generalized Linear Models for Poisson distributed data. The choice of the log-linear model is justified upon the categorical nature of the variables of interest, for which the conditional association is considered by taking the natural logarithm of the cell frequencies within a five-way contingency table. The five-way contingency table is formulated by the following variables:

- Child poverty (P): 1 = poor and 2 = nonpoor (i = 1, 2)
- Welfare regime (W): 1 = social-democratic, 2 = liberal, 3 = conservative-corporatist and 4 = South European (j = 1, 2, 3, 4)
- Father's occupation (O): 1 = higher-skilled nonmanual, 2 = lower-skilled nonmanual and 3 = manual (k = 1, 2, 3)

- Father's education (FE): 1 = low, 2 = medium, and 3 = high (l = 1, 2, 3)
- Child's education (CE): 1 = low, 2 = medium and 3 = high (m = 1, 2, 3)

We present the saturated model that includes all possible effects of the aforementioned variables:

$$\ln(F_{ijklm}) = \mu + \lambda_i^P + \lambda_j^W + \lambda_k^O + \lambda_l^{FE} + \lambda_m^{CE} + \lambda_{ij}^{PW} + \lambda_{ik}^{PO} + \lambda_{il}^{PFE} + \lambda_{im}^{PCE} + \lambda_{jk}^{WO} + \lambda_{jl}^{WFE} + \lambda_{jm}^{WCE} + \lambda_{kl}^{OFE} + \lambda_{km}^{OCE} + \lambda_{lm}^{FECE} + \lambda_{ijk}^{PWO} + \lambda_{ijl}^{PWFE} + \lambda_{ijm}^{PWCE} + \lambda_{ikm}^{PFECE} + \lambda_{jkl}^{WOFE} + \lambda_{jkm}^{WOCE} + \lambda_{klm}^{OFECE} + \lambda_{ijkl}^{PWOFE} + \lambda_{ijkm}^{PWOCE} + \lambda_{ijklm}^{PWOFECE}$$

(1)

where each vector represents, respectively,

$\ln(F_{ijklm})$ = the natural log of the expected cell frequency of the cases for cell ijklm in the contingency table
μ = the grand mean of the log of the expected frequencies
λ = the effects that the variables have on the cell frequencies
P, W, O, FE, CE = the variables of interest
i, j, k, l, m = the categories within the variables of interest.

The overall goodness-of-fit of the model is assessed by comparing the expected frequencies to the observed frequencies. We make use of the likelihood ratio to test the fit of the model, which follows a chi-square distribution and the degrees of freedom equal the number of lambda parameters set equal to zero. We run separate tests of the hypothesis that K-Way and higher-order effects are zero. The results indicate that a suitable model to represent the data will encompass no higher than three-order interaction terms. The next step is to test the lower-order terms by employing the partial associations (i.e., the differences between the two likelihood ratio statistics for the models with and without the tested effect).

The purpose of the log-linear analysis is to determine the most parsimonious (nested) model that provides a good fit of the data. In the pursuit of parsimony, it appeared that the variables of the father's education and of the children's education, which had been kicked into the log-linear model to allow us to assess some of the human capital theory's arguments on the effect of education, do not have any statistically significant association with the offspring's poverty risk. Thus, the nested model that fits the data well with a likelihood ratio value of 7.464 at 0.825 significance level takes the following form:

$$\ln(F_{ijk}) = \mu + \lambda_i^P + \lambda_j^W + \lambda_k^O + \lambda_{ij}^{PW} + \lambda_{ik}^{PO} + \lambda_{jk}^{WO} + \lambda_{ijk}^{PWO} \quad (2)$$

Table 3: Lambda parameters for the log-linear model

Lambda Parameter	Estimate	Std. Error	Sig.
Constant	10.063	0.007	0.000
[P = 1]	−1.368	0.014	0.000
[W = 1]	−2.216	0.021	0.000
[W = 2]	−0.254	0.010	0.000
[W = 3]	−1.561	0.016	0.000
[O = 1]	−1.411	0.015	0.000
[O = 2]	−1.061	0.013	0.000
[P = 1] * [W = 1]	−1.233	0.056	0.000
[P = 1] * [W = 2]	−0.442	0.055	0.000
[P = 1] * [W = 3]	−0.551	0.025	0.000
[P = 1] * [O = 1]	−0.694	0.036	0.000
[P = 1] * [O = 2]	−0.453	0.038	0.000
[W = 1] * [O = 1]	0.803	0.025	0.000
[W = 1] * [O = 2]	0.060	0.035	0.085
[W = 2] * [O = 1]	0.774	0.033	0.000
[W = 2] * [O = 2]	0.036	0.048	0.446
[W = 3] * [O = 1]	0.543	0.018	0.000
[W = 3] * [O = 2]	0.043	0.022	0.054
[P = 1] * [W = 1] * [O = 1]	0.566	0.092	0.000
[P = 1] * [W = 1] * [O = 2]	0.173	0.138	0.211
[P = 1] * [W = 2] * [O = 1]	0.340	0.096	0.000
[P = 1] * [W = 2] * [O = 2]	0.289	0.134	0.031
[P = 1] * [W = 3] * [O = 1]	0.160	0.054	0.003
[P = 1] * [W = 3] * [O = 2]	0.029	0.066	0.660

Source: Authors' estimates based on EU-SILC 2011 UDB

Table 3 shows that parental background affects the offspring's poverty risk but to a differing extent among the four welfare state regimes. Based on calculations of the combined effects of the main and the interaction terms, it appears that the lowest influence that the parental background has on an offspring's poverty risk is in the countries of the social-democratic welfare state regime, independently from the remaining parameters.[12] Undeniably, the universal and still generous social protection system of the countries representing the social-democratic welfare state regime comes as the most effective in mitigating the intergenerational poverty transmission.

What is more, Table 3 shows that there is a moderating effect of the welfare state on the association between the family background and the children's poverty risk (as indicated by the statistically significant three-way interaction terms). This means that the welfare state can alter the strength of the association by empowering less well-off families and their children so that they can attain better future outcomes. This finding signifies the importance of the welfare state in mitigating the intergenerational poverty transmission in all EU-15 welfare clusters. Thus, a reorientation toward welfare state provisions, in cash and in kind, is necessitated in order to intercept social inheritance and level the playing field for disadvantaged children and adolescents.

Conclusions

The aim of this chapter was to assess child poverty and its intergenerational transmission in the EU-15 countries from a social policy perspective. The most robust findings can be summarized as follows: Child poverty is particularly high in South European and Anglo-Saxon countries, while it is particularly low in Nordic countries. In the analysis, we identified a link between social protection systems and child poverty rates in the EU-15. More specifically, social transfers (i.e., various welfare, family, unemployment, and other benefits in cash—except pensions) appear to greatly predict the variability of child poverty rates across the EU-15. In the Nordic countries, generous and less strongly targeted social transfers greatly reduce child poverty. In contrast, in South European countries the impact of this category of social transfers on child poverty is rather low. This is due to meager welfare and other social transfers (except pensions), mostly provided through means-testing. Pensions predominate in social transfers (particularly in Italy and Greece) and given the prominent role of family and kin as providers of welfare, pensions tend to have a noticeable impact

---

12   The lambda parameters are the logarithms of the odds for the main effects and odds ratios for the interactions of the estimated frequencies.

on child poverty. Continental European states stand in between the Nordic and South European countries in terms of the efficacy of social transfers (except pensions) in reducing child poverty. Redistribution is comparatively limited in the countries of the liberal regime (United Kingdom and Ireland) due to the low generosity of social transfers and extensive reliance on means-testing and market-oriented models of family policy.

In our analysis, we also examined the link between social spending (on cash benefits—except pensions—and service provision) and child poverty. This better captures the combined effect of income transfers and services to families. A robust relationship is found that indicates the overall positive effect of a high total generosity of family policies on child poverty in the Nordic countries (supporting dual-earner transfers and extensive social services to families). Complemented by generous parental leave schemes (with earnings-related benefits), this welfare state regime achieves a family-work balance that encourages female employment. This constitutes an additional source of income in the family that further contributes to the reduction of child poverty. The lowest efficacy of social spending in reducing child poverty is exhibited by South European countries due to scarce social services and very modest family benefits. Continental European countries (notably Germany and Austria) exhibit medium generosity of benefits to families and limited service provision conducive to traditional gender divisions of labor. The efficacy of family policy arrangements in reducing poverty remains modest. The United Kingdom and Ireland opt for a residual strategy of social support to families targeted at the very poor households. This has no significant positive impact on child poverty reduction. In a nutshell, the variation in child poverty across Europe is largely attributed to the impact of the social protection system that each country has developed. By contrast, economic growth as approximated by GDP seems to have smaller interpretative ability of the variability of child poverty.

The intensity of the intergenerational poverty transmission among welfare clusters was also empirically investigated and our analysis further corroborates the previously mentioned findings. The EU countries of the social-democratic welfare state regime seem to have gone a long way in mitigating the influence of the family of origin on children's current and future welfare. The analysis has shown that the social protection system plays a crucial role in reversing the intergenerational transmission of poverty. This is contrary to what some human capital proponents believe when it comes to the importance of education for future socioeconomic outcomes and attainments. In effect, more universal and citizenship-based social provisions appear to be an adequate response to the continuing crisis that threatens to destabilize the societal structures of modern EU countries. Generous and universal public spending on family benefits and social services supporting families with children from the early childhood years and throughout childhood can have a substantial social return, as costly interventions in the future due to an extensive intergenerational transmission of poverty will be avoided. Even under conditions of fiscal consolidation in Europe, family support budgets should take priority and reforms should opt for a combination of benefits, services, paid leave for parents (as well as working time arrangements facilitating a family/work balance) that enhance equalizing coverage in a most cost-effective manner.

Finally, the findings of our analysis are also crucial in respect to policy transferability to developing countries. As the available literature shows (e.g., Grant et al., 2011: 97–102), North to South welfare policy transfer is subject to a wide range of constraints, such as the nature of poverty in the developing world (absolute or relative) and how this affects intergenerational transmission, the role of the state and the political context, and very limited resources due to low levels of domestic tax and difficulties in raising aid budgets for funding universal social security systems. Nevertheless, lessons drawn from the developed countries in respect to the positive impact of universal schemes (universal child support schemes and free access to health and welfare services) in intercepting the intergenerational transmission of poverty, as opposed to strictly conditional schemes, are highly relevant even at an early stage in the development of social protection.

References

Bäckman, Olof and Ferrarini, Tommy 2010 "Combating child poverty? A multilevel assessment of family policy institutions and child poverty in 21 old and new welfare states," *Journal of Social Policy* (Cambridge), Vol. 39, No. 2, 275–296.

Bonoli, Giuliano 1997 "Classifying welfare states. A two-dimension approach," *Journal of Social Policy* (London), Vol. 26, No. 3, 351–372.

Bracking, Sarah 2003 *The political economy of chronic poverty* (Manchester: University of Manchester).

Conger, Rand and Donnellan, Brent 2007 "An interactionist perspective on the socioeconomic context of human development," *Annual Review of Psychology* (Palo Alto, CA), Vol. 58, 175–199.

Corcoran, Mary 2001 "Mobility, persistence and the consequences of poverty for children: child and adult outcomes" in Danziger, Sheldon and Haveman, Robert (eds.) *Understanding poverty* (Cambridge: Harvard University Press).

Dafermos, Yannis and Papatheodorou, Christos 2013 "What drives inequality and poverty in the EU? Exploring the impact of macroeconomic and institutional factors" in *International Review of Applied Economics* (London) Vol. 27, No. 1, 1–22.

Duncan, Greg and Brooks-Gunn, Jeanne (eds.) 1997 *Consequences of growing up poor* (New Work: Russell Sage Foundation).

Engster, Daniel and Stensöta, Helena 2011 "Do family policy regimes matter for child well-being?," *Social Politics* (Oxford), Vol. 18, No. 1, 82–124.

Esping-Andersen, Gøsta 1990 *The three worlds of welfare capitalism* (Oxford: Polity Press).

Esping-Andersen, Gøsta 2002 *Why we need a new welfare state* (Oxford: Polity Press).

Eurostat 2012 *EU-SILC 2011 module on intergenerational transmission of disadvantages: Assessment of the implementation* (Luxemburg: European Commission).

Ferrarini, Tommy 2006 *Families, states and labor markets: Institutions, causes and consequences of family policy in post-war welfare states* (Cheltenham: Edward Elgar Publishing).

Ferrera, Maurizio 1996 "The southern model of welfare in social Europe," *Journal of European Social Policy* (London), Vol. 6, No. 1, 17–37.

Foucault, Michel 1991 *Discipline and punish: The birth of a prison* (London: Penguin).

Grant, Ursula, Moore, Karen, Royston, Sam and Vieth, Hele 2011 "Policies for interrupting the intergenerational transmission of poverty in developed countries", *Working Paper No. 199* (London: Chronic Poverty Research Centre).

Hagenaars, Aldi, de Vos, Klaas and Zaidi, Asghar 1994 *Poverty statistics in the late 1980s: Research based on micro-data* (Luxembourg: Office for Official Publications of the European Communities).

Hariss-White, Barbara 2005 *Poverty and capitalism* (Oxford: Oxford University).

Janta, Barbara and Henham, Marie-Louise 2014 "Social protection during the economic crisis. How do changes to benefits affect children?" in <http://www.rand.org/pubs/research_reports/RR555.html> accessed 11 September 2015.

Kahn, Alfred and Kamerman, Sheila 1994 *Social policy and the under-3s. Six country case studies. A resource for policy makers, advocates and scholars* (New York: Columbia University).

Kahn, Alfred and Kamerman, Sheila 2002 "Social exclusion: A better way to think about childhood deprivation?" in Kahn Alfred and Kamerman Sheila (eds.) *Beyond child poverty: The social exclusion of children* (New York: Columbia University).

Kangas, Olli and Palme, Joakim 2000 "Does social policy matter? Poverty cycles in OECD countries," *International Journal of Health Services* (London), Vol. 30, No. 2, 335-352.

Korpi, Walter 2000 "Faces of inequality: Gender, class and patterns of inequalities in different types of welfare states," *Social Politics* (Oxford), Vol. 7, No. 2, 127-191.

Liebfried, Stephan 1992 "Towards a European welfare state? On integrating poverty regimes into the European community" in Ferge, Zsuzsa and Kolberg Jon-Eivind (eds.) *Social policy in a changing Europe* (Frankfurt: European Center for Social Welfare Policy and Research).

Murray, Colin 2001 *Livelihoods research: Some conceptual and methodological issues* (Manchester: Institute for Development Policy and Management, University of Manchester).

Myrdal, Gunnar 1962 *An American dilemma: The negro problem and modern democracy* (New York: Harper & Row).

Papatheodorou, Christos 1997 "Poverty and family background in Greece: The role of father's occupation and education", *Welfare State Programme No. WSP/133, LSE-STICERD* (London: London School of Economics).

Papatheodorou, Christos 2014 "Economic crisis, poverty and deprivation in Greece: The impact of neoliberal remedies" in Mavroudeas, Stavros (ed.) *Greek capitalism in crisis: Marxist analyses* (London: Routledge).

Papatheodorou, Christos and Dafermos, Yannis 2010 *Structure and trends in economic inequality and poverty in Greece and the EU, 1995-2008* (Athens: Observatory on Economic and Social Developments, Labor Institute, Greek General Confederation of Labor, in Greek).

Papatheodorou, Christos and Papanastasiou, Stefanos 2010a *Intergenerational transmission of poverty in Greece and the EU: Theoretical approaches and empirical analysis* (Athens: Observatory on Economic and Social Developments, Labor Institute, Greek General Confederation of Labor, in Greek).

Papatheodorou, Christos and Papanastasiou, Stefanos 2010b *Intergenerational transmission of poverty in the EU: An empirical analysis* (Crete: Paper presented at the 1st International Conference in Political Economy) in <http://www.iippe.org/wiki/images/f/f3/CONF_GREEKPOVERTY_Papanastasiou.pdf> accessed 16 October 2015.

Papatheodorou, Christos and Petmesidou, Maria 2004 "Inequality, poverty and redistribution through social transfers: Greece in comparative perspective" in Petmesidou, Maria and Papatheodorou, Christos (eds.) *Poverty and social exclusion* (Athens: Exantas, in Greek).

Papatheodorou, Christos and Petmesidou, Maria 2005 "Inequality, redistribution and welfare regimes: Comparing Greece to other EU countries" in Argitis, Georgios (ed.) *Economic changes and social opposition in Greece: The challenges at the beginning of the 21st Century* (Athens: Tipothito, in Greek).

Petmesidou, Maria 2013 "Crisis and austerity: A painful watershed for the Greek welfare state" in <https://www.psa.ac.uk/insight-plus/blog/crisis-and-austerity-painful-watershed-greek-welfare-state> accessed 8 November 2015.

Petmesidou, Maria 2014 "From the golden age to the current crisis" in (the Greek translation of) Esping-Andersen, Gøsta *The three worlds of welfare capitalism* (Athens: Topos, in Greek).

Pfenning, Astrid and Bahle, Thomas 2000 *Families and family policies in Europe: Comparative perspectives* (Frankfurt: Peter Lang).

Richardson, Dominic and Bradshaw, Jonathan 2014 *Family-oriented anti-poverty policies in developed countries* (Paris: OECD).

Sen, Amartya (1992) *Inequality reexamined* (Oxford: Oxford University Press).

Thévenon, Olivier and Neyer, Gerda 2014 "Family policies and diversity in Europe: The state-of-the-art regarding fertility, work, care, leave, laws and self-sufficiency", *Working paper No.7* (Stockholm: Families and Societies Working paper series).

UNICEF (2005) *Childhood under threat: State of the world's children* (New York: UNICEF).

Venturini, Lorenzo 2008 "Poor children in Europe: An analytical approach to the study of child poverty in the European Union between 1994 and 2000," *Child Indicators Research* (Berlin), Vol. 1, No.4, 323–349.

Vilaplana-Lopez, Cristina 2013 "Children were the age group at the highest risk of poverty or social exclusion in 2011" in <http://ec.europa.eu/eurostat/statisticsexplained/index.php/Children_at_risk_of_poverty_or_social_exclusion> accessed 15 October 2015.

CHILD POVERTY, CHILD RIGHTS IN SMALL ISLAND DEVELOPING STATES (SIDS): The Case of the Caribbean

Aldrie Henry-Lee

In 2014, we celebrated the 25th anniversary of the Convention on the Rights of the Child (CRC). In 2015, we reached the deadline for the fulfillment of the Millennium Development Goals (MDGs) which established defined targets for quality of life of children. Now we have committed ourselves to the Sustainable Development Goals (SDGs). Of the three countries under discussion, Haiti was the first to ratify the CRC on June 8, 1990. Barbados ratified the CRC on October 9, 1990 and Jamaica on May 14, 1991. The CRC calls for adequate provision and protection of all children and underscores the right of children to participate in policy decisions that affect them. But are all children afforded these rights? The answer is no and especially not the children living in poverty.

Children living in poverty in Small Island Developing States (SIDS) are particularly at risk. This is because the countries in which they live are extremely vulnerable to global and international shocks. This chapter argues that SIDS cannot end child poverty because they are themselves trapped in a vicious cycle of high levels of poverty and inequality and grappling indebtedness. Unless the vulnerability of SIDS is reduced, elimination of child poverty will continue to be elusive.

This reluctance to tackle child poverty head-on, internationally, regionally, and locally is disturbing as it is well known that investment in children will bring about the best returns of investments. While many international commitments, for example, MDG and A World Fit for Children continue to promise much to our children, barriers at the macro, meso (institutional), and micro levels impede progress in the fight against poverty.

This chapter examines child poverty in three Caribbean countries. These countries were especially selected because they record various levels of human development and national poverty. National monetary poverty rates in Barbados, Jamaica, and Haiti are recorded as 9.3%, 19.9%, and 56% (Table 3). Barbados and Jamaica record high human development, while Haiti records low human development.

Research Questions

- What are the dimensions of child poverty in the Caribbean?
- What are the determinants of child poverty in the Caribbean?
- What are some of the recommendations for the reduction of child poverty?

These questions will be answered using secondary data (e.g., poverty assessment reports, research on poverty in the Caribbean, etc.) and available data sets from the three countries. The extent to which the characteristics of SIDS impede the reduction of child poverty will also be examined.

SIDS: The Case of the Caribbean

According to UNDESA (United Nations Department of Social and Economic Affairs [2014]), the Caribbean forms part of the group of countries called Small Island Developing States. Some of the main characteristics of SIDS include limited productive sectors and heavy reliance on imports; significant susceptibility to economic and environmental shocks; small labor markets, compounded by limited skilled labor, high unemployment and an impending large increase in the size of the elderly population, and tourism as a driving force of the economy (Williams et al., 2013:9). While all developing countries are vulnerable, SIDS experience high levels of vulnerability of their natural, economic, and social systems to external shocks. The intrinsic characteristics of SIDS—such as small size, insularity, vulnerability to demand- and supply-side shocks, a narrow resource base, high population densities, and indirect impacts of global environmental factors—impact negatively on the well-being of the populations living in SIDS. These three countries under discussion in this chapter exhibit the characteristics of SIDS.

In spite of the high levels of vulnerability, some SIDS record high levels of human development. In fact, all the Caribbean countries except Haiti (low human development) have UNDP high human development indicators (HDI). Barbados's HDI value for 2013 is 0.776—*in the high human development category*—positioning the country at 59 out of 187 countries.¹ Jamaica's HDI value is 0.715—*in the high human development category*—positions the country at the 96th position.² Haiti's HDI value is 0.471—*in the low human development category*—with a position of 168. Haiti is one of the poorest and least-developed countries in the world, and there are many grave social and economic problems in the country.

Table 1: Socioeconomic data for selected Caribbean countries

Indicator	Barbados	Jamaica	Haiti
NonincomeHDIvalue[a]	0.776	0.715	0.471
HDIrank[a]	59	96	168
Surface area (square kilometers)[b]	430	10,991	27,750
Urban population (%)	45.4	52.2	56.1
GDP, Gross domestic product (million current US$) 2012[b]	4,533	14,796	7,187
GDP per capita (current US$)[b] (2012)	16,004.3	5343.1	706.5
GDP growth rate at constant 2005 prices (annual %)[b] (2012)	0.7	−0.5	2.8
Gross public debt as a % of GDP[c] (2012 projections)	70.4	143.3	29.9 (2014 estimates)
Unemployment rate	11.6[1]	14.9[2]	40.6[8]
Youth unemployment rate	30[3]	37.7[4]	17.4[9]
Homicide rate[5]	11.3[6]	41.2[7]	6.9

Source:
[a] http://hdr.undp.org/sites/default/files/hdr14-report-en-1.pdf (retrieved September 10, 2015).
[b] http://unstats.un.org/unsd/pocketbook/WSPB2014.pdf (retrieved September 10, 2015).
[c] http://www.imf.org/external/np/pp/eng/2013/022013b.pdf(retrieved September 10, 2015).
[1] The Barbados Ministry of Labour Website – https://labor.gov.bb/
[2] STATIN Labor Force Press Release- "The LaborForce in October 2013". Retrieved from http://statinja.gov.jm/PressReleases/pressreleaselaborforce.aspx
[3] The Barbados Ministry of Labor Website – https://labor.gov.bb/
[4] STATIN Labor Force Press Release- "The LaborForce in October 2013". Retrieved from http://statinja.gov.jm/PressReleases/pressreleaselaborforce.aspx (youth aged 14-24)
[5] Homicides per 100,000 population; http://data.un.org/Data.aspx?d=UNODC&f=tableCode%3a1
[6] 2010
[7] 2011
[8] http://data.worldbank.org/indicator/SL.UEM.TOTL.ZS (retrieved September 10, 2015)
[9] http://www.theglobaleconomy.com/Haiti/Youth_unemployment/(retrievedSeptember 10, 2015)

---

1   UNDP (2013a)
2   UNDP (2013b)

Table 1 presents some selected socioeconomic data for the three countries. According to the World Bank classification (2014), Barbados with a GDP per capita of US$16,004 is deemed as a "high income" country; Haiti with US$706.5 is "low income"; and Jamaica with US$5343 is "upper middle income." Some of the characteristics of SIDS become evident. These countries have not experienced significant growth rates recently with only Haiti recording a growth rate of 2.8 due to international aid and support. High levels of indebtedness cripple economic growth (Table 1). Unemployment rates are high, with Haiti recording the highest at 40.6%. Youth unemployment is also very high with Barbados recording the highest at 30.4%, reflecting limited productivity by the youthful population. Jamaicans live in a violent environment with a homicide rate of 41.2%. The other social and economic challenges of these SIDS will be examined in the section on determinants of child poverty.

Children in the Caribbean Context

Children form a significant proportion of the populations of these SIDS. In Barbados, children aged 0–14 years make up 18.9% of the population. In Jamaica, children account for 27.1% while in Haiti children aged 0–14 years form up to 35% of the population (Table 2).

Table 2: Some child-related data for selected Caribbean countries

Indicator	Barbados	Jamaica	Haiti
Population in 2013 (estimated, 000)[a]	285	2 784	10.317
% of population aged 0-14 years[a] (2011)	18.9	27.1	35
Life expectancy[c]	75	75	63
Fertility rate[a]	1.8	2.3	3.1
Under 5 mortality rate (per 1000 live births)[b] 2012	18	17	76
Under 5 mortality rank[b]	100	80	31
Maternal mortality ratio (per 100,000 live births)[a]	51	110	350
Births attended by skilled health personnel (%) (2012)[d]	100	99[1]	37
Measles immunization (% of 1-year-olds)[e]	90	94	65
Low birth weight babies % of births (2011)[f]	12	11	23[2]
Prevalence of HIV, total % of population ages 15-49[a]	0.9	1.8	2.0
Enrollment at primary Schools (2011)[g]	105	90.1	57
Percentage of repeaters (primary)[j]	0.00[j]	3.21	Na
Survival rates to grade 5[h]	94	88	34
Percentage of repeaters (secondary)[i]	0.00[j]	1.19	Na
Primary to secondary transition rate[i]	99.01	90.29[2]	Na

Source:
[a] http://www.who.int/gho/countries/en/index.html (retrieved September 10, 2015).
[b] http://www.unicef.org/infobycountry (retrieved September 10, 2015).
[c] http://data.worldbank.org/indicator/SP.DYN.LE00.IN (retrieved September 10, 2015).
[d] http://data.worldbank.org/indicator/SH.STA.BRTC.ZS (retrieved September 10, 2015).
[e] http://data.worldbank.org/indicator/SH.IMM.MEAS (retrieved September 10, 2015).
[f] http://data.worldbank.org/indicator/SH.STA.BRTW.ZS (retrieved September 10, 2015).
[g] http://data.worldbank.org/indicator/SE.PRM.ENRR (retrieved September 10, 2015).
[h] http://data.worldbank.org/indicator/SE.PRM.PRS5.ZS (retrieved September 10, 2015).
[i] http://data.uis.unesco.org/index.aspx?queryid=150 (retrieved September 10, 2015).
[j] http://www.quandl.com/barbados/barbados-education--data (retrieved September 10, 2015).
[1] 2011.
[2] 2012.

Based on the available data, in Table 2; in general, the status of children seems best in Barbados and worst in Haiti. Infant mortality rate is very high (76 per 1000) in Haiti and lowest in Jamaica at 17 per 1000 live births. Children can expect to live to 75 years in Barbados but only 63 years in Haiti.

Barbados is the only country in which 100% of all births are attended by skilled health personnel. In Haiti, only 37% of births are attended by skilled personnel. Haiti also records the highest proportion of its children born with low birth weight (23%), with Jamaica and Barbados recording about 11% and 12%, respectively. Maternal mortality rates vary from 380 per 100,000 in Haiti to 52 per 100,000 in Barbados. Immunization of children against measles is highest in Jamaica (94%) and lowest in Haiti (65%).

Haiti has the lowest primary school enrolment at 57% and Barbados the highest at 105%. Survival rates to grade 5 are fairly high in Barbados and Jamaica except for Haiti where only 34% of all children survive to grade 5 (Table 2). Again, primary to secondary school transition rates are high in Barbados and Jamaica. In 2014, it was reported that 17% of the eligible cohort in Haiti was not attending primary school.[3]

The data indicate that except for Haiti, children have high levels of immunization, enjoy fairly good access to primary school education, most of them transition to secondary school, and most of them can expect to live to at least 70 years. These data compare reasonably well with global indicators for children and that is possibly why, except for Haiti, Barbados, and Jamaica record high levels of human development.

However, these macro data mask the vulnerabilities of the poorest children in these countries who do not have adequate access to basic social services, even in Barbados. As we will see in the section on child poverty, the situation of children in Haiti worsened since the 2010 earthquake. The rights of children who live in poverty in these countries are violated every day. In the next section, we will begin to examine poverty in these countries.

Poverty in the Caribbean

The experience of poverty usually includes deprivation, lack of access to basic social services, social exclusion, vulnerability, and unsustainability of livelihood. Amartya Sen in Sen (1999:3) defines poverty as capability failure. He goes beyond the issue of income to include issue of deprivation in health and education and lack of freedoms that are intrinsically good. Skirbekk and St. Clair (2000) believe that the first stage to sustained development is the freedom from poverty. According to Sen (1999:3) "development requires the removal of major sources of un-freedom: poverty as well as tyranny, poor economic opportunities as well as systematic social deprivation, neglect of public facilities as well as intolerance or over

---

3   Education Policy and Data Centre (2014).

activity of repressive states." In the 1997 Human Development Report (UNDP, 1997), poverty is described as a lack of access to choices and opportunities and results in insecurity, powerlessness and exclusion of individuals, households and communities. These and other features of poverty are present in the Caribbean.

The macro vulnerabilities of SIDS are linked to the poverty situation in these countries. We argue that unless these macro-level vulnerabilities are reduced, national poverty and child poverty will remain at high levels. The issue of poverty and its impact on these small populations need to be given serious policy attention. Sustained development will not be obtained if large proportions of the productive sector remain impoverished and their basic human rights compromised.

Table 3: Poverty indicators for selected Caribbean countries

Country	Year	Poverty Line	Headcount Poverty (%)		Poverty gap at	Severity of Poverty
			Indiv.	H/hold		
Anguilla[a]	2009	US$6055	5.8	n.a.	1.06	0.24
Antigua/Barbuda[b]	2006	US$2366	18.3	n.a.	6.63	3.75
Bahamas[c]	2001	US$2863	9.3	5.1	n.a.	n.a.
Barbados[d]	2010	US$3931	19.3	15.0	6.0	3.2
Belize[e]	2009	US$1700	33.5	n.a.	11	n.a.
Brit Virgin Is[f]	2008	US$633	22.0	16.0	4.1	n.a.
Dominica[g]	2009	US$2307	28.8	22.8	8.6	4.0
Grenada[h]	2008	US$2164	37.7	n.a.	10.13	4.03
Guyana[i]	1999	n.a.	35.0	n.a.	12.4	n.a.
Haiti[j]	2004	n.a.	56	n.a.	31	n.a.
Jamaica[k]	2012	US$1545[4]	19.9	14.4	5.8	0.024
St. Kitts/Nevis[l]	2008	US$2714/$3625	23.7/15.9	14.8/10.1	2.5/2.72	0.89/1.0
St.Lucia[m]	2006	US$1905	25.1	28.8	9.0	4.1
St. Vin/Gren[n]	2008	US$2045	30.2	20.8	7.5	3.0
Trin/Tobago[o]	2005	US$483	16.7	11.0	4.6	1.9
Turks/Caicos[p]	2012	US$2463	21.6	15.9	4.0	n.a.

---

[4] Calculated using the BOJ 2012 exchange rate of $93.01-
http://www.boj.org.jm/foreign_exchange/fx_historical_rates.php

Sources:
Note: All Poverty line figures are quoted in their current US dollar equivalent.
a http://www.caribank.org/uploads/2012/12/Anguilla-CPA-Main-Report-Final-Submitted.pdf
b http://www.unicef.org/easterncaribbean/spmapping/Planning/national/Antigua%20and%20Barbuda/2007_AntBarbCPAMainReport.pdf
c http://www.cepal.org/celade/noticias/paginas/9/46849/Bahamas.pdf
d http://www.caribank.org/uploads/2012/12/Barbados-CALC-Volume-1-MainReport-FINAL-Dec-2012.pdf
e http://www.caribank.org/uploads/2012/12/Belize-2009-Report-Vol1.pdf and http://www.pnpbelize.org/2009-poverty-assessment.pdf
f http://www.paho.org/saludenlasamericas/index.php?gid=119&option=com_docman&task=doc_view and http://www.cepal.org/portofspain/noticias/paginas/6/37516/British_Virgin_Islands_MDG_Plan_of_Action_2008.pdf
g http://www.caribank.org/uploads/publications-reports/economics-statistics/country-poverty-assessment-reports/Dominica+CPA+-+Main+Report+Final+(Submitted).pdf
h http://www.gov.gd/egov/docs/reports/Grenada_CPA_Vol_1_Main_Report_Submitted.pdf
i https://www.imf.org/External/NP/prsp/2002/guy/01/052302.pdf
j http://fafo.no/~fafo/media/com_netsukii/755.pdf
k Planning Institute of Jamaica 2012 Survey of Living Conditions (Kingston: Planning Institute of Jamaica)
l http://www.caribank.org/uploads/2012/03/St.-Kitts-and-Nevis-CPA-Vol.-2-St.-Kitts-Final-Report.pdf, http://www.caribank.org/uploads/2012/03/St._Kitts_Nevis_Final_Report2001.pdf
and http://www.caribank.org/uploads/publications-reports/economics-statistics/country-poverty-assessment-reports/St.+Kitts+and+Nevis+CPA+-+Vol.+3+Nevis+Final+Report.pdf
m http://www.caribank.org/uploads/2012/03/SLUCPAMainReport.pdf and http://archive.stlucia.gov.lc/docs/AssessmentOfPovertyInStLucia/Assessment_of_Poverty_in_St_Lucia_Volume_3_Quantitative_Assessment_of_Poverty.pdf
n http://www.stats.gov.vc/LinkClick.aspx?fileticket=gxP733Q3EZk%3D&tabid=60
o http://www.cepal.org/portofspain/noticias/paginas/0/40340/41_SLC_Analysis_of_the_Trinidad_and_Tobago_Survey_of_Living_Conditions.pdf
p https://www.caribank.org/uploads/2014/09/TCI_CPA-2012-Volume-1.pdf

Note:
All Poverty line figures are quoted in their current US dollar equivalent
n.a - not available

Table 4: Some of the Main Characteristics of Household Poverty in the Caribbean

Indicator	Characteristics
Household composition	Poor households are characterized with a significant percentage of female heads of households and a large number of dependents (children and the elderly); Poor households have more members than nonpoor households; Poor households contained different generations of persons, thus indicating some degree of intergenerational poverty; The incidence of poverty among the elderly (60 years and over) tends to be high; In some countries, child poverty is significantly more than the national average
Residential	A larger proportion of households in the rural areas live below the poverty line than those in the urban areas
Housing conditions	Poor households are subject to poor housing conditions with overcrowding being a problem and restricted access to public utilities; Squatting is a common feature among the poor in larger countries leading to environmental challenges
Human capital and labor market issues	The human capital (education and training) base of the poor is quite low;
Labor market issues	The unemployment rate is highest among members of poor household; Poor household tend to participate more in the secondary or informal labor market (employment in low-paying jobs partly reflects the low human capital base of the poor, that is, the working poor); The poor tend to be employed in elementary occupations, rural small-scale enterprises and in a range of informal sector activities; When poverty is concentrated in identifiable communities, there is evidence of stigmatization which results in discrimination in employment and labor market segmentation; The poor have been greatly affected by the seasonality of production in the region (agriculture, tourism, construction) and external shocks such as increase in prices and declining export sale

Source: Adapted from Downes (2010, pp. 4–5)

Caribbean countries suffer from high levels of poverty and inequality. The proportion of persons living below the poverty line in the Caribbean ranged from 56% in Haiti to 9.3% in Bahamas while Jamaica recorded 19.9% (Table 3). In Haiti, the average income of the monetary poor would have to increase by 31% to allow them to be at the poverty line while in Barbados it would have to be increased by 6% to reach the country's poverty line.

Most of the data on poverty is derived from country poverty assessments (CPA). These CPAs provide statistics on the proportion of households or individuals who live below an estimated national poverty line (the headcount index). The CPAs also estimate the depth or severity of national poverty. The Foster-Greer Thorbecke (FGT) P2 measures the severity of poverty, and the poverty gap measures the depth of poverty (World Bank, 2005b). The poverty gap measures the distance of the poor to the poverty line. The intensity or severity of poverty measured by the FGTP2 can be thought of as the sum of two components: an amount due to the poverty gap and an amount due to the inequality of the poor (World Bank, 2005b).

The assessment of poverty in the Caribbean can be done based on household composition; residence; housing conditions, human capital, and labor market issues (Table 4). Monetary poverty is mainly a rural phenomenon, with those living with income below the poverty line having a low human capital base and limited access to decent paying jobs in the labor market. Poor households generally live in poor housing conditions. Poverty of the adult population is intricately related to poverty of children in the SIDS. In the next section we will discuss the dimensions of child poverty.

Dimensions of child poverty

The UN General Assembly defines child poverty as:

> Children living in poverty are deprived of nutrition, water and sanitation facilities, access to basic health-care services, shelter, education, participation and protection, and that while a severe lack of goods and services hurts every human being, it is most threatening and harmful to children, leaving them unable to

enjoy their rights, to reach their full potential and to participate as full members of the society. (UNICEF Press Centre, 2007)

This multidimensional nature of child poverty links very well with the definitions of poverty offered in the previous section: child poverty like adult poverty is a situation in which a child lacks opportunities, whose choices are limited, and whose rights are denied. The UN recognized that child poverty is about more than just a financial deprivation but also entails a denial of a range of rights laid out in the UN CRC. Each deprivation that a child suffers exacerbates the effects of others and when two or more deprivations coincide, the effect can be catastrophic for those children (UNICEF, 2004).

In Latin America and the Caribbean, a total of 70 million children, that is, two in five children, are poor (ECLAC, 2013). In this section, we examine the multidimensional nature of child poverty in Haiti. Jamaica has an annual survey of living conditions and therefore would have time-series data on children living in monetary poor households. Barbados has relatively less data.

In Barbados, the poverty assessment report stated that persons under 15 years of age are overrepresented in poor households with 29.2% of the indigent poor falling in that age category (Sir Arthur Lewis Institute of Social and Economic Studies, 2012:29). The qualitative data analyzed in the most recent country poverty assessment in Barbados revealed that poverty among children was clearly associated with the intergenerational poverty of their parents and families. The characteristics of their poverty and social exclusion were reported as follows:

- Poor health and diet, hunger
- Poor living conditions in homes
- Irregular school attendance or attrition
- Family neglect, abuse, and violence
- Psychological effects of loneliness and sadness (Barbados Country Assessment of Living Conditions 2010, Volume 1, 2012, 2010b: 11)

In 2012, the annual Survey of Living Conditions in Jamaica (Table 5a), records that the overall percentage of children living in monetary poor households is 25%; this underscores the continued increase in this rate over the years; a 14% increase from 2010 and a 23% increase from 2009.

The survey showed that in 2012, a larger portion of boys than girls lived in monetary poor households (Table 5b). The rural and Kingston Metropolitan areas recorded the highest proportion of children living in poverty (26.1%) and poor households reported larger household sizes (Table 5b). Using the criteria for severe deprivation employed in the Bristol and London School of Economics Global Child Poverty Study and data from the 2009 survey of living conditions, the most severe deprivation of Jamaican children was estimated for health, (9%), followed by water (5%). No Jamaican child was reported to be severely deprived of education, and only a marginal 1% was severely deprived of sanitation (Witter 2009).

Table 5a: Poverty prevalence by age group, 2004–2012

Age Group	2004 (%)	2007 (%)	2009 (%)	2010 (%)	2012 (%)
0–17 years	20.6	12.0	20.4	21.9	25.0
18–35 years	14.7	8.9	13.3	15.4	19.4
36–59 years	14.0	7.8	14.0	14.4	16.5
60 years and over	15.2	10.2	17.1	15.9	14.6
Total	16.9	9.9	16.5	17.6	19.9

Source: JSLC 2012 data set

Table 5b: Characteristics of child poverty in Jamaica

		Percentage
Gender of child *(n = 3,238)*	Male	26.2
	Female	23.8
Residential area *(n = 3,238)*	KMA	26.1
	Other towns	20.9
	Rural areas	26.1
Mean household size (HH with children 0–17)	Poor households	5.4 persons *(n = 871)*
	Nonpoor households	4.1 persons *(n = 3,724)*

Source: JSLC 2012 data set

Gordon and Nandy (2007:11) indicate that more than 4 in 10 children in Haiti live in multidimensional child poverty. The same study indicates that 7 out of 10 children (2.66 million) experience at least one form of deprivation related to food, health, education, water, sanitation, shelter, or information. Balsari et al. (2010: 1) reveal that extreme poverty has driven poor families to place their children in residential care facilities with some families returning to find that their children have been given away for adoption.

Poor children usually live in poor sanitary conditions. In Jamaica, 64% of poorest quintile of households in Jamaica are using pit latrines with a slab cover; 30% have no drinking water available on their premises; more than half of all (Haitian) children (54%, 2.1 million) were severely shelter deprived (Gordon and Nandy, 2007:11). Being severely deprived means that their homes were made from mud, or severely overcrowded, with more than five persons per room.

The importance of early child development to long-term health and productivity has long been established. In Jamaica, only 54.7% of children under the age of 5 are living in households that have at least 3 children's books present (UNICEF, 2011). This falls to 30% for 10 or more books. Children in the richest households are twice as likely to have 3 or more children's books as those in the poorest. Fathers in the richest households are more engaged: children in the poorest households are 3 times less likely to have their father engaged in activities that support learning. The percentages of children aged 3--5 years who are developmentally on track for dedicated domains show wealth differentials: 79.1 for the poorest quintile and 97.1 for the richest quintile (UNICEF, 2011).

Child poverty affects access to secondary education. In Jamaica, children in the poorer households are less likely to attend secondary school (87.6%), (UNICEF, 2011). Overall 91.5% of children ages 12-16 are attending secondary school. In the poorest households, attendance rate was 87.6% with rural areas attendance rate at 89.5%. Among the children in the poorest quintile, 88.2% of them were only educated to the primary level and there are concerns about high levels of drop out, absenteeism, violence in schools, and literacy/numeracy skills (UNICEF, 2011).

The 2013 MDG Report: Haiti states that the country has steadily boosted net enrolment rate in primary education from 47% in 1993 to 88% in 2011, achieving equal participation of boys and girls in education (MDG 2). However, 4 out of 10 people in Haiti cannot read or write (Verner, 2008: 49) and 20% of children suffer from malnutrition (Verner, 2008: 24).

Early pregnancy impacts negatively on the life chances of adolescents—especially those with limited education. In Jamaica, girls in the poorest households are 10 times more likely to have a child before the age of 18 than those in the richest quintile. The birth rate among adolescents who have no education or only primary level (17.7%) is more than twice the rate of adolescents who have a tertiary education—8.7% (UNICEF, 2011).

Violence against children is a serious health issue. In 2010 in Barbados, there were 846 cases of child abuse reported to the Child Care Board. Of these, 72 (44%) were due to neglect, 191 (22.8%) to physical abuse, 185 (21.9%) to sexual abuse, and 95 (11.2%) to emotional abuse. In the Caribbean, the law permits corporal punishment and parents can legally apply physical punishment.

In Jamaica, children in the poorest households are 8 times more likely to be involved in child labor than those in the richest households (UNICEF, 2011). As seen in the earlier section, there is a high prevalence of violence in Jamaica. Figures from the Statistics Department of the Jamaica Constabulary Force (JCF) indicate that since January 2013 and May 2014, 60 children were murdered and 99 were shot and injured.[5]

Haiti is a source, transit, and destination country for human trafficking. Haiti has also become known for its use of restaveks, that is, child laborers. These restaveks are often unpaid, denied education, and physically and sexually abused. Child advocates in Haiti warn that a number of unaccompanied minors remaining in camps after the 2010 earthquake are vulnerable to this form of forced labor or to trafficking. Much of Haiti child trafficking involves girls, from low-income households sent to live with other families in the hope they will be cared for in exchange for performing light chores.[6] Restaveks make up a large proportion of Haiti's population of street children, who are forced into prostitution, begging, and street crime by violent gangs.[7] The data reveal that children living in poverty are usually children whose parents are themselves faced with several challenges daily. Children unable to fend for themselves suffer the impact of poverty to a greater extent.

---

5   http://www.jamaicaobserver.com/news/60-children-murdered--99-shot-and-injured-in-past-16-months
6   Human Rights Watch (2012).
7   CIA Fact Book 2016.
    https://books.google.com.jm/books?iforced%20into%20prostitution%2C%20. Accessed July 28, 2016

Determinants of child poverty in SIDS

What are the causes of child poverty? The Social Selection Theory (Huston et al., 1994) states that children born into poor families are disadvantaged because they have parents who have lower levels of human capital. The children themselves will, in turn, have relatively poor intellectual and social skills as a result of both family and environmental influences provided by their parents. Social Causation Theory states that economic and social institutions and structures offer opportunities and barriers that lead to poverty or affluence (Huston et al., 1994). Poorer persons have less availability of jobs paying high wages to escape poverty.

Bradshaw (2006) outlines some other theories of poverty: (1) individual deficiencies, (2) cultural belief systems that support subcultures in poverty, (3) political-economic distortions, (4) geographical disparities, or (5) cumulative and circumstantial origins. The Individualistic Theories (e.g., Herrnstein and Murray, 1994 and Rainwater, 1970) blame the individuals for their conditions. These theories have been criticized for their myopic view of poverty and their lack of understanding of the impact of the conditions that the children find themselves. Cultural theories state that poverty has roots in the "Culture of Poverty." While not blaming the individual for their individual attributes, they believe that poverty is created by the transmission over generations of a set of beliefs, values, and skills that are socially generated (Bradshaw 2006:8). Cultural theories believe that individuals are not necessarily to be blamed because they are victims of their dysfunctional subculture or culture.

> Once the culture of poverty has come into existence it tends to perpetuate itself. By the time slum children are six or seven they have usually absorbed the basic attitudes and values of their subculture. Thereafter, they are psychologically unready to take full advantage of changing conditions or improving opportunities that may develop in their lifetime. (Scientific American, October 1966 quoted in Ryan, 1976: 120)

The concern about the cultural theories is what causes and constitutes the subculture of poverty (Bradshaw, 2006: 9).

The third group of poverty explanations outlines the aspects of economic, political, and social systems that cause people to have limited opportunities and resources with which to achieve income and well-being. The geographical theories of poverty call attention to the fact that people, institutions, and cultures in certain areas lack the objective resources needed to generate well-being and income, and that they lack the power to claim redistribution. Some writers speak about the geography of poverty being a spatial expression of the capitalist system (Shaw, 1996:29).

The final set of theories (Cumulative and Cyclical Interdependencies theories) combine the individual and structural theories and propose that individual and their communities are caught in a spiral of opportunity and problems, and that once problems dominate they close other opportunities and create a cumulative set of problems that make any effective response nearly impossible (Bradshaw, 2006:16). Bradshaw (2006:14) looks explicitly at individual situations and community resources as mutually dependent, with a faltering economy, for example, creating individuals who lack resources to participate in the economy, rendering their economic survival more difficult.

None of these theories/studies comprehensively explain the existence of child poverty in the Caribbean. Child poverty in the Caribbean has its roots in global and local spheres. Perhaps the Cumulative and Cyclical Interdependencies theories come closest in explaining the complexity of the poverty situation in the Caribbean. We now examine determinants of poverty at the macro level, meso (institutional), and micro levels.

At the macro level, high indicators of human development did not shelter any of the islands from manifesting the characteristics of SIDs. The three islands illustrate the vulnerability of SIDs: they are very susceptible to external shocks, given their small physical size and populations, SIDs rely heavily on imports and have limited domestic production and a larger percent of their GDPS is spent on imports, Caribbean SIDs average between 45% and 65% expenditure of GDP on imports, and significant amounts of the imports are focuses on food and fuel. For example, Haiti imports 52% of its food, including over 80% of its rice (World Bank, 2013a). This has implications for social protection responses as food expenditures comprise a much higher share of income for the poor compared to other income groups. As a result, SIDS in general and specifically poor households in SIDs face high exposure to global food price variability.

In SIDs, export earnings are mostly derived from primary commodities. These commodities no longer benefit from economies of scale and competitive pricing now that preferential trade agreements have expired. For example, the agreement between the African Caribbean and Pacific (ACP) Group of States and the European Union (EU) has had a very negative impact on poverty levels in the SIDS. The loss of competitiveness has resulted in increased unemployment. The heavy reliance on primary commodities and the trends in global trade present significant macro-level vulnerabilities that impact the levels of child poverty. When earnings from trade decrease, public poverty increases.

Public poverty manifests in high debt-to-GDP ratio as shown earlier in Table 1. Most of the countries' revenue is spent on paying debt. Little is left for investment in basic social services. Access to good basic social services is important in the fight against poverty. High levels of inequality (measured by the Gini coefficient) indicate that the disparity between the income of the poor and the rich is very wide. The Gini coefficients for Barbados, Jamaica, and Haiti were 0.47, 0.38, and 0.59 respectively.[8]

Natural disasters are unpredictable and cause huge financial and human loss when they occur. For example, the earthquake in Haiti cost 122% of GDP (Cavallo et al., 2010). In poverty-stricken countries, natural disasters can stall the implementation of the poverty-reduction agenda and ultimately affect the general wellbeing of children.

At the meso level, there are some institutional weaknesses that negatively affect the delivery of social services to the poor. In their study of Social Protection in SIDS with focus on the Caribbean, Williams et al. (2013: 2) found that many groups are underserved, there is duplication of efforts, and evidence of inefficiency and the systems show limited responsiveness to shocks. Globally, countries generally spend a mean of 1.9% of GDP on Social Safety Nets (SSNs). The average for Latin America and the Caribbean was 1.3% (Williams et al., 2013). A World Bank study found that many SSN programs in the Caribbean are characterized by problems of limited coverage, weak targeting, and ineffective mechanisms for determining eligibility (World Bank, 2005).

---

[8] Gini coefficients for Barbados and Jamaica from their country poverty assessment report and Haiti from the World Bank (2014).

In Barbados, there are public assistance programs that provide support to the needy and indigent. In Jamaica, The Programme of Advancement through Health and Education (PATH), a conditional cash transfer (CCT) program funded by the government through support from the World Bank has become the main social assistance program, which has over 400,000 registered beneficiaries as of 2014. In Haiti, an Integrated Social Protection Mechanism has been established. This delivers social services directly to families through household development agents (HDAs). They work with at least 100 households (World Bank, 2013b). The HDAs utilize a three-pronged strategy to: (1) raise awareness and increase knowledge of health, nutrition, hygiene, and sanitation practices; (2) provide a package of basic commodities and services; and (3) where possible, refer families to relevant social services (World Bank, 2013b).

Household and individual characteristics can cause child poverty. Poverty studies in the Caribbean highlight four factors that cause monetary poverty in the region: unemployment, large families and single parenting, lack of education and/or skills, and low pay (Frank, 2007; Downes, 2010: 6). These features impact a child's well-being. Witter et al. (2009: 84) state that households with children are more likely to be poor than households with no children. The probability of being poor is much higher for rural households and their members than for their urban counterparts. These factors reflect human capital formation—labor market and demographic explanations for poverty in the Caribbean (Downes, 2010: 6).

As stated before, research has shown that high levels of poverty are caused by high levels of unemployment. Unemployment rates are high in the Caribbean. Unemployed heads of households cannot adequately provide for their children. Unemployment rates vary from 11.5% in Barbados to 40.6% in Haiti; Jamaica's unemployment rate is 13.4.[9]

Generally the poor receive poor services, and the services are not always available (World Bank, 2004). Table 6 summarizes some of the main deficiencies of the social assistance programs. These include inadequate value of the benefit, limited coverage, and inadequate staff. Weak social policy environment with low accountability, limited social dialogue, and democratic and participatory governance make it difficult for effective and efficient delivery to the poor to take place (Henry-Lee, 2002).

---

9   Rates are for March 2014 from ieconomics.com (accessed October 11, 2014).

Table 6: Selected poverty reduction programs in the three countries

Country	Program	Targets	Observations
Barbados	o Public assistance o School feeding program o Housing welfare program o Skills training program	o The needy and indigent—some recent efforts at gender-based targeting o The elderly and the disabled o School children o Youth	o Limited due to insufficiency of funds, staffs and adequate office space o Recent establishment of Ministry of Social Transformation intended to increase funds and improve targeting o Skills training—largely limited to low skill areas
Jamaica	o PATH o SIF o Macro Investment Development Agency o Self-Start Fund o Food Stamp Program o Public Assistance and School Feeding Program o Special Training and Empowerment program o Revitalization of Inner City o Minimum Wage Legislation	o Children, lactating mothers, elderly o Unemployed youth, the aged, women, the disabled o Human resource devt, and social and physical infrastructural devt, in economically deprived communities o Rural communities, small and microenterprises o Children under 6 yrs and pregnant and lactating mothers, the elderly, poor, single member households o Needy students o Bussiness devt, in urban communities	o Some successful geographical targeting o Inadequate value of benefit o Operations limited by low purchasing power of food stamps and low lending limits for enterprise dev. o Neglect of low-income households not in target groups o Strategy needed to address one unintended consequence of the minimum wage legislation—namely increased unemployment

Haiti	○ Universal education ○ Improving the supply and distribution of water ○ Interdepartmental corporation ○ Reforestation ○ Minimum wage	○ Equal access to education ○ Better productivity from workers and a healthier labor force ○ Repair the damages caused by decades of deforestation	○ Most children are not enrolled in either private or public schools ○ Drinking water supply in most areas tend to be very limited, with availablity being dependent on individual initiative

Sources:
a. Downes, S. A. 2010. "Poverty and its Reduction in the Small Developing Countries of the Caribbean."
b. Haiti: Interim Poverty Reduction Strategy Paper

While there is universal access to school at the primary level and access to secondary schools is fairly high, there are indications that the quality of education is questionable in Jamaica and Haiti. In Jamaica, 70% of the labor force is uncertified (Downes 2010: 8). In Haiti, while there is increased access to secondary school, more than 60% of 24 year olds have still not completed grade 9. All this has implications for the alleviation of poverty in these countries.

Of course, employment and relief from poverty are not mutually exclusive (Brown, 1995) and there is the phenomenon of the "working poor." Their low wages and unsatisfactory working conditions do not alleviate their poverty. The poor can also be found working in the informal sector. This sector is composed of those who have no recourse but to be (self-)employed outside of the mechanisms that defend their rights to decent work and a minimum standard of living (and whose employers pay no taxes and/or do not respect minimum safety, environmental and other standards and regulations) as well as some people who are associated with illegal activities. The intricate link between these informal activities and crime has been well established.

The coping strategies of the poor themselves can further entrench their various vulnerabilities. Coping strategies used by the poor include: to forego basic needs; to increase or maintain existing levels of debts; using savings or assets; to seek help from relatives or friends; or to seek extra work or hustle and pray (Anderson, 2001: 49). Another coping strategy that promotes intergenerational poverty is the cutbacks on education. Sixty percent of poor households reported that they would not send their children to school when they experienced financial difficulty (Anderson, 2001: 49).

All these factors at the macro, meso, and micro levels determine the levels of child poverty in SIDS. Reduction in child poverty would necessitate the implementation of strategies at all three levels.

The Way Forward

High HDIs mask the true vulnerability of children in SIDS. Notwithstanding the level of human development of the countries, children face the same challenges (even though at different levels). As the world prepares for the developmental agenda beyond 2015, there needs to be increased focus on the vulnerability of SIDS to secure their sustainable development. It is only through sustainable development that will a significant reduction in child poverty will be obtained. As we end 2015, the "MDG 8: Global Partnership for Development" has not been fully realized and there needs to be improvement in the responsiveness to economic and environmental shocks of SIDS. There have been few achievements in the Programme of Action for Sustainable Development of SIDS since its adoption in 1994. Advocates for this initiative also ask that the resources be used with greater efficiency and equity.

Table 6 lists some of the main programs in the countries under discussion. However, there are proposals for the improvement of social protection programs in SIDS. For example, Williams et al. (2013:3) suggests the following: (1) harmonize SP systems and policies across the region to better respond to increased regional mobility; (2) consolidate SP programs within countries to improve efficiency; (3) foster key human capital improvements among the poor to break inter-generational transmission of poverty; (4) improve monitoring and evaluation systems and data collection capacity to facilitate more responsive SP programs; and (5) increase partnerships with civil society and private sector. Williams et al(2013:2) also called for improved efficiency and effectiveness of social safety net programs, in particular cash transfer programs; tailoring labor market interventions to respond to constraints faced in the SIDS context; and reforming social insurance schemes, particularly pension schemes, to address current deficiencies and ensure readiness to respond to impending ageing.

At the meso (institutional) level, the UNICEF/UNDP 20/20 initiative should be instituted. This initiative advocates that developing countries allocate, on average, 20% of the local budget and 20% of official development assistance (ODA) to these basic social services.

As advocated by the Programme of Action for Sustainable Development of SIDS at the micro level, there must be a promotion of human resources development programs, including education, training, and skills development. Strategies should be put in place to ensure that more students are certified and reduce the number of students who graduate without a certificate. Given the high rates of unemployment, labor market opportunities need to be provided to reduce these high rates.

For the children themselves, social investment in all groups of children (i.e., an approach based on equity) is key in breaking the cycle of poverty. Children need good quality early childhood education to secure a firm foundation in their academic pursuits. Nutrition programs at schools will ensure that children are not hungry while trying to learn. Affordable and accessible good quality care for all children, even those in the most rural areas, must be a priority. There are some children whose parents confront several challenges (e.g., drugs, imprisonment, and abuse) and they need multiple well-targeted interventions to reduce the deleterious effects of all these challenges. The children who receive less policy attention (e.g., children with disabilities, street children, children infected with and affected by HIV/AIDS) should be targeted to reduce their vulnerabilities and lift them out of poverty. Only then would we be able to see a sustained reduction in child poverty.

References

Anderson, Patricia 2001 "Poverty in Jamaica: Social target or social crisis," *Souls: A Critical Journal of Black Politics, Culture and Society* Vol.3, No. 4.

Balsari, Satchit, Lemery, Jay, P. Williams, Timothy and D. Nelson, Brett 2010 "Protecting the children of Haiti," *New England Journal of Medicine*, Vol. 362 No. 9.

Bradshaw, Ted K. 2006 "Theories of poverty and anti-poverty programs in community development," *RPRC Working Paper No. 06-05* in <http://www.rupri.org/Forms/WP06-05.pdf> accessed 21 January 2016.

Brown, D. 1995 *Profile of the poor in Jamaica* (Kingston, Planning Institute of Jamaica).

Cavallo, Eduardo A., Powell, Andrew and Becerra, Oscar 2010 "Estimating the direct economic damages of the Earthquake in Haiti", *The Economic Journal*, Vol. 120, No. 546, F298–F312.

CIA The World Factbook *Central America and Caribbean: Haiti* in <https://www.cia.gov/library/publications/the-world-factbook/geos/print_ha.html>

Downes, Andrew S. 2010 *Poverty and its reduction in the small developing countries of the Caribbean* in <http://www.chronicpoverty.org/uploads/publication_files/downes_caribbean.pdf>

ECLAC 2013 *Social panorama* (Santiago de Chile: ECLAC) Education Policy and Data Center 2014 *Haiti – National Education Profile. 2014 Update* in <http://www.epdc.org/sites/default/files/documents/EPDC%20NEP_Haiti.pdf> accessed 18 December 2015.

Equity for Children 2012 "UNICEF and ECLAC present guide to estimating child poverty" in <http://www.equityforchildren.org/unicef-and-eclac-present-guide-to-estimating-child-poverty/>

Frank, C. 2007 "Some new findings from CPAs in the Eastern Caribbean" in Melville, Juliet and Wint, Eleanor (eds.) *A new perspective on poverty in the Caribbean*, 24–57 (Kingston: Ian Randle Publishers).

Gordon, Gordon and Nandy, Shailen 2007 *Absolute child poverty in Haiti in the 21st century* (Bristol: University of Bristol/UNICEF Haiti) in <http://www.bristol.ac.uk/media-library/sites/sps/migrated/documents/rx9144finalreportenglish.pdf>

Henry-Lee, Aldrie 2002. "Economic deprivation and private adjustments: the case of security guards in Jamaica", *Social and Economic Studies,* Vol. 51, No. 4,:181–209.

Human Rights Watch 2012 "World report 2012: Haiti – events of 2011" in <https://www.hrw.org/world-report/2012/country-chapters/haiti>

Herrnstein, Richard J. and Murray, Charles 1994. *The Bell Curve* (New York: The Free Press).

Huston, Aletha C., McLoyd, Connie C. and Garcia Coll, Cynthia 1994. "Children and poverty: Issues in contemporary research", *Child development* Vol. 65 No. 2: 275–282. In <http://ieconomics.com> accessed October 11, 2014.

Kairi Consultants 2010 "Dominica – Reducing poverty in the face of vulnerability", *Caribbean development bank country poverty assessment report* in <http://www.caribank.org/uploads/publications-reports/economics-statistics/country-poverty-assessment-reports/Dominica+CPA+-+Main+Report+Final+(Submitted).pdf>

Kairi Consultants 2009 "Final report country poverty assessment – St. Kitts and Nevis 2007/08: Living conditions in a Caribbean small island developing state, volume 2", *Caribbean Development Bank Country Poverty Assessment Report* in <http://www.caribank.org/uploads/2012/03/St.-Kitts-and-Nevis-CPA-Vol.-2-St.-Kitts-Final-Report.pdf>

Kairi Consultants 2009 "Final report country poverty assessment – St. Kitts and Nevis 2007/08: Living conditions in a Caribbean small island developing state, volume 3", *Caribbean Development Bank Country Poverty Assessment Report* in <http://www.caribank.org/uploads/publications-reports/economics-statistics/country-poverty-assessment-reports/St.+Kitts+and+Nevis+CPA+-+Vol.+3+Nevis+Final+Report.pdf>

Kairi Consultants 2009 "Final report country poverty assessment – St Vincent and the Grenadines 2007/08: Living conditions in a Caribbean small island developing state, volume 1", *Caribbean Development Bank Country Poverty Assessment Report* in <http://www.stats.gov.vc/LinkClick.aspx?fileticket=gxP733Q3EZk%3D&tabid=60>

Kairi Consultants "County poverty assessment 2007/2009 volume 1: Main report", *Caribbean Development Bank country poverty assessment report* in <http://www.caribank.org/uploads/2012/12/Anguilla-CPA-Main-Report-Final-Submitted.pdf>

Kairi Consultants "Final report – country poverty assessment: Grenada, Carriacou and Petit Martinique. volume 1: Main report 2007/2008", *Caribbean Development Bank country poverty assessment report* in <http://www.gov.gd/egov/docs/reports/Grenada_CPA_Vol_1_Main_Report_Submitted.pdf>

Kairi Consultants 2007 "Trade adjustment and poverty in Saint Lucia 2005/06, volume 1: Main report", *Caribbean Development Bank country poverty assessment report* in <http://www.caribank.org/uploads/2012/03/SLUCPAMainReport.pdf>

Kairi Consultants 2007 "Living conditions in Antigua and Barbuda – Poverty in a services economy in transition", *Caribbean Development Bank country poverty assessment report* in <http://www.unicef.org/easterncaribbean/spmapping/Planning/national/Antigua%20and%20Barbuda/2007_AntBarbCPAMainReport.pdf>

Kairi Consultants 2006 "Draft report, The assessment of poverty in St Lucia, Volume 111: Quantitative Assessment of Poverty in St. Lucia", *Caribbean Development Bank Country poverty assessment report* in <http://archive.stlucia.gov.lc/docs/AssessmentOfPovertyInStLucia/Assessment_of_Poverty_in_St_Lucia_Volume_3_Quantitative_Assessment_of_Poverty.pdf>

Kairi Consultants 2001 "St. Kitts and Nevis poverty assessment report", *Caribbean Development Bank country poverty assessment report* in <http://www.caribank.org/uploads/2012/03/St.-Kitts-and-Nevis-CPA-Vol.-2-St.-Kitts-Final-Report.pdf>

Pan American Health Organization (PAHO) 2012 *"Health in the Americas 2012"* in <http://www.paho.org/salud-en-las-americas-2012/index.php?option=com_docman&task=doc_view&gid=114&Itemid=>

Planning Institute of Jamaica 2012 *Survey of Living Conditions* (Kingston: Planning Institute of Jamaica).

Pelling, Mark and I. Uitto, Juha 2001 "Small island developing states: natural disaster vulnerability and global change", *Global environmental change part B: Environmental hazards Vol. 3* No. 2: 49–62.

Rainwater, Lee 1970 "Neutralizing the disinherited: Some psychological aspects of understanding the poor" in Allen, V. L. (ed.) *Psychological factors in poverty*, 9-28 (Chicago: Markham).

Ryan, W. 1976 *Blaming the victim* (New York: Vintage Books).

Sen, Amartya 1999 *Development as freedom* (Oxford: Oxford University Press).

Shaw, Wendy 1996 *The geography of United States poverty* (New York: Garland Publishing).

Sir Arthur Lewis Institute of Social and Economic Studies 2012 "Barbados country assessment of living conditions 2010 volume 1: Human development challenges in a global crisis: Addressing growth and social inclusion" *Caribbean Development Bank country poverty assessment report* in <http://www.caribank.org/upl oads/2012/12/Barbados-CALC-Volume-1-MainReport-FINAL-Dec-2012.pdf> accessed 26 May 2014.

Skirbekk, Gunnar and St. Clair, A. 2001 *A philosophical analysis of the World Bank's conception of poverty in a critical review of the World Bank report: Attacking poverty, world development report, 2000/2001,* Comparative Research Programme on Poverty.

Statistical Institute of Jamaica (STATIN) "The labour force in October 2013" News Release in <http://statinja.gov.jm/WUPS/(201404)LFSNews.pdf>

Statistical Institute of Jamaica 2004 *Jamaica labour force survey* (Kingston: The Statistical Institute of Jamaica).

UN Data "Intentional Homicide, number and rate per 100,000 population" in <http://data.un.org/Data.aspx?d=UNODC&f=tableCode%3a1>

UNDESA 2014 in <https://www.un.org/development/desa/en/> accessed 28 January 2016.

UNDP 1997 "Human development report 1997" in <http://hdr.undp.org/sites/default/fil es/reports/258/hdr_1997_en_complete_nostats.pdf>

UNDP 2014 *Haiti. A new look.* 2013 MDG Report – Executive Summary. In http://www.latinamerica.undp.org/content/dam/rblac/docs/Research%20an d%20Publications/MDG%20Reports/UNDP-RBLAC-HT-ExecSummaryMDGRe port-2014.pdf > accessed 26 May 2014.

UNDP 2013a "The rise of the South: Human progress in a diverse world", *Human development report 2013 – Explanatory note on 2013 HDR composite indices Barbados* in <http://hdr.undp.org/sites/default/files/Country-Profiles/BRB.pdf> accessed 26 May 2014.

UNDP 2013b "The rise of the South: Human progress in a diverse world" in *Human development report 2013 – Explanatory note on 2013 HDR composite indices Jamaica* in <http://hdr.undp.org/sites/default/files/Country-Profiles/JAM.pdf> accessed 26 May 2014.

UNDP 2014 "Sustaining human progress: Reducing vulnerabilities and building resilience" in *Human development report 2014* in <http://hdr.undp.org/sites/default/files/hdr14-report-en-1.pdf>

UNESCO1998 "Statement of commitment for action to eradicate poverty adopted by Administrative Committee on Coordination" in <http://www.unesco.org/most/acc4pov.htm> accessed 8 February 2016.

UNICEF 2011 *Jamaica: Multiple cluster indicator survey 2011* in <https://mics-surveys-prod.s3.amazonaws.com/MICS4/Latin%20America%20and%20Caribbean/Jamaica/2011/Final/Jamaica%202011%20MICS_English.pdf>

UNICEF Press Centre 2007 "UN General Assembly adopts powerful definition of child poverty", News Note, January 10, 2007 in <http://www.unicef.org/media/media_38003.html> accessed 4 October 2014.

UNICEF 2004 "The multiple dimensions of child poverty", Myriad Editions Limited. In <http://www.unicef.org/sowc05/english/map2.html>

UNICEF "Information by country and programme" in <http://www.unicef.org/infobycountry/>

United Nations Statistics Division 2014 "World statistics pocketbook – 2014 edition" in <http://unstats.un.org/unsd/pocketbook/WSPB2014.pdf>

United Nations Statistics Division 2014 "World Statistics Pocketbook- 2014 Edition". In <http://unstats.un.org/unsd/pocketbook/WSPB2014.pdf>

Verner, Dorte 2008 "Making poor Haitians count – Poverty in rural and urban Haiti based on the First Household Survey for Haiti", *World Bank policy research paper* 4571.

Williams, Asha, Cheston, Timothy, Coudouel, Aline and Subran, Ludovic 2013 "Tailoring social protection to small island developing states – Lessons from the Caribbean" in *Social protection & labor discussion paper, No. 1306*. In <http://www-wds.worldbank.org/external/default/WDSContentServer/WDSP/IB/2013/08/07/000356161_20130807153340/Rendered/PDF/801050NWP0P11707980OB00PUBLIC001306.pdf> accessed 26 May 2014.

Witter, Michael, Dixon Hamil, Kelly-Ann and Spencer, Nekeisha 2009 "Child poverty and disparities in Jamaica" in <http://www.unicef.org/jamaica/Child_Poverty_and_Disparity_in_Jamaica.pdf>.

World Bank 2014 *World Development Indicators*, on-line database (Washington: World Bank) in < http://data.worldbank.org/indicator/NY.GDP.MKTP.CD>

World Bank 2013a *Social Protection Discussion Paper Tailoring Social Protection to Small Island Developing States Lessons Learned from the Caribbean* in < http://documents.worldbank.org/curated/en/2013/08/18086868> accessed 28 July 2016.

World Bank 2013b *Tailoring Social Protection to Small Island Developing States Lessons Learned from the Caribbean* in <http://documents.worldbank.org/curated/en/286351468290980780/text/801050NWP0P117079800B00PUBLIC001306.txt> accessed 28 July 2016.

World Bank 2005a *Caribbean Social Protection Strategy Paper* (Washington: World Bank).

World Bank 2005b *Poverty manual* in <http://siteresources.worldbank.org/PGLP/Resources/povertymanual_ch4.pdf> accessed 28 July 2016.

World Bank 2004 *World Development Report* (Washington: World Bank).

World Health Organization 2014 "Global Health Observatory: Country statistics" in <http://www.who.int/gho/countries/en/> accessed 28 May 2014.

PART II:
YOUTH (UN)EMPLOYMENT AND SOCIAL EXCLUSION: TRENDS AND POLICY ISSUES

PART II

UNPACKING THE NEETs OF LATIN AMERICA AND THE CARIBBEAN: Methodological challenges and surprising results*

Alberto Minujín, Diego Born, María Laura Lombardía, and Enrique Delamónica

The situation, issues, expectations, and dangers faced and imagined by adolescents and youngsters (A&Y) have gained recognition and prominence among academics as well as in the public policy agenda in the last decades (Breakwell, 1982; Bridgeland et al., 2006; UNICEF, 2011). While there is recognition of their potential as drivers of social change there is also a growing concern about specific social problems particularly affecting this age group, in particular adolescent girls and young women (Chen, 2011; Cusworth et al., 2009; ILO, 2012; OECD, 2010; Perisic et al., 2012).

Thus, a category—NEETs, or not in education, employment or training—has emerged and occupied a central place in political, journalistic, and academic debates (Bynner and Parsons, 2002; Furlong, 2006, 2007; Bendit and Hahn-Bleibtreu, 2008; ; Eurofound, 2011). However, this is a complex category that hides (and misses) various phenomena—some more acute than other ones. For instance, a youngster who works in extremely unsafe conditions, at an informal job, and is exploited by being paid below the minimum wage (or the level required to subsist) would not be considered a NEET—whether the youngster is attending school or not. Moreover, the unemployed are not counted in the NEET category either, given

---

* This chapter is based on a study that some of the authors carried out for the Regional Office of UNICEF for Latin America and the Caribbean, *Análisis cuantitativo de la situación de los adolescentes y los jóvenes en América Latina y el Caribe en base a encuestas recientes*. We want to thank Luz Angela Melo, Vicente Teran, Francisco Benavides, Joaquin Gonzalez, and all the regional advisors for their comments and collaborations.

the standard definition, which causes confusion among the lay audience.[1]

In addition, almost four out of five NEETs are females. Their background is usually rural, from the lowest quintiles of wealth distribution, and daughters of parents with little formal education. Most of their time is used caring for children (theirs or those of others). Gender stereotypes confuse the picture. Thus, an adolescent girl who instead of attending school spends 10 to 12 hours a day caring for a child would be considered a NEET while an adolescent boy who is not attending school but works at an informal job for 4 to 6 hours a day would be considered gainfully employed and thus not a NEET.

The main purpose of this chapter, after reviewing recent trends, achievements, and challenges in education and youth employment, attempts to unpack the NEET category, in particular among adolescents. This is done, on the one hand, by exploring the quantitative evidence on NEETs for 18 Latin American and Caribbean countries and, on the other hand, by introducing a new measurement of adolescent and youth vulnerability. We call this measurement VEL (Vulnerability in Education and Labor) as it incorporates the highest level of formal education achieved and the type of labor market engagement (unemployed, informally employed, and formally employed) of adolescents and youngsters. Thus, this measure goes beyond a simple (dichotomous) classification based on whether or not A&Y participate in school and the labor market, presenting a more nuanced and complete depiction of the problems faced by A&Y. The percentage of A&Y with high vulnerability in education and labor is twice as high (almost 30%) than the proportion of NEETs (almost 15%[2]). We also describe subregional and country-by-country differences.

Analytical framework and data sources

There is consensus about the importance of identifying adolescence as an important transitional period in the lifecycle. It is a period of

---

[1] Although in this case employed and unemployed have been distinguished, in most analyses of this kind adolescents and youngsters are classified as active or inactive, not separating among the former whether they are working or unemployed.

[2] This estimate is slightly lower than the one reported by Espejo and Espindola (2015). Their estimate includes an older age group (up until 29 years of age) and is for a more recent year (2012).

physical and emotional development (UNICEF, 2002). However, its limits are imprecise. There is no exact age or moment when a child becomes an adolescent or an adolescent becomes a youngster. This is due to the social constructions (some translated into legislation) framing the various aspects of the life and experience of A&Y. These various aspects or dimensions are related to, for instance, the minimum age for voting, driving, participating in the military, consuming alcohol, getting married, working, facing criminal charges, or signing contracts. Moreover, even within the same country, it is often the case that the minimum age is different for these activities and there is no standard rule to be applied internationally (UNICEF, 2011).

In this chapter, while recognizing the limits imposed by these considerations, the A&Y population will be categorized in three distinct, age-based groups. This approach enables the construction of data, facilitates their analysis, allows inter-country comparisons, and highlights the situation of different age groups within the A&Y.

According to the United Nations, the period between ages 15 and 24 is considered "youth." Consequently, this category includes the adolescent period, which ranges between 10 and 19 years of age (UNICEF, 2011). For the descriptive and analytical purposes of this chapter, A&Y will be divided in three groups covering five years each: the early part of adolescence (between ages 10 and 14), the latter part of adolescence (between 15 and 19 years old), and youth (between 20 and 24 years of age).

Using these definitions, there are about 163 million A&Y (between 10 and 24 years old) in Latin America. This group constitutes 27.5% of the total population of the region. About two-thirds of them (close to 115 million) are adolescents between 10 and 18 years old.

The age groups belong also to different stages of the lifecycle. According to the Convention of the Rights of the Child (and as a result of its translation to national statues under most national legislation in Latin America and the Caribbean, employment of children in the early part of adolescence is outlawed.[3] For the latter part of adolescence the national legislation is more diverse. Employment of adolescent in hazardous activities is mostly deemed illegal. Even when working is not outlawed, it should

---

3   Thus, the 10–14 years age group is not part of the analysis of the labor market, NEETs, and VEL.

contribute to the growth and development of the child and not interfere with education (and also leisure) time and activities. The age of 18 is usually the age of maturity, consequently no legislation forbids or restricts employment for youth nor are they covered by even the most expansive legislation on the gratuity and mandatory years of schooling (which in the best cases covers up to the end of secondary school, i.e., until children are 17 or 18 years old).

Figure 1 captures schematically this situation. The horizontal axis measures time (ages between 10 and 24), while the vertical axis measures the distribution of A&Y by type of activity (only in school, only working, both, or NEETs). While the vast majority of children aged 10–14 years are in school (as they should), a few them are also or only working. A few of them are excluded both of school and the labor market. This groups start to increase as children age (of course, it need not be the same children, as they can cross in and out from one category to another one and back). Also, as they grow older, the likelihood of exiting the school system increases and the insertion in the labor market (attending school or not) increases. Both of these processes accelerate in the late adolescence. For youngsters (ages 20–24) the opportunities to attend school (i.e., a university, the superior or third level of formal education) are drastically reduced and the majority of them are inserted in the labor market. Gender has a fundamental imprint in this process. While the majority of A&Y who participate in the labor market are males, the vast majority of NEETs are female (Figure 2), as we describe empirically later in the chapter (showing that part of this imbalance is due to categories and classifications that may need revision).

Figure 1: Age distribution of the education–labor relationship through the life cycle

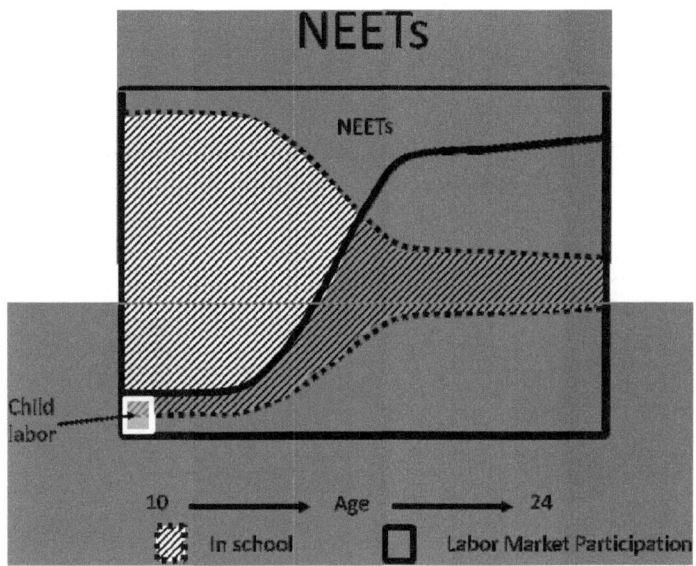

While these figures show the all-important employment and education aspects of A&Y (and the gender inequities therein), it must also be remembered that both adolescence and youth are categories that are not only (or mainly) defined by age but by fluid and changing social relationships. As it was mentioned earlier, as most A&Y transit from school to work and other go in and out of them (in an entwining of individual and collective stories and trajectories), other aspects related to their identity and their social standing are also being shaped, transformed and determined during these years (Lister, 2006; Llobet and Minujin, 2011). One of these is the autonomy/dependence from their parental household[4] in terms of income/resources as well as emotionally. Another important dimension is sexuality and gender relations. The latter, as already mentioned earlier, are fundamental in the unpacking and description of the NEETs in Latin America. Besides these personal and family-based dimensions, there are wider

---

4   As we explore empirically, education and employment achievement (or not, the NEETs) of A&Y, the socioeconomic position of the parents is shown to be a major determinant of inclusion/exclusion.

social interactions with peers and the rest of society, including cultural and political participation. All of these aspects affect the success, and even the perceived definition of success, in the life of these A&Y as well as the policies aimed and helping, supporting, empowering, and emancipating them (Montes and Sendón, 2006; Bustelo, 2007).

Figure 2: Gender, labor markets, and NEETs in Latin America and the Caribbean

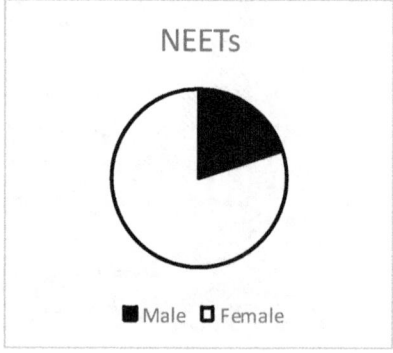

Source: Multiple Indicators Cluster Survey (MICS-4) and Demographic Health Survey (DHS), accessed at http://mics.unicef.org/

For this study we used a standardized database with national household survey (HSS) from most of the Latin American countries. These surveys are carried out by the respective national statistical offices to regularly monitor the standard of living of the population with a particular emphasis on labor market conditions. We used the homogenous microdatasets prepared by SITEAL/UNESCO (Sistema de Información de Tendencias Educativas en América Latina/United Nations Educational, Scientific and Cultural Organization). The information contained in this dataset is crucial for the analysis of education and labor in the 18 countries under consideration.

School attendance and completion

In this section, the outcomes in terms of schooling for A&Y are described. The data cover 18 countries with comparable information. These 18 countries represent 150 (out of the 163) million A&Y in the region.[5]

Medium-term trends

Figure 3 shows the progress in terms of literacy rates and secondary school completion according to an individual's age for the region as whole.[6] These trends portray a clear historical process of expansion of the school system. Secondly, this process has been more inclusive of women than men.

Illiteracy rates have declined *pari passu* with the expansion and completion of schooling. Thus, while one-third of people in their 80s are illiterate, this rate is less than 5% for those in their 20s and less than 2% for teenagers. Concomitantly, only about 20% of the persons above 60 years old have completed secondary education in contrast with people in their 20s, among whom 55% completed their secondary studies.

---

5   The countries included in this study are: Argentina (urban), 2010; Bolivia, 2007; Brazil, 2009; Chile, 2009; Colombia, 2010; Costa Rica, 2009; Dominican Republic, 2009; Ecuador, 2009; El Salvador, 2009; Guatemala, 2010; Honduras, 2009; Mexico, 2008; Nicaragua, 2005; Panama, 2009; Paraguay, 2009; Peru, 2009; Uruguay, 2009; and Venezuela, 2009.

6   Assuming that a person aged between 17 and 20 years should have finished secondary school, whoever was 50 years old in 2010 gives information about secondary school completion about 30 years ago, that is, approximately in 1980.

Figure 3: Illiteracy and secondary school completion by age and gender HHS, circa 2009

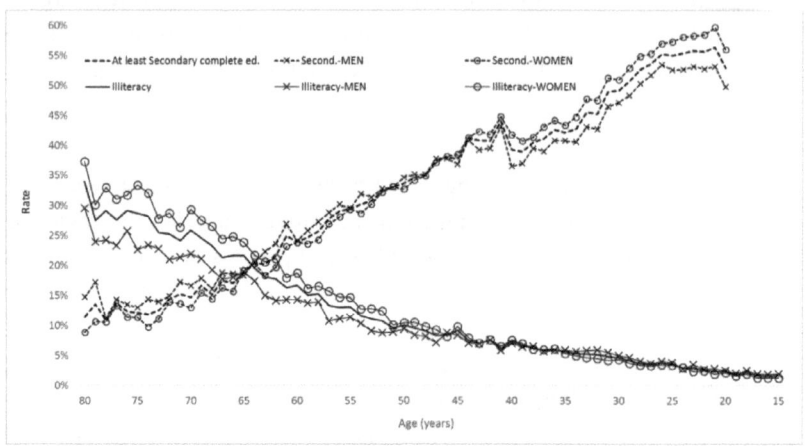

Source: Own estimates based on household surveys

Current situation: School attendance

One out of six (16.2%) A&Y between the ages of 10 and 19 who have not completed their middle school are not currently attending any type of formal schooling.[7] As expected the situation is worse among 15–19-year-old adolescents than among 10–14-year- old ones. As shown in Figure 4 and male A&Y in rural areas, those coming from poorer families, and those whose parents have little or no formal education are the most affected.

---

7   Espejo and Espindola (2015) estimate secondary school dropout at 15.5%.

Figure 4: Out-of-school adolescents by age, sex, parents' education, and household income. countries with HHS, circa 2009

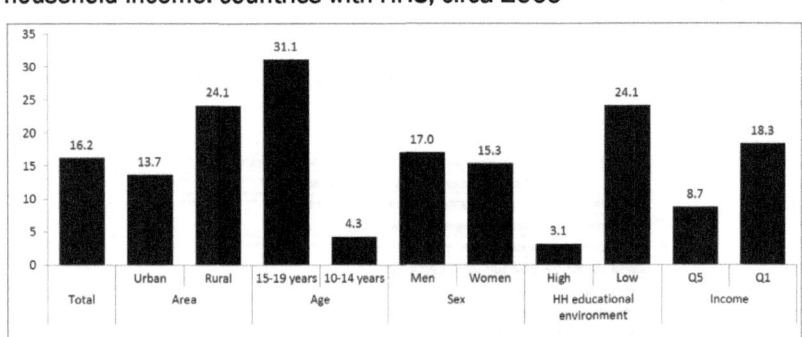

Source: Own estimates based on household surveys

Slightly more than 20% of rural A&Y do not attend school. In contrast, less than 15% of urban A&Y fail to attend school. The gender differences are small, with a slight disadvantage against boys (who do not attend school at a rate of 17% compared to 15.3% for girls[8]).

A major determinant of school attendance seems to be the parents' education. A&Y whose parents have little or no formal education are eight times more likely to fail to go to school than children whose parents have finished secondary school. There are also income differentials but not as high as those exhibited by parents' level of education.

School attendance by country can be observed in Figure 5. In Honduras, Nicaragua, Guatemala, Mexico, and El Salvador, more than 20% of the A&Y are not attending school. At the other end of the spectrum, less

---

[8] All differences among countries or groups within countries highlighted in the text are statistically significant (confidence intervals are not presented throughout the chapter in order to facilitate reading). Nevertheless, it is important to remember that as household surveys have an average of 400,000 observations, confidence intervals around national estimates are very narrow (in general, a small fraction of 1%). When large sub-national groups, as the ones presented in this chapter (e.g., urban/rural, male/female, etc.), are used the confidence intervals are still less than a percentage point above and below the point estimate. If simultaneous stratification were used (e.g., geographic location *and* level of education), the confidence intervals would be higher. However, simultaneous stratifications are not analyzed in this chapter.

than 13% of A&Y are not attending school in Chile, Peru, Dominican Republic, Brazil, Argentina, Bolivia, and Venezuela.

Figure 5: Out-of-school adolescents and repetition; countries with HHS, circa 2009

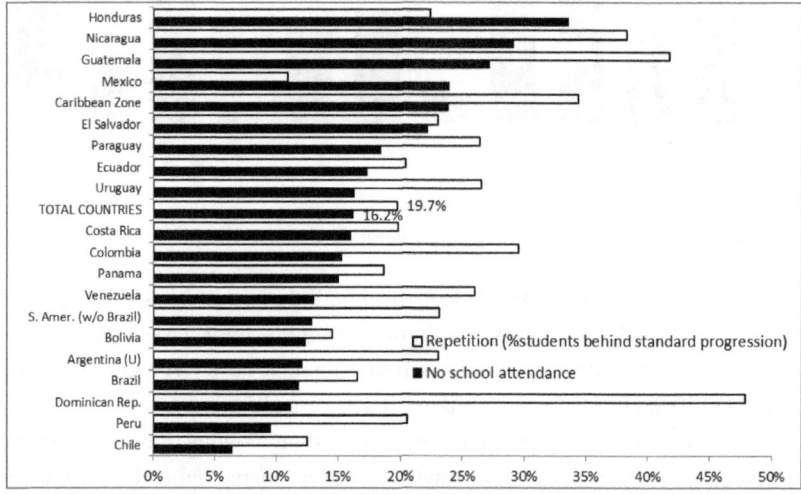

Source: Own estimates based on household surveys

School achievement among 20—24-year-old youngsters

In all countries in the region, by age 20 all students should have finished their secondary education. However, region-wide, almost half of youngsters between ages 20 and 24 have not completed their middle schooling[9] and more than 70% of them never started their post-secondary education (Figure 6). In other words, among those who completed middle (secondary) school and could have continued on to a university or college, half dropped out of the formal school system.

While girls are a little better off (almost 48% of boys fail to finish middle school compared to 42% of girls), there are still too many of them out of school. The differential in terms of location is more pronounced. Youngsters in rural areas complete their middle (secondary) school at half the rate of urban youngsters.

---

9   Espejo and Espindola (2015) report similar estimates.

Income differentials are even starker. Among youngsters from the poorest quintile, not completing middle (secondary) school reaches a rate of 70%, but it is less than 20% for youngsters in the richest quintile. This 50-percentage-point gap results in the poorest youngsters being three and half times more likely not to finish middle school than the richest youngsters.

The situation is worse for youngsters whose parents have little or no formal education. Barely more than 1 in 10 of them finishes middle (secondary) school. Youngsters whose parents completed secondary education or higher finish middle school at a rate of almost 95%. Moreover, less than 2% of youngsters whose parents have little or no formal education move on to attend post-secondary schooling compared to 80% of youngsters whose parents completed secondary education or higher.[10]

---

[10] In all Central American countries (except in Panama) more than half of youngsters 20–24 years old have not completed their middle (secondary) schooling. In Nicaragua and Honduras this is the case for 70% of youngsters while in Guatemala for the figure is 80%. Clearly, given these rates, more than 80% of youngsters have never attended a college or university. At the other extreme, Chile and Peru can be found with "only" 20% and 30% of youngsters who have not completed their middle (secondary) schooling. However, even in these "better off" countries, more than 50% of youngsters have never attended a university or college.

Figure 6: Youngsters (20-24 years old) who have not finished secondary schooling and who have never enrolled in tertiary education by geographic location, sex, parents' education, and household income. countries with HHS, circa 2009

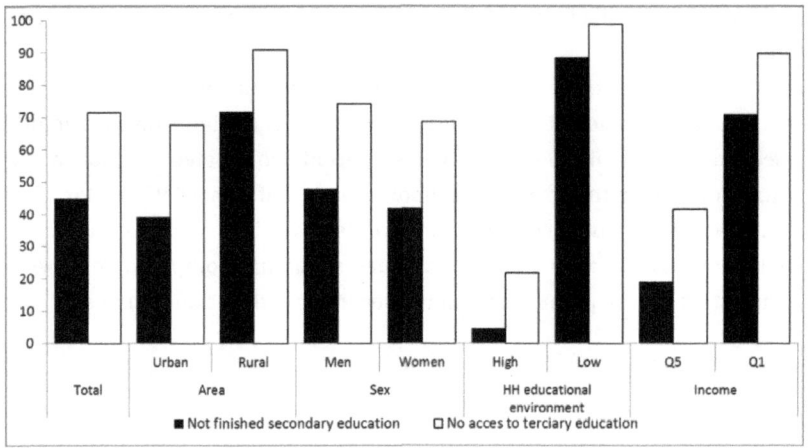

Source: Own estimates based on household surveys

While the gender differences in school attention and completion (for the different age segments of the A&Y group) is minimal, it is clear that there are shortcomings in rural areas, which are related to low amount of investment in education (compounded by its uneven and unfair geographic distribution) and availability of schools. A high correlation would be expected between low household income and low level of education among the adults in the household (which could be evidenced by the similar levels of school attendance and achievement of A&Y from households in the bottom quintile and in households where the parents have not completed primary education). Both low parental levels of education and low income are concentrated in rural areas. All of this implies the poorest, rural A&Y have few opportunities for schooling. Thus, an integrated set of policies comprising of investment in schools (and their proper staffing), scholarships, and other incentives are needed. In addition, policies geared toward bridging the cultural and digital divides, allowing (forbidding exclusion of) adolescents who are pregnant or mothers from attending school, incorporating gender considerations school curricula, providing nontraditional schooling options of high quality, promoting inclusion of indigenous and afro-descendant adolescents, and aligning the type and content of education with employment skills will also contribute to enhance education outcomes, reduce drop outs, and bring back out-of-school children into the education system (Guerrero et al., 2006; Lopez, 2011; Aikman and Rao, 2012; Sunkel and Trucco 2012; IIPE-UNESCO, 2012; Rico and Trucco, 2014; ECLAC, OIJ and IMJUVE, 2014).

Labor market

Youngsters and adults[11]

Among the 18 countries for which comparable data are available, the participation rate[12] of A&Y is 54%.[13] This is considerably lower than among adults (25–60 years old) who participate at a rate of 78%. In addition, the probabilities of finding a job are lower for A&Y and, if they do find employment, it is under worse conditions than among adults.

Consequently, unemployment rate[14] among A&Y almost triples the rate of adults (14.9% and 5.2%, respectively). Among the employed, informality[15] reaches 61.3% among A&Y and 44.2% among adults (Figure 7).

The highest participation rate for A&Y is found in Brazil (62.7%), where, partly as a consequence of this, the gap in participation rates between A&Y and adults is the smallest. Brazil also exhibits the highest unemployment rate for A&Y in the region. Mexico enjoys the lowest unemployment among its A&Y population. However, these A&Y have the highest rate of informality in the region.

---

11 As mentioned earlier, children under 15 years of age are not supposed to be working. Consequently, they are not included in the labor market analysis.
12 The proportion of persons between 15 and 24 years of age participating in the labor market whether employed, underemployed, or unemployed (i.e., actively looking for a job).
13 For the slightly larger and older group analyzed by Espejo and Espindola (2015), they report basically the same figure (50%).
14 The proportion of persons between 15 and 24 years of age participating in the labor market who are actively looking for a job.
15 The proportion of persons between 15 and 24 years of age employed without a contract, workers in a family business without a fixed wage, and other similar categories of workers. It also includes the self-employed who have not completed their secondary education. For the cases in which there was no information about the type (or lack of) contract, those workers who had not finished their secondary school studies were considered informal workers. All of this clearly points to an incomplete agenda on labor rights and decent work in the region.

Figure 7: Labor market participation rate, unemployment rate, and participation in informal labor rate; adult and youngsters differences; countries with HHS, circa 2009

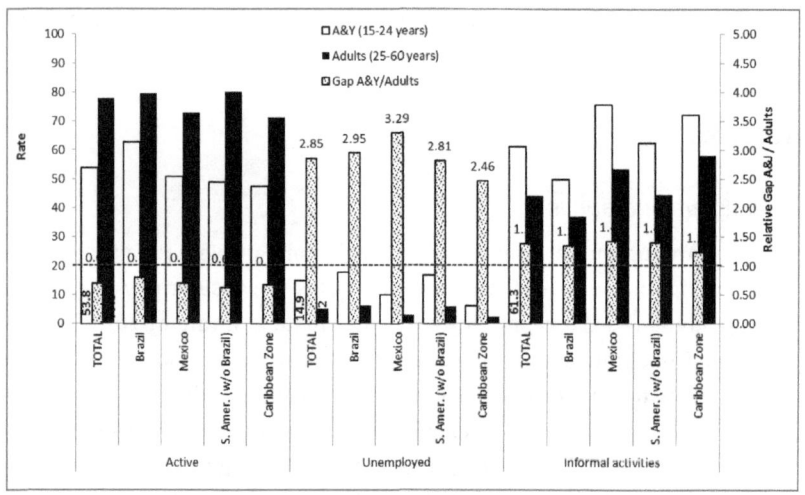

Source: Own estimates based on household surveys

Differences among adolescents and youngsters

The characteristics of the labor market participation for each country are presented in Figure 8. The heterogeneity is evident. Paraguay, Peru and Brazil have the highest participation rates (above 60%), while Chile and Dominican Republic present the lowest levels, closely followed by Argentina and Venezuela.

The unemployment rate among A&Y is highest in Chile and Colombia (exceeding 25%). In some Central American countries, such as Nicaragua and Guatemala, it is less than 5%.

Informality among A&Y is highest in Guatemala (87%) and Paraguay (85%). Nevertheless, there many countries where informality surpasses 70% (Ecuador, Honduras, El Salvador, Mexico, Dominican Republic, and Bolivia).

In Guatemala, Honduras, and El Salvador, low unemployment rates are combined with high informality. This means that while A&Y can easily find a job, it is almost impossible for them to obtain formal employment. The situation is reversed in Chile, Costa Rica, and Uruguay where informality is lower but unemployment is higher.

Figure 8: Employment conditions of Y&A; countries with HHS, circa 2009

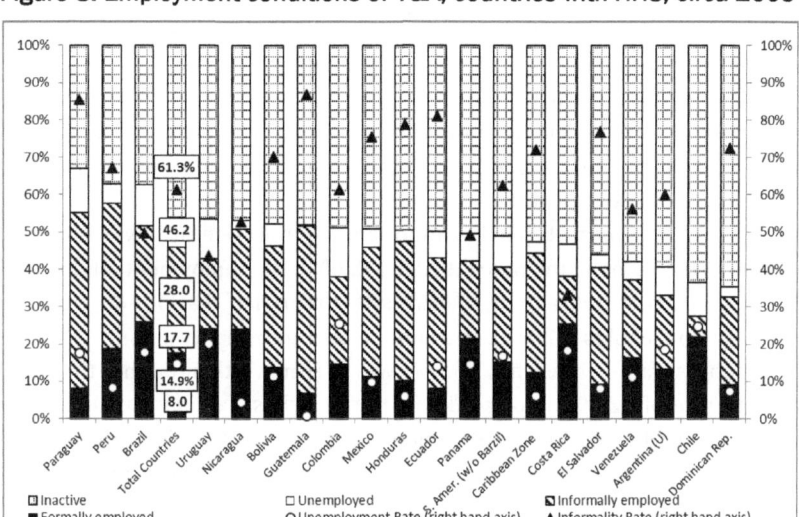

Source: Own estimates based on household surveys

The socioeconomic characteristics of A&Y labor market participation are summarized in Figure 9. It can be observed that rural A&Y usually have higher participation rates than urban A&Y. Nevertheless, this situation is not the same in every country. For instance, in Bolivia, the participation rate of rural A&Y is 72% higher than among urban A&Y, but in Chile urban A&Y participate in the labor market at a higher rate than rural A&Y. While unemployment is higher among urban A&Y (17%) than among rural ones (7%), informality is worse among rural A&Y.

The participation rate of adolescents between 15 and 19 years old (39.4%) is about half of that among youngsters between the ages of 20 and 24 years (69.9%). However, among the younger group, unemployment and informality are higher. The unemployment rate for the younger group is about 30% higher. In Brazil and Mexico, it is 50% higher. Similarly, the rate of informality among 15–19-year-old adolescents is almost 60% higher than among 20–24-year-old youngsters.

The participation rate of female A&Y is significantly lower than for male A&Y. However, female A&Y suffer higher unemployment than male ones. For instance in Honduras and Nicaragua, it is double than of male A&Y.

A&Y whose parents have little or no formal education participate at higher rates in the labor market than those whose parents completed secondary or higher levels of education. Unemployment is higher among A&Y whose parents completed secondary or higher levels of education, with wide variations across countries. Among those A&Y whose parents have little or no formal education, informal employment reaches 60%, whereas it is 40% among A&Y whose parents completed secondary or higher levels of education. Chile, Costa Rica, and Panama show the highest disparity in these indicators.

Labor market participation among the richest A&Y is higher (54.4%) than among the poorest A&Y (45.6%). Unemployment among A&Y from the richest households (9.6%) is less than half that of A&Y from the poorest households (22.3%). In a similar vein, informality among A&Y from the poorest families reaches 89.5%, which is more than double the informality rate of 42.8% among A&Y from the richest families. In Dominican Republic, Chile, and Venezuela, unemployment for A&Y from the poorest quintiles is four times higher than for A&Y from the richest quintile. Uruguay, Costa Rica, and Panama exhibit four-fold differences in terms of informality between the poorest and richest A&Y.

To summarize, in spite of the variety of experiences and situations across countries in terms of labor market participation rates, unemployment, and informality, a few clear patterns emerge. A&Y are less active in the labor market than adults. This is expected as some of these A&Y are too young to be lawfully employed in many of these countries.[16] However, when they are employed they are usually hired informally. In addition, female A&Y have lower participation rates than male ones. A&Y from relatively richer households or with better-educated parents enjoy better working conditions.

All of this speaks of the need for, on the one hand, macroeconomic policies to promote full employment and, on the other hand, stronger regulation of labor markets to eliminate informality. These could be coupled with special training programs, efforts to match training with employment prospects (especially in terms of rural contexts and rural to urban migration), establishing internship programs, special programs to promote "first job" without undermining labor rights of contributions to social security (e.g., a higher share of government contributions in the earlier years of

---

16 Or can only be hired for some jobs under special circumstances depending on their age. For instance, at no age can they engage in hazardous jobs or activities that prevent them from attending school. The ages at which they can work in non-hazardous jobs that allow them to study, as was mentioned above, varies from country to country.

employment), and recognizing (in particular for social security and pension purposes) nonpaid housekeeping work and in the care economy (Finnegan, 2006; Jacinto, 2008; Jacinto and Zangani, 2009; ILO, 2013; Soto et al., 2015).

Figure 9: Labor market participation rate, unemployment rate, and participation in informal labor rate by geographic location, age, sex, secondary school completion, parents' education, and household income; countries with HHS, circa 2009

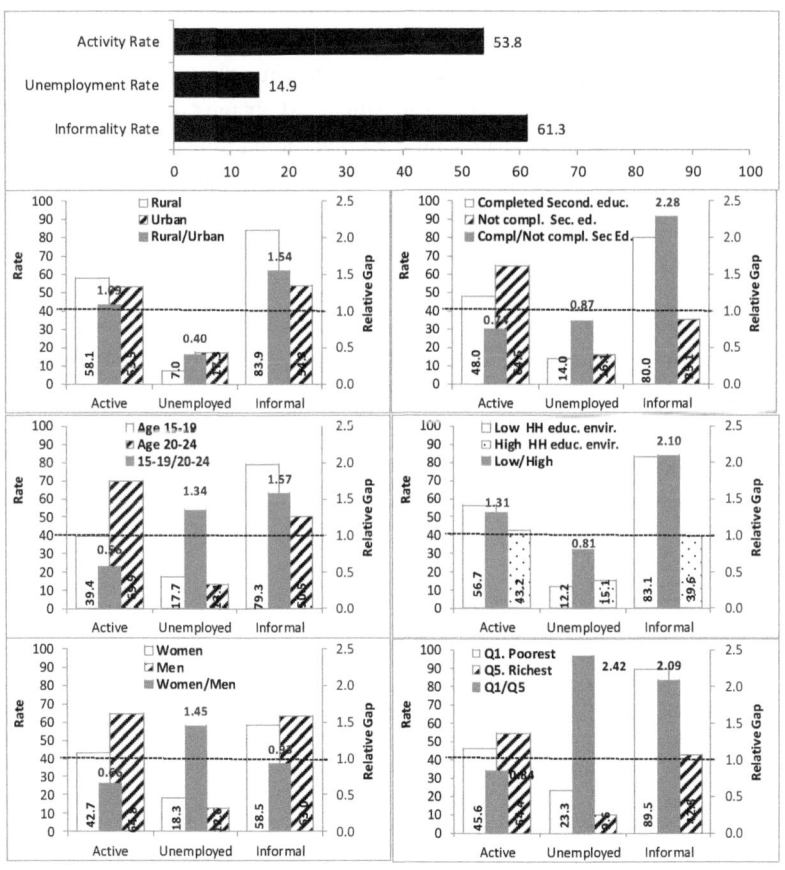

Source: Own estimates based on household surveys

Education and employment

NEETs

> I must be with Agustin [her son] and take care of my mother. I can't leave them alone.
>
> –Daniela P. (21), pregnant at the age of 19.[17]

Most NEETs are female.[18] Contrary to the stereotypical image portrayed by the media (and some academics) of a bunch of drunk or drugged youngsters wasting life away or preparing for their next crime, 8 out of 10 NEETs are adolescent girls or young women doing household chores and taking care of children. This is partly the result of the sexual division of labor, whereas constrains women to the reproductive and care activities while men are the only ones supposed to earn income by joining the labor market.[19]

However, domestic work is hidden under the NEET category. A young woman who stays at home to take care of children (either her own or younger siblings or cousins) so that her husband or brothers can go to work (even if at informal jobs) is considered "doing nothing." Thus, she is classified as a NEET. Thus, it is important to distinguish young women who make a conscious choice to take time off to take care of their babies, after completing their formal studies, from adolescent girls who cannot afford to

---

17 From the Chilean newspaper *El Mercurio*, Friday, October 3, 2014
18 According to Espejo and Espindola (2015), they represent 73.5% of all NEETs (between 15 and 29 years of age) in the region.
19 About 40% of male NEETs live in households where at least one member is under 10 years old. This proportion is the same for the other categories. However, among female NEETs, this proportion is 70%. This proportion is not only higher than for male NEETs but also for women in the other categories (about 50%). Further supporting the point made earlier regarding the male-dominated sexual division of labor, it is useful to note that while almost 9% of male A&Y are considered "head of household," only less than 4% female A&Y are classified as head of household. In contrast, almost 15% of women are classified as spouse, while less than 1% of males are considered as spouse. Furthermore, half of the women considered spouse are neither working nor studying.

continue and finish their studies or have to drop out of them due to early, unplanned, or undesired pregnancies (or other reasons). Although, obviously, aspects of a male-dominated society are present in both scenarios, the situations (and the degrees of freedom and empowerment) of women are starkly different in each case. In Guatemala, Honduras, and Nicaragua, the percentage of female A&Y who are classified as NEETs exceeds 35%, while in Bolivia, Peru, and Uruguay it is about 15%. Moreover, the highest relative gap between female and male NEETs occurs in Guatemala (almost 13 female NEETs per male one), Mexico (7.5 female NEETs per male one), and Paraguay (more than 6 female NEETs per male one). In addition, while in Guatemala, more than 90% of NEETs are female, in Chile and Dominican Republic female A&Y represent about two-thirds of all NEETs.

The distribution of A&Y according to their schooling and labor situation (and their combinations) in the 18 countries with comparable information is presented in Figure 10. Region-wide, almost one-third (31%) of the A&Y are dedicated only to their studies. While less than 3 % of A&Y are studying and looking for work, almost 15% are simultaneously working and attending school.[20] These three groups account for almost half of A&Y. Another third (32.8%) is only working. While almost 6% is not working but looking for employment, there are 15% of A&Y who are not in education, neither employed nor in training—the NEETs.[21]

In Mexico, the NEETs account for 18% of all A&Y and in the Caribbean countries for which there is information, they represent slightly more than 20% of A&Y. As in Spanish-speaking South America, the proportion of A&Y who are only studying is above the regional average the "space" for NEETs is relatively small. Similarly, in Brazil, where more A&Y either just work or both study and work, there is also "less room" for NEETs than in Mexico or the Caribbean.

In Chile, Dominican Republic, Argentina, Venezuela, and Costa Rica, about 40% of A&Y only study and are not participating in the labor market. Nevertheless, the percentage of NEETs in the A&Y population

---

20 As we are highlighting the situation of adolescents, our estimates for those who are only studying or studying and working are slightly higher than the ones by Espejo and Espindola (2015) whose sample includes youngsters up to age 29.

21 Various ILO reports make reference to the growing concern about NEETs. More recently, the category has been expanded to include those looking for a job (NLEETs).

ranges from 19% (Dominican Republic), above the regional average, to 13.7% (Costa Rica), below the regional average.

The highest incidence of NEETs is found in Honduras, Nicaragua, Guatemala, and El Salvador. In all of these countries NEETs represent more than 22% of all A&Y. The lowest incidence occur in Ecuador, Uruguay, Paraguay, Peru, and Bolivia.

Figure 10. Youngsters, employment situation, and schooling; countries with HHS, circa 2009

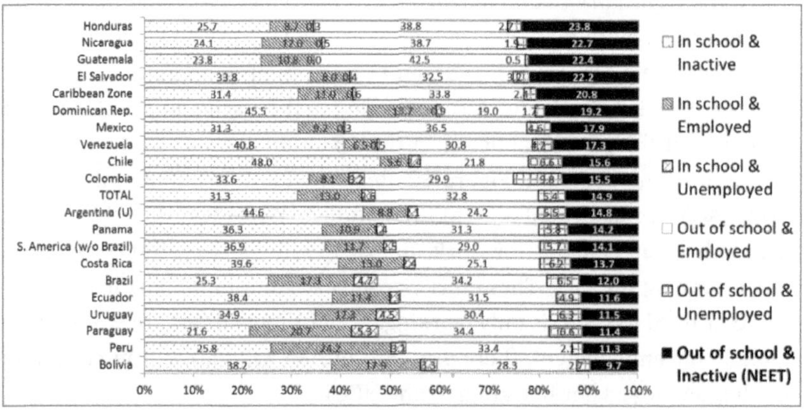

[Figure showing horizontal stacked bar chart with the following categories: In school & Inactive, In school & Employed, In school & Unemployed, Out of school & Employed, Out of school & Unemployed, Out of school & Inactive (NEET). Countries listed: Honduras, Nicaragua, Guatemala, El Salvador, Caribbean Zone, Dominican Rep., Mexico, Venezuela, Chile, Colombia, TOTAL, Argentina (U), Panama, S. America (w/o Brazil), Costa Rica, Brazil, Ecuador, Uruguay, Paraguay, Peru, Bolivia.]

Source: Own estimates based on household surveys

As mentioned in the previous section, school attendance is lower (while labor market participation is higher) in rural than in urban areas. In Figure 11, it can be observed that only a bit more than 20% of rural A&Y use their time only to study, compared to a third of A&Y in urban areas.

As expected, there are age differences with the A&Y category. Among adolescents 15–19 years old, those who are only attending school reaches almost 50%, while just over 12% of the 20–24-year-olds only study. In almost a mirror image, the labor market participation rate for the first group is 18% and almost 50% in the second group. In terms of NEETs, they represent 12% of the first group and 18% of the second one.

Among the A&Y who are not attending school, more than 40% are employed. However, less than one in four adolescent girl or young woman who is not attending school is employed. Female NEETs constitute almost a quarter of all female A&Y (23.6%). This value is four times the rate of male NEETs (6.2%): In Figure 12, it can be seen that, with different intensity, this situation is repeated among all the countries. The incidence of NEETs among adolescent girls and young women is even higher in rural areas, among the poorest families, and for those whose parents have little or no formal education.

A&Y from households where the parents have little or no formal education attend school at a rate that is half of those whose parents have completed secondary or higher education. Their participation rate in the labor market is also lower, as it was discussed in the previous section. The proportion of NEETs among A&Y whose parents have little or no formal education is 20%—two and a half times higher than among A&Y whose parents have completed secondary education or higher (8%). In Uruguay and Costa Rica, the proportion of NEETs in the first group is five times higher than in the second one. Venezuela and Peru are the countries where this relative gap is the lowest.

As with parents' education, A&Y from household with higher income also attend school and participate in the labor market at higher rates than A&Y from poorer families. Partly as a result of this, almost one in four (23%) A&Y from the lowest quintile is classified as NEET. This rate is more than triple the one for A&Y from the richest quintile (7%). In Brazil and Mexico, the rate of NEETs among the poorest A&Y quadruples the one for the richest A&Y.

Figure 11: Youngsters' labor situation and schooling, by geographic location, age, sex, secondary school completion, parents' education, and household income; countries with HHS, circa 2009

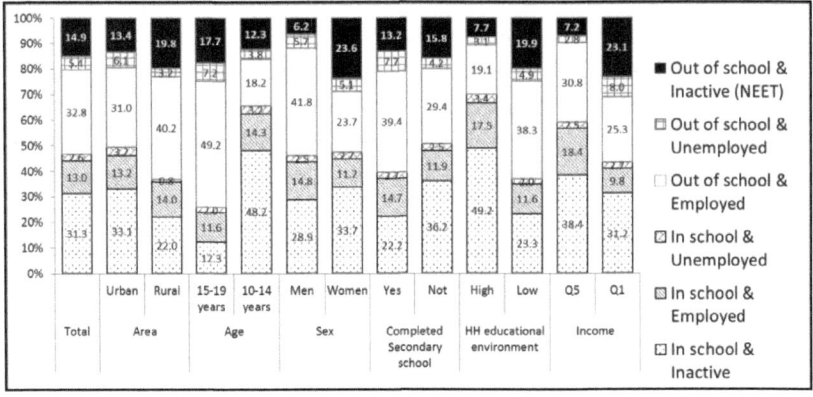

Source: Own estimates based on household surveys

Figure 12: NEETs by sex and by country; 18 countries with HHS, circa 2009

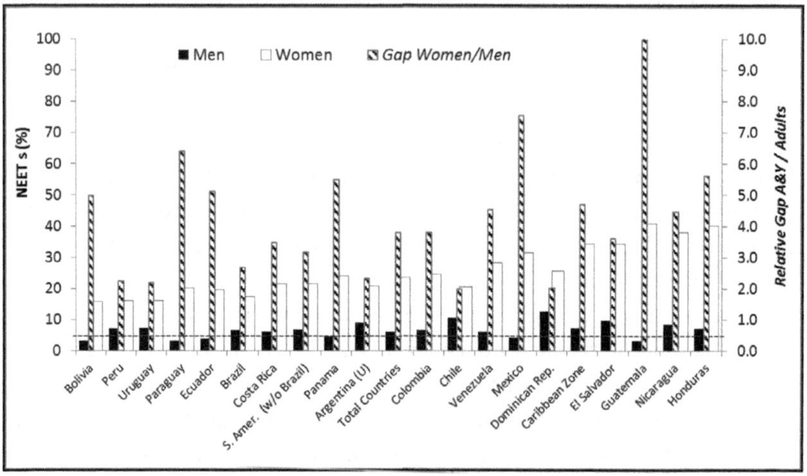

Source: Own estimates based on household surveys

Vulnerability in Education and Labor

Given the problems highlighted earlier, it seems useful to unpack the NEETs. This would allow to avoid the gender bias in the construction and measurement of this category. In addition, it important to capture the weak social inclusion of A&Y who are not only out of school but also unemployed or in very precarious and informal employment. Thus, a measure combining both educational as well as labor vulnerabilities is presented. This is accomplished by introducing two additional variables: secondary school completion and formal employment.

A three-way classification is proposed. Combining school attendance (and completion) and type of employment (unemployed, informal employment, and formal employment), A&Y can be categorized as suffering high or medium vulnerability in education and labor, or not suffering vulnerability.

Concretely, we would speak of high vulnerability in education and labor (high VEL) when describing A&Y who satisfy the following conditions:

- They are not attending school
- They have not completed secondary education

- They are outside the labor market
- They are in the labor market but they are unemployed or they have an informal job

Conversely, A&Y without vulnerability in education and labor (no or low VEL) are those who satisfy the following conditions:

- They are attending school and they do not participate in the labor market (this labor market condition applies to A&Y under age 19)
- They are attending post-secondary school (independently of their employment situation)
- They have finished secondary school and they are not attending post-secondary school but they are formally employed
- They are formally employed and attending school

The A&Y who cannot be classified as either suffering high vulnerability in education and labor (because they do not satisfy all four conditions simultaneously) or who are not considered without vulnerability, belong to the medium vulnerability in education and labor (medium VEL) category.[22]

Figure 13 depicts the different possible combinations of school attendance/completion and type of employment with the ensuing classification as high, medium, or no vulnerability in education and employment. The proportion of A&Y region-wide in each subgroup is also included, which shows that roughly half of A&Y in Latin America and the Caribbean do not suffer from vulnerability in education and employment, while about a quarter of them suffer from medium VEL and another quarter suffer from high VEL.

---

22 This proposed classification, of course, could be adjusted, adapted, and modified. For instance, the proportion of overage students (a leading indicator of dropping out) could be incorporated. The presence and number of children in the household could also be used to obtain a better idea of the care activities of adolescent girls and young women.

Figure 13: VEL among A&Y; classification framework and basic results; countries with HHS, circa 2009

		15 - 19 years Not completed Secondary School		20 - 24 years Not completed Secondary School		15 - 24 years Completed Secondary School		TOTAL
Vulnerability in education and labor (VEL)	**Low**	Student & inactive	22,3%			Student & inactive	7,8%	46,6%
		Student & formally employed	0,7%	Student & formally employed	0,4%	Student & formally employed	3,1%	
			23,0%		0,4%	Student & informally employed	2,1%	
						Student & unemployed	0,9%	23,2%
						Not a student & formally employed	9,3%	

Medium	Student & informally employed	5,7%		Student & inactive	1,1%		
	Student & unemployed	1,4%	**8,1%**	Student & informally employed	0,9%		Not a student & informally employed	4,6%
	Not a student nor formally employed	1,0%		Student & unemployed	0,3%	**5,5%**	Not a student & unemployed	2,7%	**12,0%**
	Not student & informal employed	6,2%		Not a student & formally employed	3,3%		Not a student & inactive	4,7%
	Not a student & unemployed	1,3%	**12,5%**	Not a student & informally employed	8,5%				**25,7%**
High	Not a student & inactive	5,0%		Not a student & unemployed	1,4%	**15,2%**		
				Not a student & inactive	5,2%			**27,7%**

Source: Own estimates based on household surveys

Caribbean countries have a higher than average rate of high VEL (41%), considerably higher than the regional average (Figure 14). Guatemala and Honduras are the individual countries with the highest incidence of high VEL, over 50% in both countries. Mexican A&Y also suffer high VEL, almost 40%. Brazil, Costa Rica, Panama, and Dominican Republic are countries where the high VEL incidence is lower than the regional average. Finally, in Spanish-speaking South America, the incidence of high VEL is also below the regional average.

It is also interesting to consider the incidence of low VEL. For instance in countries like Argentina and Costa Rica, where the incidence of high VEL is about average, the incidence of low VEL is among the highest (second after Chile) in the region (over 50%).

Figure 14: Adolescents and youngsters with VEL; countries with HHS, circa 2009

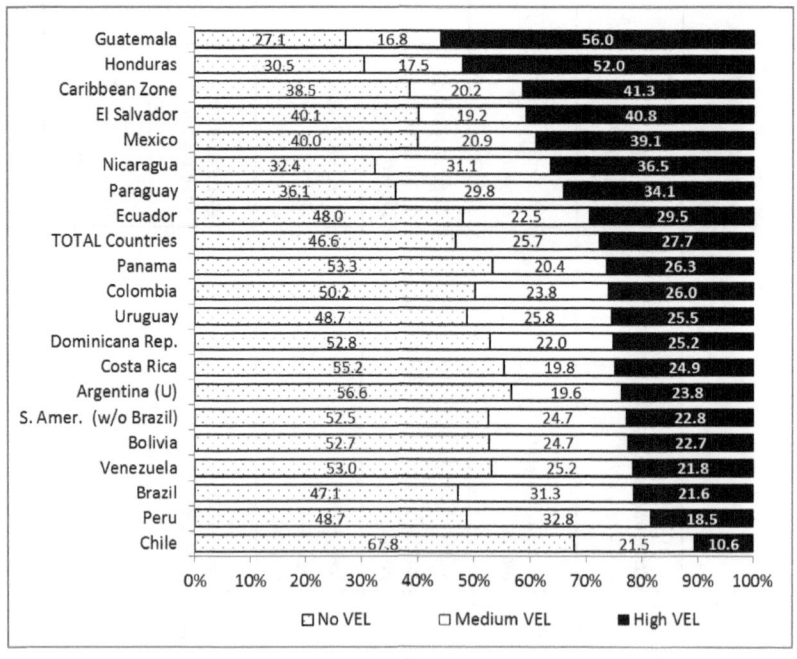

Source: Own estimates based on household surveys

The socioeconomic background of the A&Y suffering from high or medium VEL (or not suffering VEL at all) is presented in Figures 15 and 16.

Almost half of rural A&Y suffer from high VEL, while less than a quarter of urban A&Y suffer high VEL. On average, rural A&Y suffer twice as much from high VEL than urban A&Y. In Brazil, Mexico, and the Caribbean countries, this proportion is lower while it is higher in Spanish-speaking South American counties, in particular Bolivia, Colombia, and Peru. The percentage of A&Y suffering medium VEL is roughly the same (about 25%) in both urban and rural areas.

Older A&Y (i.e., those who are 20–24 years old) have a higher proportion of high VEL (about a third) than younger ones. High VEL affects almost one in four adolescent 15–19-year-olds. The highest age-group differences are found in Brazil and Spanish-speaking South America (except Uruguay, which joins Costa Rica, Honduras, and Mexico as the countries with the lowest age group differences).

As mentioned earlier, the NEET category is embedded in a stereotypical perspective about gender roles. As the VEL was constructed partly to compensate for this, it is interesting to note that there are almost no differences between male and female A&Y in either high or medium VEL. This is not the case in every country, which shows that, on the one hand, some of the gender bias of the NEET measurement has been corrected but, on the other hand, the VEL category can still pick up unfair disparities between the male and female A&Y.

In most Spanish-speaking South American countries and in Brazil, there is an advantage for adolescent girls and young women, while the situation is reversed (at roughly the same magnitude) in Mexico and in Caribbean countries. For instance, in Argentina, Dominican Republic, and Venezuela, the incidence of high VEL among male A&Y is 20% than among female A&Y. In contrast, among female A&Y in Bolivia, Nicaragua, and Guatemala, the incidence of high VEL is 20% above the one for male A&Y.

Figure 15: VEL among A&Y by geographic location, age, sex, parents' education, and household income; countries with HHS, circa 2009

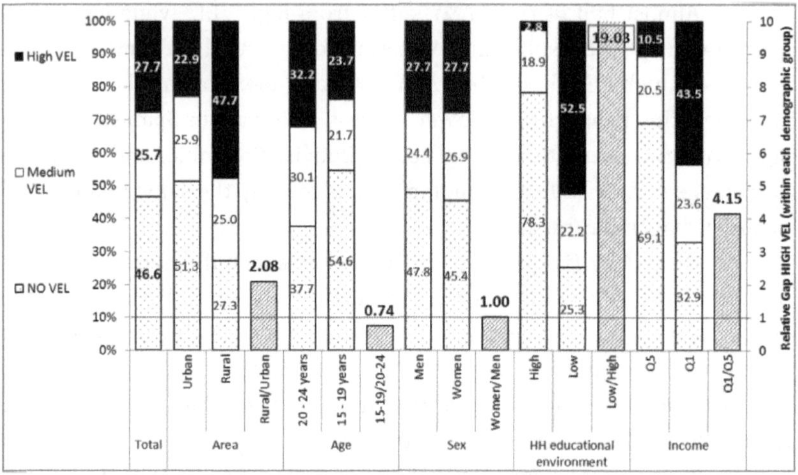

[Chart showing High VEL, Medium VEL, and NO VEL percentages across categories: Total, Area (Urban, Rural, Rural/Urban), Age (20-24 years, 15-19 years, 15-19/20-24), Sex (Men, Women, Women/Men), HH educational environment (High, Low, Low/High), Income (Q5, Q1, Q1/Q5). Values visible include: Total: 27.7/25.7/46.6; Urban: 22.9/25.9/51.3; Rural: 47.7/25.0/27.3; Rural/Urban: 2.08; 20-24 years: 32.2/30.1/37.7; 15-19 years: 23.7/21.7/54.6; 15-19/20-24: 0.74; Men: 27.7/24.4/47.8; Women: 27.7/26.9/45.4; Women/Men: 1.00; High: 18.9/78.3/2.8 (shown as 2.8 at top); Low: 19.03/22.2/52.5 (with 19.03 labeled); Low/High: 25.3; Q5: 10.5/20.5/69.1; Q1: 43.5/23.6/32.9; Q1/Q5: 4.15]

Source: Own estimates based on household surveys

For each A&Y in the richest income quintile who suffers high VEL, there are more than four A&Y in the lowest quintile suffering high VEL. Spanish-speaking countries in South America show similar values to this regional average. However, it is a bit higher in Mexico, and twice as large in Brazil. This relative gap is lower in Caribbean countries (where it is about two instead of more than four).

However, the highest disparities exist between A&Y whose parents have little or no education and those whose parents have completed secondary or higher education. While one out of four A&Y whose parents have little or no education suffer no VEL, about three out of four A&Y whose parents have completed secondary or higher education suffer no VEL. The disparity is even higher when analyzing A&Y suffering high VEL. More than half of A&Y from the first group but less than 3% in the second group suffer high VEL. Thus, for the region as a whole, the incidence of high VEL in the first group is almost 20 times larger than in the second group. The highest divergence occurs in South America (both in Brazil and in Spanish-speaking countries). In no country is this ratio less than 10. The lowest relative gaps take place in Mexico (about 13 times) and in Guatemala and Honduras (12 times).

Figure 16: A&Y with high VEL by geographic location, age, sex, parents' education, and household income; countries with HHS, circa 2009

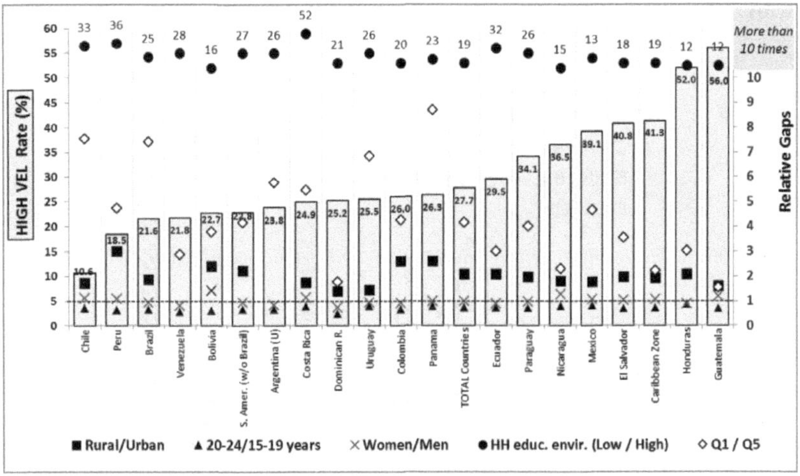

[Chart showing HIGH VEL Rate (%) and Relative Gaps across countries: Chile, Peru, Brazil, Venezuela, Bolivia, S. Amer. (w/o Brazil), Argentina (U), Costa Rica, Dominican R., Uruguay, Colombia, Panama, TOTAL Countries, Ecuador, Paraguay, Nicaragua, Mexico, El Salvador, Caribbean Zone, Honduras, Guatemala. Legend: ■ Rural/Urban, ▲ 20-24/15-19 years, × Women/Men, ● HH educ. envir. (Low/High), ◇ Q1/Q5. Values above bars: 33, 36, 25, 28, 16, 27, 26, 52, 21, 26, 20, 23, 19, 32, 26, 15, 13, 18, 19, 12, 12 (More than 10 times).]

Source: Own estimates based on household surveys

A comparison between NEETs and high VEL is offered in Figure 17. The proportion of A&Y with high VEL almost doubles the proportion of NEETs (28% against 15%). The relative disparities among A&Y suffering high VEL are higher than for NEETs when comparing rural and urban A&Y as well as income levels or the parent's education. The relative disparities are lower for age groups and they almost disappear between male and female A&Y.

Figure 17: NEETs and A&Y with high VEL, differences by geographic location, age, sex, parents' education, and household income; countries with HHS, circa 2009

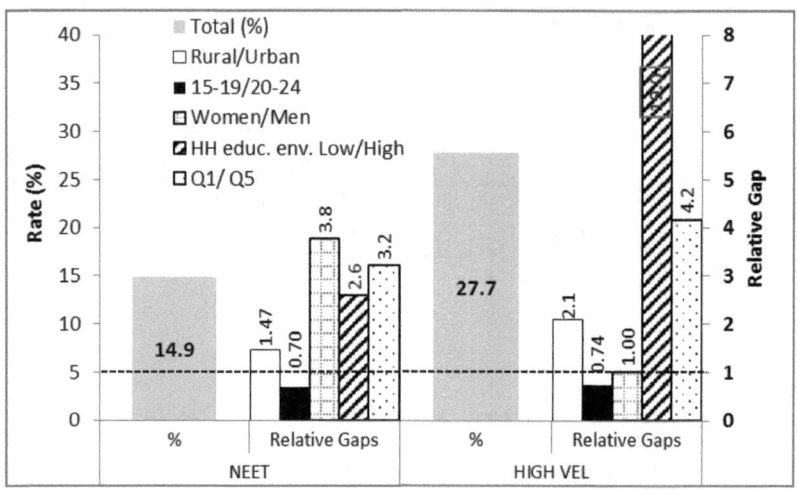

Source: Own estimates based on household surveys

Although the VEL has been introduced as a way to surmount some of the limitations of the NEETs category, they do share some of the same basic information. Thus, it is not surprising they are correlated. Of course, the correlation is not one to one and it is worthwhile to explore where there are divergences between the two indicators.

In Honduras, Guatemala, El Salvador, Nicaragua, and Mexico, A&Y suffer both high incidence of NEETs and of high VEL (Figure 18). The situation is reversed in Bolivia, Brazil, Peru, and Uruguay. Colombia, Costa Rica, and Panama show average levels for both measurements.

However, Ecuador and Paraguay show a divergence. Their A&Y do not have a high incidence of NEETs but they do suffer from high VEL. It is the opposite in Chile where A&Y classified as NEETs exceed the regional average but where the incidence of high VEL is half the regional average value. A similar pattern (with less extreme values) is found in Argentina, Venezuela, and Dominican Republic.

Figure 18: NEETs and A&Y with high VEL by country; countries with HHS, circa 2009

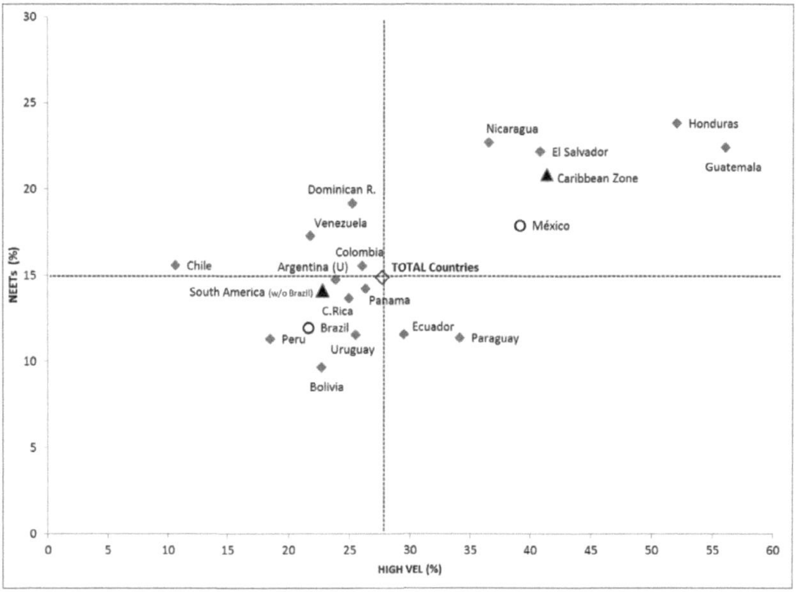

[Scatter plot with x-axis "HIGH VEL (%)" from 0 to 60 and y-axis "NEETs (%)" from 0 to 30. Data points labeled: Honduras, Nicaragua, El Salvador, Guatemala, Caribbean Zone, Dominican R., Venezuela, México, Colombia, Chile, Argentina (U), TOTAL Countries, South America (w/o Brazil), Panama, C.Rica, Brazil, Peru, Ecuador, Uruguay, Paraguay, Bolivia.]

Source: Own estimates based on household surveys

As the measurement of VEL combines education achievement with labor market conditions, it is clear that policies aimed at improving education outcomes and labor inclusion would contribute to reduce the estimated VEL. However, more than this can be done. First, calculating VEL highlights the importance of integrating education and labor policies for A&Y. Second, it provides guidance in terms of specific inclusion efforts for the most disadvantaged A&Y in order to break the intergenerational transmission and geographic-specific patterns of social exclusion. In other words, "generic" policies will have natural limits or may take inordinately long (thus failing the current generation of NEETs—and perhaps even the next one). Consequently, universal policies to ensure good-quality education for all and full employment may need reinforcements with specific actions to promote the inclusion of NEETs.

In addition, third, adolescent development policies geared toward addressing some of the underlying constraints A&Y, in particular the most disadvantaged, confront will also help to address the limitations of traditional education and labor policies. Several years ago, Roth and Brooks-

Gunn (2003) developed a framework to design these type of policies and interventions. The objectives are to build competencies (social, cultural, etc.) among A&Y, to strengthen their confidence (so A&Y feel their lives matter and they can hope for a better future); to further their connections (to family members, mentors, etc.); to reinforce their character (highlighting positive behaviors and distinguishing right and wrong), and promoting caring (relying on their compassion to further empathy for themselves and toward others). Clearly, none of them, singly or combined with the other ones, will solve the problems of low-quality schooling and underperforming labor markets. However, they can be fundamental in providing A&Y tools and skills to make the most of the opportunities offered to them. This is an important contribution to increase the efficiency and effectiveness of (singly focused, silo-type) education and labor policies.

Conclusions

Four main conclusions come out of the previous analysis and description. First, NEETs are mainly girls and young women. For Latin America and the Caribbean as a whole, 80% of NEETs are female (this ranges between more than 90% in Guatemala and less than 70% in Chile and Dominican Republic). Gender dynamics and stereotypes (translated into analytical categories) explain most of this imbalance. Among the former is the fact that girls and young women inherit the primary care responsibility from their mothers, all too often at a very early age—either because they themselves become mothers or they have to take care of somebody else's children. Thus, given the prevailing gender dynamics and norms, they are counted as "doing nothing," that is, not engaged in productively in the labor market. This is when the second elements come to play. While an informally employed young male is counted as working (in spite of him having extremely low income, no job security, and probably being engaged in a very low productivity activity for a few hours a day), a young woman who toils 10–12 hours a day fulfilling important activities without which society would not be able to reproduce itself is considered a NEET. That means the category needs to be revised.

Second, to respond the need to revise the NEET category, the measure of Vulnerability in Education and Labor (VEL) has been proposed as a better descriptor of the risks and challenges faced by A&Y in Latin America and the Caribbean. The VEL does not look just at whether an adolescent or youngster is in (out of) school or (un)employed. It takes into account the completion (or attendance to) of secondary schooling, on the one hand, and, on the other one, the type of employment (formal/informal/unemployment). This allows for a richer description of the situation of A&Y in the region. Clearly, the measurement of VEL is a tool which is just being developed and could certainly be improved (e.g., including data on repetition, completion of tertiary education, or other indicators). Compared to NEETs (about 15% of the A&Y population), VEL is twice as high (almost 30%). Moreover, there is no gender imbalance in VEL. This does not imply that all A&Y are equally likely to suffer from VEL.

Third, although the VEL shows no major gender discrepancies (the female/male relative gap is around 1, meaning equality in most countries except Bolivia where it is almost 2 and Dominican Republic where it is 0.8), other disparities are quite prominent. The major inequities are concentrated in rural areas and among A&Y whose parents have low education and low income. Clearly, all these three axes of disparity are related, which points to a particular kind of exclusion which the younger generations are still struggling to break.

Thus, finally, a set of policies have been highlighted in the chapter that could contribute to open the doors of inclusion to these A&Y. These policies include higher and more equitable investment in education. Higher education investment would not only increase the quality and efficiency of education systems, it would also provide A&Y from rural and poorer household the skills required to find decent (i.e., productive, well-paid, safe, and secure) jobs. As education may not be sufficient to succeed in the labor market, in particular for A&Y from excluded families and with low social capital (and because the education investments may take several years to bear fruit while many A&Y must enter the labor force right now) specific employment programs and policies focused on A&Y employability (without promoting child labor) would be needed. Given the importance of care activities among adolescent girls and young women, it is also important to address gender issues in schools as well as recognizing the importance of the (unpaid) care economy within the social security system. In order to enhance the impact of labor and education policies, they have to be complemented with adolescent development policies to promote competencies, connections, and confidence among A&Y, as well as addressing other root causes of exclusion (e.g., ethnicity). Clearly, none of these policies will be sufficient if macroeconomic, trade, and productive policies do not provide a context of full employment with decent jobs. Thus a combination of social and economic policies is necessary (although not sufficient) to guarantee not only the rights of A&Y but also to offer opportunities for their social inclusion, the means (material and sociocultural) required for the full development of their creativity, and the liberty to shape a better future for themselves and, consequently, for all of us.

References

Aikman, Sheila and Nitya, Rao 2012 "Gender equality and girl's education: investigating frameworks, disjunctures and meanings of quality education," *Theory and Research in Education*, Vol. 10, No. 3.

Bendit, Rene and Hahn-Bleibtreu, Marina (eds.) 2008 *Youth transitions: Processes of social inclusion and patterns of vulnerability in a globalised world* (Opladen, Germany: Barbara Budrich Publishers).

Breakwell, Glynis M. 1982 "Aspects of the social psychology of young people in and out of work," *Bulletin of the British Psychological Society*, Vol. 35: A86.

Bridgeland, John M., DiIulio, John J. and Burke Morison, Karen 2006 *The silent epidemic: Perspectives of high school dropouts, A report by Civic Enterprises in association with Peter D. Hart Research Associates* (Seattle: Bill & Melinda Gates Foundation).

Bustelo, Eduardo 2007 *El Recreo de la Infancia* (Buenos Aires: Siglo XXI editors).

Bynner, John and Parsons, Samantha 2002 "Social exclusion and the transition from school to work: The case of young people not in education, employment," *Journal of Vocational Behaviour*, Vol. 60, No. 2, 289–309.

Chen, Yu-Wen 2011 "Once a NEET always a NEET? Experiences of employment and unemployment among youth in a job training programme in Taiwan," *International Journal of Social Welfare*, Vol. 20, No. 2, 33–42.

Cusworth, Linda, Bradshaw, Jonathan, Coles, Bob, Keung, Antonia and Chzhen, Yekaterina 2009 *Understanding social exclusion across the life course: Youth and young adulthood* (London: Cabinet Office).

ECLAC, OIJ and IMJUVE 2014 *Invertir para transformar, La juventud como protagonista del desarrollo* (Santiago de Chile: ECLAC, Organización Iberoamericana de Juventud and Instituto Mexicano de la Juventud).

El Mercurio, Friday 3 October 2014 in <http://impresa.elmercurio.com/pages/LUNHome page.aspx>.

Espejo, Andrés and Espindola, Ernesto 2015 "La llave maestra de la inclusión social juvenil: educación y empleo" in Trucco, Daniela and Ullmann, Heidi (eds.) *Ju-*

ventud: realidades y retos para un desarrollo con igualdad, Libros de la CEPAL, No 137 (LC/G.2647-P) (Santiago de Chile: ECLAC).

Eurofound 2011 *Young people and NEETs in Europe: First findings* (Dublin: Eurofound).

Finnegan, Florencia 2006 Reseña de políticas educativas públicas de articulación de la educación media con la formación para el trabajo en América Latina. Los casos de Colombia, Uruguay, México, Brasil y Chile (Buenos Aires: IIPE-UNESCO).

Furlong, Andy 2006 "Not a very NEET solution: Representing problematic labour market transitions among early school-leavers," *Work, Employment and Society*, Vol. 20, No. 3, 553-569.

Furlong, Andy 2007 "The zone of precariety and discourses of vulnerability: NEET in the UK," *Journal of Social Sciences and Humanities*, No. 381, 101-121.

Guerrero, Elizabeth, Patricia Provoste and Alejandra Valdés 2006 "Acceso a la educación y socialización de género en un contexto de reformas educativas" in *Equidad de género y reformas educativas. Argentina, Chile, Colombia, Perú* (Santiago de Chile: Hexagrama Consultoras, Facultad Latinoamericana de Ciencias Sociales and Instituto de Estudios Sociales Contemporáneos, Universidad de Bogotá).

IIPE-UNESCO 2012 *La escolarización de los adolescentes: desafíos culturales, pedagógicos y de política educativa* (Buenos Aires: IIPE-UNESCO).

ILO 2012 *Global employment trends for youth 2012* (Geneva: International Labour Organization).

ILO 2013 *Trabajo decente y juventud en América Latina* (Lima: International Labour Organization).

Jacinto, Claudia and Zangani, Mireille 2009 "Un dispositif d'insertion des jeunes: contextes et acteurs dans les nouvelles stratégies d'action publique. Le cas du programme « pro-jeunes » en Uruguay" in *Formation emploi No. 107*, 41-55.

Jacinto, Claudia 2008 "La transición laboral de los jóvenes y las políticas públicas de educación secundaria y formación profesional en América Latina: ¿qué puentes para mejorar las oportunidades?" in Espinosa, Betty, Estéves, Ana and Pronko, Marcela (eds.) *Mundos del trabajo y políticas públicas en América Latina* (Quito: FLACSO).

Lister, Ruth 2006 "Children (but not women) first: New labour, child welfare and gender," *Critical Social Policy*, Vol. 26, No. 2, 315-335.

Llobet Valeria and Minujin Alberto 2011 "Transferencias Condicionadas de Ingresos para Adolescentes y procesos de ampliación de derechos. Una relación contradictoria," *ALAS* No. 4: 253-268.

Lopez, Nestor 2011 *Informe sobre tendencias sociales y educativas en América Latina 2011. La educación de los pueblos indígenas y afrodescendientes* (Buenos Aires: IIPE-UNESCO and OEI).

Montes, Nancy and Sendón, Maria 2006 "Trayectorias Educativas de Estudiantes de Nivel Medio: Argentina a comienzos del siglo XXI," *Revista Mexicana de Investigación Educativa,* Vol. 11, No. 29, 381–402.

OECD 2010 *Off to a good start? Jobs for youth* (Paris: OECD).

Perisic, Mima, Komarecki, Marina and Minujin, Alberto 2012 *Adolescent girls, cornerstone of society: Building evidence and policies for inclusive societies* (New York: UNICEF).

Rico, Maria Nieves and Trucco, Daniela 2014 "Adolescentes: Derecho a la educación y al bienestar futuro," *Serie Políticas Sociales,* No 190 (LC/L.3791) (Santiago de Chile: ECLAC and UNICEF).

Roth, Jodie and Brooks-Gunn, Jeanne 2003 "Youth development programs: Risk, prevention and policy," *Journal of Adolescent Health,* Vol. 32, 170–182.

Soto, Humberto, Trucco, Daniela and Ullmann, Heidi 2015 *Hacia la inclusión social juvenil: Herramientas para el análisis y el diseño de políticas* (Santiago de Chile: ECLAC).

Sunkel, Guilermo and Trucco, Daniela (eds.) 2012 *Las tecnologías digitales frente a los desafíos de una educación inclusiva en América Latina. Algunos casos de buenas prácticas (LC/L.3545)* (Santiago de Chile: ECLAC).

UNICEF 2002 *Adolescence: A Time that Matters* (New York: UNICEF).

UNICEF 2011 *The State of the World's Children 2011: Adolescence – An Age of Opportunity* (New York: UNICEF).

"BIOGRAPHICAL DUALISM": Youth employment and poverty patterns in Spain

Luis Garrido,* Rodolfo Gutiérrez, and Ana M. Guillén

Introduction

The economic crisis has resulted in a dramatic situation for youth employment in Spain. At the end of 2013, the unemployment rate amounted to 75.5% among young people aged 16–19, 50.9% among those aged 20–24, and 32.3% among those aged 25–29. Half of the young unemployed had been looking for a job for more than one year. One in four neither worked nor studied. Although the youth population has dropped, their employment problems have not improved. Over the last six years, one million more young people have joined the unemployment ranks, whereas the youth population has decreased by 1.5 million.

Recent comparative research agrees on identifying the Spanish case as one of the lowest performers in aggregate indicators of youth labor market integration and in specific dimensions of its quality, also for every youth age group and both during growth and, very prominently, during recession periods (Berlingieri et al., 2014; O'Reilly et al., 2015; Hadjivassiliou et al., 2015).

Youth unemployment is not the only problem. It is rather the consequence of other shortcomings of the Spanish labor market prior to the crisis. What has been failing for more than 30 years is the entire Spanish model of youth labor integration. Some of its characteristics are most singular in the international context. Comparative research on youth employment in Spain has emphasized two outstanding traits and associated institutional arrangements to explain the extreme singularity of this national case: on the one hand, the low quality of school-to-work transitions (STW), related to the different levels of the educational system; and, on the other,

---

*   This article is a product of the research project "Welfare capitalism in South Europe: a comparative assessment (CABISE)," funded by the Spanish Ministry of Economy (MINECO-13-CSO2012-33976).

the high intensity of the insider/outsider divide as to labor market regulations.

The analysis undertaken in this chapter is oriented by a somewhat different viewpoint from the mechanisms interpreting the Spanish case from a comparative perspective. In the Spanish case, both flexibilization and dualism show specific profiles as to the orientation of the former and the peculiar pattern of the latter. Flexibilization has been the main objective of many different labor market reforms carried out over the last 25 years. But the type of flexibilization that has been consolidated is "flexibilization at the margins," as it has mainly affected the labor market entry stages, and it has scarcely modified employment regulations for those enjoying a consolidated working position through a permanent contract. This has resulted in a very marked pattern, much more so than in any other country (including those of southern Europe), with a longitudinal type dualization. In other words, the insider-outsider dynamics have to do mainly with the working lifecycle. Thus, this type of dualization has acquired a shape peculiar to a queue rather than the typical form of two segments.

This chapter aims to analyze three major and specific traits of the Spanish case. In the first section, comparative research on youth employment regimes is addressed and discussed in relation with the Spanish case. The second section discusses the high and increasing gap of employment outcomes by educational level, which is related to the problem of (long-term) unemployment among the low-qualified youth. The third section focuses on the almost universal "temporary" pattern of incorporation into the labor market, a pattern having prevailed for three decades and that has not been modified during the long recession. The fourth section deals with recent deterioration in the traditional pattern of low poverty risk among young people. The chapter closes by gathering the research results and indicating future avenues for research.

STW and employment regimes: Situating the Spanish case

Comparative research has mainly focused on typifying clusters of countries with strong similarities in youth labor market performance and identifying the specific mechanisms and institutional arrangements that can explain the observed variety. STW regimes and employment regimes represent the two most relevant approaches in the field.

The dichotomy distinguishing between an *occupational* and an *organizational* (or internal) entry into labor markets can be seen as an initial formulation of the STW regimes (Shavit et al., 1998; Gangl, 2001, 2002; Müller and Gangl, 2003). This dichotomy is based on the assumption that the structure of education and training has important effects on the transition process between education and work. "Occupational labor market" countries exhibit extensive systems of vocational training/apprenticeship, as in Germany and other Central European countries, where young people are predominantly trained within the traditional dual vocational system. "Organizational labor markets" can be found in countries with less integrated education and employment systems, such as France, the United Kingdom and Spain, where transitions are less socially shaped and employers deploy a more extensive role of discretionary recruitment and training in shaping early labor market careers.

Following this dichotomy, relative outcomes of labor market entrants differ significantly between these two institutional arrangements. In occupational contexts, on the one hand, strict educational channeling of individuals allows for a more immediate match between qualifications and jobs, while lack of experience has low detrimental effects, so that young workers should be in a more favorable position both in employment and occupational status attainments. In organizational contexts, on the other hand, youth labor market outcomes are primarily achieved via work experience and horizontal mobility, so that young entrants are more dependent on contingencies of individual job-worker matches and both unemployment and precarious employment should exhibit a strong experience gradient.

The approach in terms of STW regimes constitutes a more ambitious attempt to include in the analysis not only educational and labor market arrangements, but also complex systems of socioeconomic structures, institutional arrangements, and cultural patterns. Based on a reformulation of Gallie and Paugam's typology of employment regimes (2000), Walther (2006) has elaborated a typology of four clusters of STW regimes: *universalistic, employment-centered, liberal,* and *subprotective.*

The *subprotective* transition regime is supposed to correspond to Southern European countries, such as Italy, Spain, and Portugal, where educational systems, labor markets, welfare provision, and youth policies have shaped a regime to render specific outcomes and patterns. The school system is structured comprehensively until the end of compulsory education and the rate of early school leavers tends to be high. Vocational training is weakly developed and largely provided by professional schools, with low involvement of companies. Higher education plays an important role in providing young people with a chance to improve status in the waiting phase, prompting risks of either dropping out before reaching the end of their degree or becoming overqualified. Labor market segmentation and lack of training contribute to very high rates of youth unemployment, especially affecting young women. Young people are not entitled to social benefits and a scarcity of public childcare facilities leads to dependency on family support and delays in individual careers. The most relevant educational policies are aimed at prolonging school participation and at integrating vocational training, whereas labor market policies are focused on incentives for employers to hire young people together with assistance and incentives for those unemployed to turn to self-employment.

The employment regimes perspective, in turn, emphasizes the institutionalized role of organized labor in decision-making at both national and workplace level and the extent to which employment practices and regulations facilitate the integration of the potentially most vulnerable labor market groups (Gallie, 2007). A distinction is drawn between "inclusive" and "dualist" regimes. In dualist regimes, such as Germany, France, and Spain, organized labor draws its strength primarily from an easier-to-mobilize core workforce of employees in large firms and its central concern is to guarantee rights to this core workforce of long-term employees (insiders). Employment regulations tend to reflect this by providing high employment protection, good working conditions, and generous welfare support for the core workforce, but much poorer conditions and significant vulnerability for those on nonstandard contracts (outsiders).

Structural change toward postindustrial labor markets has produced similar, albeit not identical, sets of insiders and outsiders across regimes (Häusermann and Schwander, 2012). Continental and Southern European regimes tend to perpetuate and even reinforce the insider–outsider divide with regard to all three dimensions of dualism: not only the labor market dimension of dualism, mainly reflected in unequal access of outsiders to job mobility and training, but also the social protection dimension, by the effect of taxes and transfers on net income differentials between both segments; and, furthermore, the political dimension, that is, the insider–outsider gap in terms of trade union membership and political participation.

There is a repeated and clear conclusion about all these comparative approaches: South European countries, and more specifically Spain, do not fit well into any framework. Gangl (2001) concludes that South European countries clearly do not line up with the patterns found in the United Kingdom and France, supposedly in the same organizational cluster, and this constitutes the most intriguing weakness of the dichotomy of occupational/organizational labor markets. The South European pattern combines one element present in the occupational system—the role of strong experience effects on employment outcomes—but also another element of the organizational system, as far as large educational differentials may be ascertained as regards outcomes. Furthermore, the position of Spain is also peculiar as it is clustered with the flexible and deregulated youth labor market system common to North European countries.

The picture for South European countries is also somewhat complex under the insider/outsider lens. Häusermann and Schwander (2012) found that labor markets are less dualized than in continental Europe, both with regard to gross wage gaps and training/promotion prospects, although the low degree of dualism may reflect poor job conditions even for insiders. The dualist effect is clearer in the dimensions of social protection and of political integration than it is in the employment dimension. Another intriguing trait of this group of countries, and particularly pertaining Spain, is that, while they have introduced many elements of policy reform similar to other countries, increased labor market flexibility has not significantly improved the employment integration of young people.

In the analysis based on the employment regimes approach, Gallie (2007) calls into question the characterization of countries in terms of the emphasis on skills specificity as a predictor or more inclusive employment patterns. Further, among supposedly dualist countries, such as France, Germany, and Spain, no particularly distinctive traits could be ascertained as regards the disadvantage associated with temporary contracts as a determinant of low-quality employment integration. There are important variations among countries falling under each of the two regimes and categorizations are, at best, broad brush. Gallie (2007: 232) closes his ambitious analysis, in the last paragraph of his book, by conceding that "regime analysis can complement, but not substitute for, the older tradition of 'societal' analysis which takes seriously the specificity of the historically derived institutional frameworks of particular countries."

The limited analytical power of the hitherto discussed characterizations reinforces the need for country case analyses paying more attention to (a) longer time periods and relevant changes in crucial institutional arrangements and (b) to longitudinal approaches in order to assess the effects of those changes on different youth generations. The following sections undertake such challenges in the analysis of the Spanish case.

The increasing salience of education in the Spanish labor market

Spain has experienced a massive "educational overturn" during the last four decades due to the substantial increase of the educational level among younger cohorts. Taking into account only those educational levels directly applicable to work (namely, professional training, university degrees, but also high school degrees, which were used by older cohorts to obtain white collar jobs), those Spanish men born between 1931–1935 enjoyed 13.5% of education/training for work while those born between 1976 and 1980 had reached 65.1% in 2014. Such an "overturn" has been even more intense among women, who, for the same cohorts, have evolved from 6.4% to 75.4%.

In this context of educational overturn, the dualization of the Spanish labor market is directly related to two very important effects for youth employment, which go in very different directions: On the one side, the likelihood of obtaining a job depends very intensely on the education level, a pattern much more intense during economic crisis cycles; on the other side, the skill wage premium has clearly deteriorated for the younger generations in recent decades.

The data included in Figure 1 show the aforementioned first effect. The employment rates have been calculated from 1976 to 2014 for young people of both sexes that have already abandoned their studies. Since young people enter the labor market at different ages, the age groups are also different for each educational level, corresponding to the first five years of their working life for each group (calculated by means of fixed ages throughout the entire period). To make the comparison more homogenous, only young Spanish people are included (i.e., those born in Spain). In other words, no immigrants are incorporated, as their entry trajectories into the labor market depend a great deal on the time of their arrival in Spain and, therefore, their experience in the labor market cannot be made to coincide with the year they complete their studies as with those born in Spain.

Data in Figure 1 further prove two facts of singular relevance. First, education levels are increasingly and intensely differentiating the employment levels of young people. At the beginning of the 70s, the education levels of young people hardly affected their employment levels: All men enjoyed full, or almost full, employment; all women had lower levels of employment and there were some inequalities due to educational levels. The tendency to greater inequality began with the oil crises at the end of the 70s but it has been maintained afterward, both during the crisis and growth cycles. Moreover, the last crisis has had the effect of intensifying an already long-term tendency. In fact, intensification has occurred to such an extent that the employment rate of the less-qualified (primary education) women aged 16–20 years amounted to 7% in 2013, that is, over 50 points lower than that of female university graduates aged 23–27 years, which was of 64%. Among young men, the difference was only slightly less pronounced, that is, 21% and 60%, respectively.

Second, the other fact to be highlighted is that the Spanish labor market also presents a long-term nonemployment tendency among the less-qualified young people. Each crisis period has lowered the employment level of the less-qualified young people a little more than the previous period, while during successive growth cycles the employment level achieved in the previous cycle has scarcely been recuperated. This tendency is much more accused among women than among men. However, the different crisis periods affected the employment level among more-qualified young people much less, especially among young university graduates in general and even less among young female graduates. During such a severe employment crisis as the current one, the employment rate of the more-qualified young women has dropped 15 percentage points between the time they achieved the highest employment level (2007–09) and the time of the lowest level (2013). Still, the employment rate of young women with compulsory secondary education levels has decreased by 35 points between the best time (2006) and the worst time (2013).

It is noteworthy that, during expansive phases, youth employment rates by educational level are very similar when compared at equal "working ages" and excluding those who are currently studying, as calculated in this chapter.[1] Hence, one may consider that labor integration of Spanish youth is relatively favorable in such economic phases. Conversely, during recessions (as can be observed in the figures with fixed labor ages), performance of the different educational levels are much more unequal, and these variations are the product of decreases in the employment rate that are much more pronounced the lower the formal educational level.

Figure 1: Youth employment rates by educational level and age in Spain, 1976–2014 (young population born in Spain and not enrolled in education)

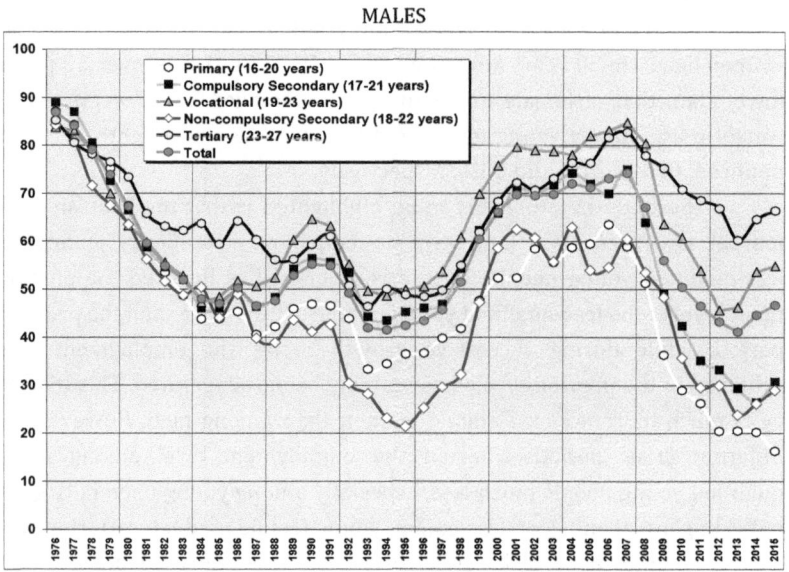

---

[1] Fixed ages have been used for each educational level as the age of studies ending is not available until 1992. Therefore, tracing the trajectory from 1976 has been considered preferable to the use of specific "working ages" for each individual (calculated as years gone by since the end of formal education). If such "individual working ages" are used and educational levels are classified into nine levels, the difference between the expansion and recession phases becomes much more evident.

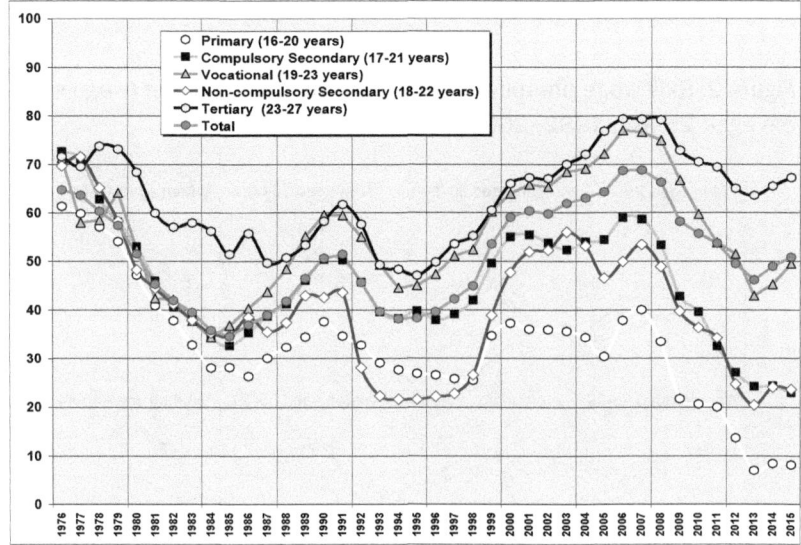

Source: Own calculations, INE, Labour Force Survey.

Despite the intensely pro-cyclical behavior of the Spanish labor market, the highly qualified young people have managed to maintain their long-term employment opportunities at a reasonably stable level, so that their position has only deteriorated moderately with the recent crisis. Nonetheless, this does not mean that their position in the labor market has not worsened in other senses, especially regarding their relative salaries. Felgueroso et al. (2010) provide the calculations for the skill wage premium (SWP) by age, cohort and gender, comparing educational or qualification groups (Figure 2). The results are quite revealing: First, at the time of entry into the labor market, the SWP has continued to fall for the cohort born after the early 60s (those entering the market after 1985); second, despite the apparent increase with age, the SWP falls with time for all the male cohorts; the differences by gender are due to a delay in the SWP fall for females. Specifically for women, a substantial increase of the SWP for the cohort born 1963–1967 (aged 43–47 in 2010) is observed. For those born after 1967, a small decrease of the SWP is detected at all ages. Alternatively, for men, the fall of the SWP starts for cohorts born between 1958 and 1962, currently aged 48–52. Note, finally, that for both genders the discrepancies between the SWP measured by educational level or occupation are larger for younger cohorts, very likely due to the increasing fraction of mismatched educated individuals in younger cohorts.

Figure 2: Skill wage premium by age, birth year, and gender (wage earners aged 25-44, 1982-2008)

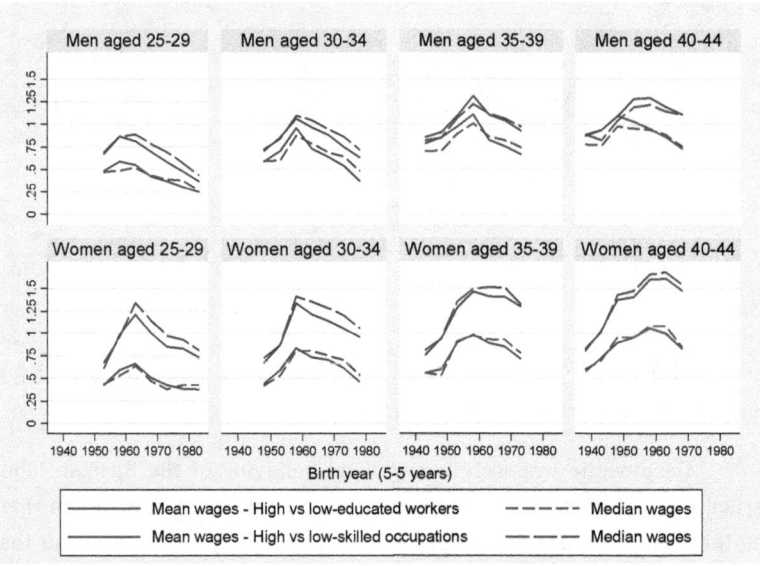

Source: Calculations by Felgueroso, Hidalgo, and Jiménez (2010), from the *Muestra Continua de Vidas Laborales (MCVL)*

Fixed-term contracts as a peculiar dualization mechanism

The main causes of the extension and severity of the liabilities of youth employment in Spain are deeply rooted (Garrido and Gutiérrez, 2011). They have to do above all with the way in which some basic problems of the Spanish labor market were addressed at the end of the Francoist dictatorship and during the early democratic transition. Some of the answers to the challenges at those critical moments were consolidated as more or less implicit, social agreements, and/or as institutional arrangements, both with powerful inertias on the capacity to generate new answers to old problems.

Spain is a country where, most paradigmatically, an institutional device of the labor market can be seen as a dualization mechanism. Since the mid-1980s, Spain has introduced successive reforms aimed at increasing labor market flexibility. Those attempts to increase flexibility have taken place through changes at the margins in the employment protection legislation. The latter liberalized the use of fixed-term (or temporary) contracts, while leaving largely unchanged the legislation affecting the stock of employees under open-ended (or permanent) contracts.

The successive changes implemented since the mid-1980s to regulate labor contracts maintained a pattern of two-tier employment protection (Guillén and Gutiérrez, 2006; Bentolila, Dolado and Jimeno, 2012). Reforms have modified all the items of temporary contracts (causality and costs of dismissals, mainly) and have encouraged open-ended contracts in all possible ways, modifying their protection only slightly.

The intensity of the 2007 crisis and the extraordinary increase in unemployment were not sufficient reason for the Spanish government to carry out labor reforms. The initial reaction was that the reforms were not necessary and that, if they were carried out, they would have to be the result of an agreement with the social partners. But those agreements never came about and the government, forced by the threats of the financial markets and the pressure of its European co-member states, changed its stance about the need for reforms, and at the beginning of 2010 began a series of actions that led to another employment protection modification phase between June 2010 and September 2011. These reforms were much more extensive and intense than the previous ones and mainly affected four areas: dismissal costs, working hours, active employment policies, and collective bargaining.

The entry in office of a new center-right wing government at the end of 2011 led to a major labor reform in 2012, which modified many aspects of employment protection and continued along the line of the reduction of severance payments for permanent contracts. Thus, the law established incentives to internal flexibility measures in order to save jobs of workers on fixed-term contracts. More recently, in 2013, the government introduced some measures on stable employment and employability primarily focused on young unemployed with little or no work experience. For instance, the Decree-Law 11/2013 of 2 August, introduced a temporary contract (*primer empleo joven*) aimed at encouraging first working experience among young unemployed under the age of 30.

It is still very early to evaluate these latest reforms and even more difficult in a period of economic recession that has brought employment creation to a standstill. The initial impression is that these reforms are moving in the direction of reducing institutional duality, but they are doing so in a very timid way. Spain was the country where young employees had the shortest tenure in their first job during the years of booming employment (2006–2007) and it still remains so during the crisis. It is not strange that new reforms in the same direction are more than likely to be required in coming years (Bentolila et al., 2012; OECD, 2013).

Despite all the efforts aimed at promoting permanent contracts and at limiting temporary or fixed-term ones, the proportion of temporary jobs in Spain has remained at very stable levels over the last 30 years. Such levels are much higher than those of other countries in the south of Europe, such as France or Italy, where there is a similar weight of strong seasonal economic activities (agriculture and tourism, mainly) as well as similar labor relations systems, leading one to believe that they would also show very similar proportions of temporary employment.

In fact, temporary employment has become an almost universal labor integration track in Spain. It constitutes more of a formal rule to shape the integration process than a factual rule regulating the actual duration of contracts. With data from the *Labour Force Survey* in 2014, 45% of those employed through fixed-term contracts have enjoyed a chain of fixed-term contracts in the same firm and 59.2% of them have been working for the same firm for almost a year. Temporary employment as a dualization mechanism does not work as a secondary segment but rather as a predominant *queue* for youth integration and consolidation in the labor market.

Equally, the overall temporary employment rate is a very limited indicator of the salience of this situation in young people's work trajectories. A longitudinal approach is required to observe these trajectories better, as offered in the data of Figure 3. The temporary employment rate curves are illustrated for the different demographic cohorts for men and women who have been part of the Spanish labor market over the last two decades. These include the cohort born between 1931 and 1935, the closest cohort to retirement age during that period, and the cohort of those born between 1991 and 1995, that is, the youngest to join the market, which can only be observed, therefore, up to 24 years of age.[2]

---

[2] We must warn that this representation is not entirely rigorous from the viewpoint of the longitudinal monitoring of the trajectory of a cohort. It must be taken into ac-

This way of presenting the temporary employment trajectories shows the biographic stability of temporality. Longitudinally, temporary contracts have become the canonical form of labor integration, with such continuity that each cohort follows a practically identical trajectory to those preceding it in the association between age and level of temporality in employment. Successive cohorts of men and women follow an upward contract stability trend that mimics that followed by their predecessors. The cyclical oscillation of employment, which as we have seen, is very intense in the Spanish case, only manages to slightly and transitorily alter what has become a consistent regularity over the last two decades.

The relevant parallelism between the trajectories of both genders makes it easier to measure the distance between them. The average trajectory rate is calculated for each gender. The difference in temporary employment of those average trajectories is obtained for each age. The average for the whole working life (from 16 to 68 years) amounts to 3.0 points. This difference is maintained for the greatest part of the trajectory with the exception of the central phase (35 to 45 years), where it rises to 4.3 points, and in the final phase (from 54 to 64 years), where it decreases to 1.1 points. This comparison clearly proves the similarity of the labor consolidation process for both genders.

Another way of measuring this difference consists of advancing female trajectories by one year. In this way, it will coincide with the trajectory of men in the entire initial part, to the extent where the average difference in the phase from 16 to 34 years is 0.0 points. This means that the difference as regards the incidence of temporary employment between men and women in the integration phase is that men "are one year ahead" in biographical terms.

---

count that the components of a cohort share the birth period but they are very different in terms of education levels and, therefore, they join the labor market at very different ages. That is why, within the younger age ranges, although they do share that same birth period, they do not represent the same group as they reach the successive ages. This is due to the fact that, as only salary earners are included, these start work at very different ages depending on their respective study levels. To this end, during the first age ranges (16–20 years), the majority are people with low qualifications and, as they grow older, the others, who have higher education levels, gradually join the labor market.

Figure 3: Percentage of employed people with fixed-term contracts by birth cohort in Spain, 1992–2014 (born-in-Spain population)

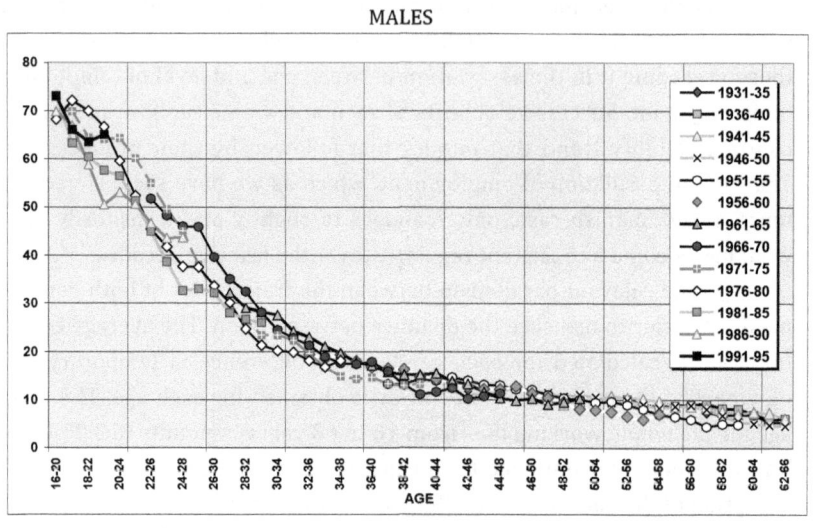

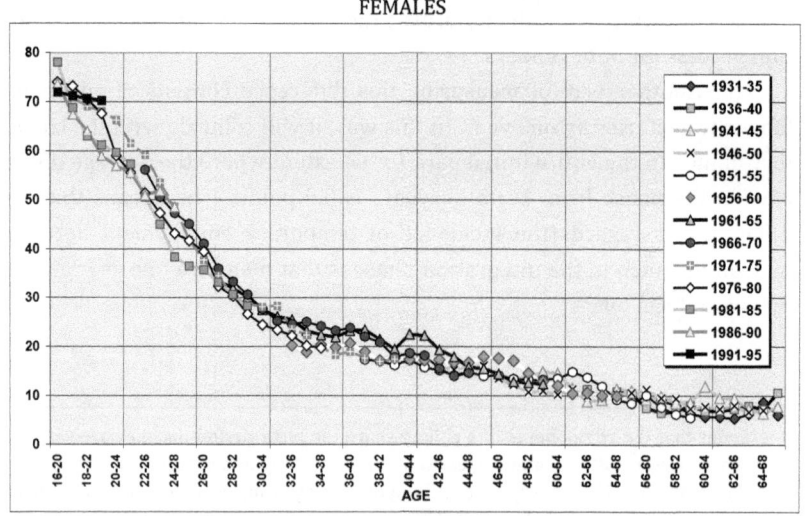

Source: Own calculations, INE, Labour Force Survey

Having verified this overlapping of trajectories, it is especially interesting to focus on what has occurred during the current crisis. The initial drop of temporary employment, as the principal way to adjust employment, has meant that the proportion of permanent employment has increased, so that the trajectories of the younger cohorts show less temporality. It must be highlighted that, during the strongest crisis phase, no cohort (except for the males born between 1986 and 1990) decreased in 2009 by 9.5 points, which is the general rate. This is due to the fact that this important drop of the temporary employment rate is the result, mainly, of the loss of employment among young people, who are those who endure temporary employment the most.

Therefore, the "departures" from the trajectories of their predecessors are less important than the total drop of temporary employment. Admittedly, it would be possible to reduce general temporality without the trajectory of any cohort being altered provided each one of them were to lose temporary and permanent employment in the same proportion, but only if the younger cohorts were to lose more jobs because the majority of the temporary jobs are held by them. As we can see in the following text, this is precisely what has happened in the end.

Indeed, the last two years show a return to the average trajectory, by going back to the previous situation where age marks the temporary employment pattern rather than changes in intensity and age composition of employment. These results show that the decrease of the general temporary employment rate is precisely an employment composition effect. The loss of jobs among young people (above all those with the lowest levels of qualification, who register the highest levels of temporary employment and who are also those that start working earlier) leads to a decrease in the general proportion, but this does not alter the biographic regularity of the trajectories. It can be deduced from this that, in the end, the proportion of both temporary and permanent jobs lost in each cohort is the same as verified previously at each age. During the first two years of the crisis, temporary jobs were the first to drop, while permanent jobs increased strongly, thus altering the trajectory in a transitory manner. However, in the next two years there were more permanent dismissals (or less stabilization of the temporary ones than was typical of each age), thus resulting in a return to the canonical trajectory.

The importance of this recovery of the trajectory is decisive with respect to the construction of the biographies of young people, above all of those young-adults who have all kinds of difficulties to consolidate their labor integration. Although it could be argued that it is early days to evaluate the results of the 2012 labor reform, its ineffectiveness to reduce that basic dualization mechanism seems clear. This is proof of the continuity of the extensive and drastic segmentation of the labor market with respect to the termination of work contracts depending on age, both as to the biographic age and the "working age," understood not as employment experience but as time elapsed since they abandoned their studies.

Youth poverty risks

Under the assumptions of the insider–outsider approach, a clear income gap should be observed between both groups. In the southern countries, a combination of poor employment outcomes and weak social protection has worsened the situation for young outsiders, further widening the net wage gap after taxes and transfers (Häusermann and Schwander, 2012).

In the case of Spain, those expectations are only partially confirmed. Youth poverty risk is comparatively high in Spain, but not as high as expected by such poor labor market outcomes (Goerne, 2011; García-Espejo and Gutiérrez, 2011). With data from EU-SILC, in 2005, at the peak of the economic boom phase, the rate of youth (18–24 years) in poverty risk was 17.0, considerably lower than in some Nordic countries (Denmark 33.9, Sweden 29.5) and also lower than in some other southern countries (Italy 22.1, Greece 21.4). At the peak of the recession period (2012), this rate amounted to 28.2 in Spain, higher than the average in EU-15 countries (23.1), but still lower than in Denmark (40.5) and Sweden (29.9).

This traditionally low level of youth poverty in Spain is clearly due to the role played by living arrangements as a protection mechanism (Ayllón 2009). The scarce labor market integration of young people in Spain has been compensated by household behavior. An increase in the number of dual-earner households, thanks to the rise in female participation in the labor market, has played a crucial role in the reduction of poverty among youth, counteracting the effect of the decline in the economic status of young people. Delayed emancipation, concentrated mostly among those families that can best afford it, also means than emancipation occurs when young individuals and couples access more secure income. Under these circumstances, a high poverty risk among young outsiders only occurs (albeit significantly) when emancipation involves childbearing.

Such pattern has remained basically stable during the recession period despite intense deterioration of employment opportunities for young Spaniards (Figure 4). Those youths who have either avoided or overcome the "integration queue," by reaching a long-term contract, enjoy a very low poverty risk, only slightly increased by the crisis. In fact, the poverty risk amounted to 6.3 in 2005, and it reached a maximum of 8.3 in 2010. It is precisely among those young people still in the "queue" where risk has grown most because of the recession: They used to triple the risk of those with permanent employment, and in 2012 they almost doubled the poverty rate they suffered in 2005.

That a return to the postponement of emancipation is the case, explains that those youths less linked to employment, namely those who are inactive, have increased very slightly their poverty risk, for they are the group that has delayed both the exit from the education system and emancipation. Even the young unemployed, with a poverty risk affecting 4 out of 10, have failed to see an increase in accordance with the predictable loss of income (as the proportion of young long-term unemployed among them has been growing and, over time, a higher portion have lost unemployment benefits).

In the Spanish case, welfare performance during the crisis has proved particularly weak for those households including low-qualified adults with minor dependents (Guillén et al., 2012; Gutiérrez, 2013). This is the population group that should be classified as subprotected, much more so than those young people who have been able to keep their poverty risk stable, that is, those having overcome the phase of outsiders, and those who have seen it only slightly increased thanks to a protracted stay within the education system and the postponement of emancipation.

Figure 4: At-risk-of poverty rate among youth in Spain, 2004–2013 (18–29 years)

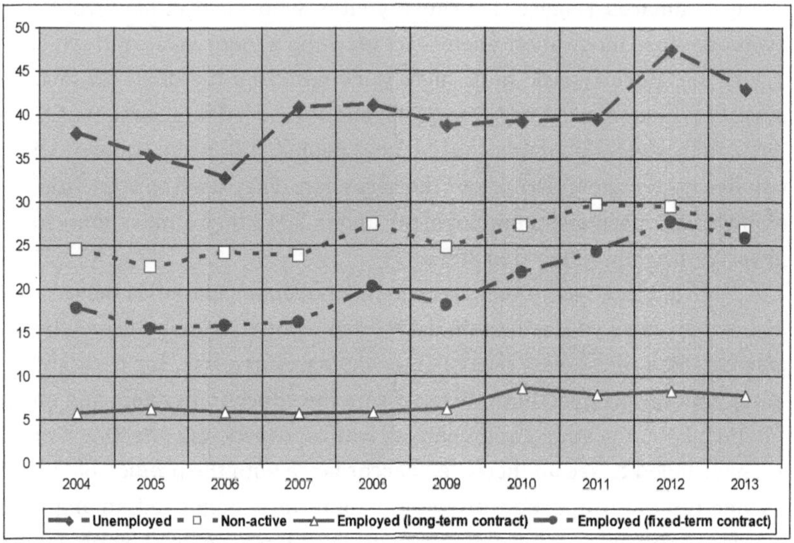

Source: Eurostat, *EU-SILC*

Conclusions

Spain has evolved as an extreme case in terms of poor performance and quality of the youth labor market, even worse in comparison to other countries in Continental or Southern European geographical areas in economic recession periods. Explaining this with reference to its belonging to a specific regime, either the subprotective or the insider–outsider, is clearly insufficient. Moreover, it can also be confusing as regards the identification of the actual institutional mechanisms behind the observed outcomes.

In this chapter, Spanish youth employment has been analyzed, during the last three decades from a longitudinal perspective, and two of the most dominant and stable traits have been ascertained, namely, the relationship between employment participation and educational levels, and temporality as an almost universal pattern of labor insertion. The risk of poverty for different labor positions has also been observed, in this case for a more recent period.

Results of the analysis show that youth employment bears a singularly cyclical behavior: (1) differences in employment are considerably reduced during expansion phases, (2) there is a tendency toward growing nonemployment among the lowest qualified youth, and (3) the skill wage gap has notoriously narrowed. This study has also presented evidence to prove the persistence of the same biographical profiles of temporality over the analyzed period of 30 years, closely linked to the incorporation of young people into the labor market, prolonging employment beyond the duration of formal contracts. Temporality seems more a universal queue shaping the entry into the labor market than a trait of a secondary segment. In spite of this, youth poverty risk is moderate and clearly linked to temporality and unemployment.

For all these reasons, the Spanish case can be better understood with the perspective of trajectories of dualism under strong pressure for flexibilization than from the perspective of employment regimes. Since the mid-1980s, the Spanish labor market has undergone successive institutional reforms aimed at increasing flexibility. Attempts with this aim have taken place through changes at the margins by modifying the employment protection legislation that liberalized the use of fixed-term (or temporary) contracts, while leaving largely unchanged the legislation affecting the stock of employees under open-ended (or permanent) contracts. Comparatively rocketing shares of temporary employment have remained as a very stable trait of the Spanish labor market and the first candidate to constitute the main mechanism of dualization.

The most accepted hypothesis among scholars assumes that temporality constitutes a "pure" mechanism of dualization: It contributes to create two separate segments in the labor market, divided by their respective sets of unequal rewards, and characterized also by low mobility among both segments. Nevertheless, findings of this study could also support an alternative interpretation of the effects of temporality dualization. The dominant profile of dualization in the Spanish labor market is of a "biographical" nature. Despite the changes in the composition and characteristics of occupation, temporality trajectories remain (practically) constant among consecutive cohorts. Temporality is closely connected to the age of workers so that it strongly decreases after the insertion phase into the labor market is completed, even if this phase is comparatively longer.

This hypothesis would also affect the interpretation of the political mechanism that explains the existence and stability of a labor market with two-tier employment protection, even though combating and overcoming this has been a declared objective of all the governments and social partners. The usual interpretation, above all in economic analyses, is based on the theory of the "average voter" of governments and unions, in other words, the stable predominance of a constituency for both, comprised of insiders. The biographical profile of temporary employment and its empirical configuration would adjust better to a hypothesis of "implicit intergenerational pact."

Insiders (adult workers with open-ended or permanent contracts and an advantageous position in the labor market despite their low educational and training skills base) and outsiders (young and young-adult workers with fixed-term contracts, disadvantaged labor and wage conditions, and a comparatively higher educational and training skills base) would live in the same households. In other words, the former are the fathers and the latter are the offspring. In this context, insiders would preferentially hold the central positions in the work and public spheres. In turn, outsiders would enjoy freedom and take advantage of "domestic" services in the parental household while extending their formative period and preparing for a long process of consolidation within the labor market.

In Spain, young workers would be made to compete against each other for labor market insertion in a sort of queue rather than being able to compete with all workers by using their productive capacities and corresponding salaries. In other words, the institutional framework of the Spanish labor market produces a very rigid differential remuneration by capacity, while flexibility to contract and dismiss is very high. This may explain overqualification and low salaries among young workers. Moreover, it is in this sense that the Spanish pattern of youth employment can be characterized as "longitudinal" or "biographic" dualism in comparative terms.

Furthermore, there are many factors that contribute to the deterioration of the skill wage premium for young workers. Atypical work has become structural (typical) for young Spaniards, supported by a sectorial and uncoordinated collective bargaining that has generated wage increases above market prices for permanent workers. Admittedly, in the presence of excess demand (and/or severe crisis) entrepreneurs have the opportunity to offer lower wages and successive labor reforms have given them the tools to perpetuate these dualizing practices. Moreover, economic uncertainty obliges many youths to accept (despite their preference for stability) temporality and overqualification, considering that, ultimately, the aforementioned intergenerational pact serves to soften their transition to permanent labor integration.

To sum up, the results of this research reinforce two salient conclusions for comparative endeavors on employment and income attainments among young people. On the one hand, more longitudinal evidences should be gathered in order to nuance the comparative panorama. Limited descriptive evidence has been offered here, with fixed ages as relates labor market entry and birth cohorts in temporality profiles. Pure longitudinal analyses are needed, based on panel data. On the other hand, it is also necessary to develop approaches incorporating an interpretation of trajectories of policy reform. In this way, a better understanding could be reached of why similar labor market flexibilization reforms are conducive to very different results as to types of dualization.

References

Ayllón, Sara 2009 "Poverty and living arrangements among youth in Spain, 1980-2005," *Demographic Research* (Rostock), Vol. 20, No. 17, 403–434.

Bentolila, Samuel, Dolado, Juan J. and Jimeno, Juan F. 2012, "Reforming an Insider-Outsider Labor Market: The Spanish Experience" in *Documentos de Trabajo Fedea* No 01, <http://www.fedea.es> accessed 26 September 2014.

Berlingieri, Francesco, Bonin, Holger, and Sprietsma, Maresa 2014 *Youth unemployment in Europe, appraisal and policy options* (Stuttgart: Robert Bosch Stiftung GmbH).

Felgueroso, Florentino, Hidalgo, Manuel and Jiménez-Martín, Sergi 2010 "Explaining the fall of the skill wage premium in Spain" in *Documentos de Trabajo Fedea* No 19. In <http://www.fedea.es> accessed 26 September 2014.

Gallie, Duncan and Paugam, Serge (eds.) 2000 *Welfare regimes and the experience of unemployment in Europe* (Oxford: Oxford University Press)

Gallie, Duncan 2007 *Employment regimes and the quality of work* (Oxford: Oxford University Press).

Gangl, Markus 2001 "European patterns of labour market entry: A dichotomy of occupationalized versus non occupationalized systems?" *European Societies* (UK), Vol. 3, No. 4, 471–494.

Gangl, Markus 2002 "Changing labour markets and early career outcomes: Labour market entry in Europe over the past decade," *Work, Employment and Society* (UK), Vol. 16, No. 1, 67–90.

García-Espejo, Isabel and Gutiérrez, Rodolfo 2011 "Spain: Persisting Inequalities in a Growing Employment Context" in Fraser, Neil, Gutiérrez, Rodolfo and Peña-Casas, Ramón (eds.) *Working poverty in Europe. A comparative approach* (Basingstoke: Palgrave Macmillan).

Garrido, Luis and Gutiérrez, Rodolfo 2011 "La reforma ineludible. Regularidades e inercias del mercado de trabajo en España", *Panorama Social* (Madrid), .No. 13, 37–54.

Goerne, Alexander 2011 "A Comparative Analysis of In-Work Poverty in the European Union" in Fraser, Neil, Gutiérrez, Rodolfo and Peña-Casas, Ramón (eds.) *Working Poverty in Europe. A Comparative Approach* (Chippenham: Palgrave Macmillan).

Guillén, Ana M., Pavolini, Emmanuele, Luque, David and Anaut, Sagrario 2012 "The role of social policy in resolving needs generated by the crisis" in Lapara, Miguel and Eransus, Begoña (eds.) *Crisis and social fracture in Europe. Causes and effects in Spain* (Barcelona: Obra Social La Caixa).

Guillén, Ana M. and Gutiérrez, Rodolfo 2006 "Social pacts in Spain: the impact on the labour market and the social protection system," *International Labour Brief*, Vol. 4, No. 3, 12–20.

Gutiérrez, Rodolfo 2014 "Welfare performance in Southern Europe: employment crisis and poverty risk," *South European Society and Politics*, Vol. 19 No. 3, 371–392.

Hadjivassiliou, Kari, Kirchner Sala, L. and Speckesser, Stefan 2015 "Key indicators and drivers of youth unemployment", STYLE Working Papers 01/2015. CROME, University of Brighton, Brighton. In <http://www.style-research.eu/publications/> accessed 10 June 2015.

Häusermann, Silja and Schwander, Hanna 2012 "Varieties of Dualization? Labor market segmentation and insider-outsider divides across regimes" in Emmenegger, Patrick, Häusermann, Silja, Palier; Bruno and Seeleib-Kaiser, Martin (eds.) *The age of dualization. The changing face of inequality in deindustrializing societies* (Oxford and New York: Oxford University Press).

Müller, Walter and Gangl, Markus 2003 "The transition from school to work. A European perspective" in Müller, W. and Gangl, M. (eds.) *Transitions from education to work in Europe. The integration of youth into EU labour markets* (Oxford: Oxford University Press).

OECD 2013 *The 2012 Labour market reform in Spain: A preliminary assessment* (Paris: OECD). In <http://dx.doi.org/10.1787/9789264213586-en> accessed 6 October 2014.

O'Reilly, Jacqueline et al. 2015 "Five characteristics of youth unemployment in Europe: Flexibility, education, migration, family legacies and EU policy," *Sage Open (US)*, January–March, 2015.

Shavit, Yossi, Müller, Walter and Tame, Clare (eds.) 1998 *From School to work: A comparative study of educational qualifications and occupational outcomes* (Oxford: Clarendon Press).

Walther, Andreas 2006 "Regimes of youth transitions. Choice, flexibility and security in young people's experiences across different European contexts," *Young-Nordic Journal of Youth Research,* Vol. 14, No. 2, 119–139.

YOUTH IN THE GREEK LABOR MARKET

Apostolos Dedoussopoulos and Eva Maria Papachristopoulou

The question of youth employment and the labor market remains a hotly debated political topic that also poses analytical and empirical issues. Though work along alternative theoretical approaches has increased our insight and understanding of this issue, empirical work lags behind, mostly because of the complicated nature of the issue itself.

The aim of this chapter is twofold: We briefly review the main theoretical currents and questions posed on the issue and provide an account of significant macro-tendencies on the basis of constructed indices for Greek society of the period between 1983 and 2013. We approach various dimensions of youth labor market problems in Greece from a longitudinal perspective and with a clear focus on gender and age-related issues.

Our empirical investigation constitutes a preliminary attempt to clear the ground for more detailed and focused empirical research. We believe that specific case studies become meaningful and add to our understanding by showing the significance of additional explanatory factors only when macro-tendencies have been clearly established. Data availability is always a factor, limiting choices and creating inevitable disjunctions between theory and empirical research. Thus, our approach in this chapter is determined by both methodological considerations and the availability of relevant data.

Youth unemployment: How important is it?

Almost 15 years ago, two of the most prominent US American economists, D.G. Blanchflower and R.B. Freeman (2000; 1997), stated in their introduction to a NBER volume dedicated to the problem of youth employment that young people in modern society were much better off in all aspects of their lives in comparison with past generations, with one notable exception: all aspects related to work, that is employment status, stability of work, career prospects, and remuneration, had been deteriorating

One may easily admit that this is a correct description, but at the same time it is somehow an absurd one. It overlooks the centrality of work in modern society and its role in shaping social identities; it ignores the social and individual costs of unemployment, precarious work, and low-level wages. Ultimately, it is a comforting statement. What Blanchflower and Freeman implied is that things are not as bad as they look.

The grievances of youth unemployment have become a key argument for the introduction and proliferation of policies such as *training without jobs*, tailor-made educational programs, flexible working time arrangements, part-time and fixed-time wage contracts, substitution of apprenticeships or stage contracts for regular work, wages under minimum standards, *national security exceptions, costless hiring and hiring procedures,* and *marginal or none unemployment benefit*. In this sense, the youth labor market has been an extremely unregulated market, a social experiment *per se* to be generalized and institutionalized.

However, unemployment rates among young persons are high as ever, with the ratio of youth unemployment being constantly double that of adults in most EU countries—with only four exceptions. To be more precise, the ratio of youth unemployment rate to total unemployment rate for all 28 EU countries stands at 2.34 with a standard deviation of 0.473. Four countries (Belgium, Italy, Luxembourg, and Romania) have a ratio exceeding the average by more than one standard deviation, while four countries (Germany, Denmark, Lithuania, and the Netherlands) have a ratio lower than the average by one standard deviation. Ireland, Croatia, and Sweden are at the margin.

Figure 1 indicates the close relationship between overall unemployment and youth unemployment rates. For EU countries, a 1% increase in total unemployment means an average rise of 2.14 in the youth unemployment rate. Though the estimated regression does not indicate any causality, it points to the existence of common determinant variables affecting the behavior of both total and youth unemployment. In fact, this evidence reinforces the validity of the conclusions reached by estimations of the so-called "Gaude regression" indicating a constant long-term relationship between youth and adult unemployment rates (Blanchflower, 1999; Gaude, 1997; O' Higgins, 1997).[1]

---

[1] The Gaude regression is expressed as $\ln(YUR)_t = a + b \ln(AUR)_t + \varepsilon_t$, connecting the youth unemployment rate to adult unemployment rate in a logarithmic form.

Figure 1: Total unemployment rates vs youth unemployment rates, EU28, 2013

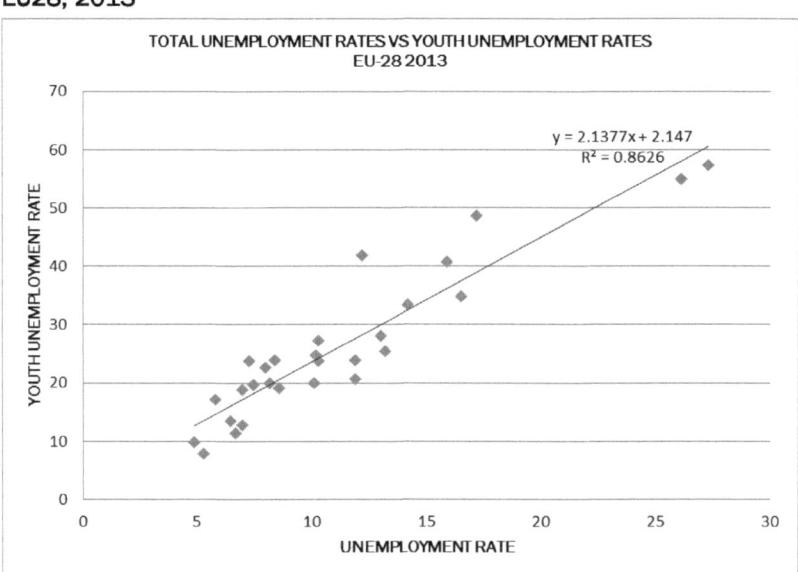

The school to work transition: Youth theories

Education has been compulsory up to a certain age in European countries since the late 19th century. Compulsory education is not only providing a minimum age separating children from persons who are considered fully able to work, it has also helped to define the category of "youth" itself. In a sense, any theory addressing the question of youth is bound to be related to a theoretical conception of education in modern society. This statement holds true for all sociological and for most economic theories.

It is not our aim to discuss in detail the various theories advanced to deal with the relationship between youth and the labor market. The table in Appendix I tries to recapitulate the main theories and themes in order to simplify the presentation (Dedoussopoulos, forthcoming; Rudd, 1997).

Summarizing essential characteristics of the various theories, one may conclude that:
- Structural–functionalist approaches implied a rather static conception of social order with limited social mobility. Within their

framework, youth employment prospects have been largely predetermined. Three factors of determination were notified, that is, social class (defined as social class in Marxist terms, or as income, wealth, education level of parents, position in the work hierarchy, groups, or any combination of them), gender and racial, ethnical, or religious groups, representing social inequalities. Transition from education to work positions was considered being instantaneous, so that the relationship between the educational system and work was an immediate one. On a whole, system rationality prevailed over individual rationality, with the individual having to either adjust consensually to pre-determined jobs, or be excluded (anomy).

- Individualistic approaches flourished after unemployment and, long-term unemployment, in particular, has been an established permanent feature of modern societies since the last quarter of the 20th century. The time spent in unemployment (unemployment duration) increased and unemployment spells became more frequent. As a result, attention was directed to individual actions aiming at "filling the void" per se or *acquisition*, either real or frictional, of occupational skills, through training programs, part-time employment, fixed time contracts, or low-paid temporary schemes, stage employment, and in-firm training. Baethge (1989) notes that the concept of individualization questions the existence of "youths" as a specific social category.

- "Reflective modernity," according to Beck, or "rationalization" (Furlong, 2003) indicates a phase of reconsideration, self-evaluation, and adjustment to future opportunities and risks of the inherently rational individual. Thus, re-orientation and new actions are evoked after a previous stage of planning and acting. The individual moves from "station to station," from education to various forms of jobs, training schemes, idle time, or combinations of the above, following individualized trajectories, paths, or routes, materializing a transition process, until a satisfactory job is obtained.

- Though "the individualization project" has been developed in view of explaining a reality of increased complexity and uncertainty, the empirical outcome has not been promising. Empirical work has either taken the form of specific case studies, the conclusion of which could hardly be generalized, or ended up reaffirming the explanatory power of the dominant three factors, celebrated by the structural–functional approaches: the role of social class, gender, and race (Vickerstaff, 2003). Individual choices and available opportunities are confined within a well-specified area of social action, determined by social structures and procedures, indicating the need for a new approach combining the concept of transition with structural conceptions of society.

- State policy has contributed to a large degree in both the proliferation and the shaping of these "station posts" and, hence, of patterns of transition. Flexibilization of the labor market, marginal social protection of the youth, active labor market policies, and activation policies have created the institutional setting of the so-called "transitional labor markets" (Brzinsky-Fay, 2010), and inspired a large volume of theoretical and empirical work in the last 15 years. Yet, as Ch. Brzinsky-Fey observes, "bridging the micro-macro gap remains a problem that has not been solved satisfactorily" (2010: 17). Social class is commonly omitted from the explanatory factors of the transitional labor markets project, though policy and social institutions are incorporated in the analysis. Hence, transitional labor markets tend to contribute to a broader conception in comparison to the simple supply-side fixation of the individualistic approach. Though the evidence is still inconclusive, some indication exists that part-time jobs, mini-jobs, or temporary contract jobs for young persons may lead to a permanent trap rather than creating a bridge to better jobs, unless they contribute to the acquisition of firm-specific and/or occupational skills. Such a conclusion is also consistent with traditional human capital theory.
- Economic approaches, on the other hand, tend to concentrate on explanations based on lower-than-average individual labor productivity of youth, resulting in lower wage rates, unemployment, or frequent unemployment spells. Supply-side considerations are prominent in human capital, skill mismatch, employability, structural unemployment, or inadequate social skills variations. The demand side is reflected in approaches based on "ports

of entrance," which may lead to inferior job traps, if coupled with segmentation theories and/or institutional approaches of labor market organization.
- Transitions in economic approaches are treated as a sequence of independent decisions taken by a rational, utility maximizing individual when faced with two or more alternative situations. Decisions are always made in the present, with future costs and benefits converted to their present value. This has been the clear pattern in most of the literature concerning transitional labor markets.

In conclusion, sociological research has contributed to our understanding of youth as *a transitional social category*, that is, a social group in the process of transition from education to the labor market. Such a transition is not an instantaneous one, as simplified in structural–functionalist approaches, nor a series of decisions made by rational agents, as supported by economic theory. Transition is characterized by uncertainties and risks and the final outcomes, though structured, are not predetermined. Paths and trajectories do not describe a step-by-step advancement toward a given end, but involve regression, stagnation, and shifts, while the target is continuously redefined.

Furthermore, structural analyses underline the importance of major social factors that divide youth and determine their prospects in the labor market. "Youth" is not a homogeneous category; it is a highly differentiated, heterogeneous group.

Hence, the relationship of youth, as a transitional social category, with the labor market, cannot easily be quantified with the use of the usual labor market indices. This observation has to be kept in mind throughout the analysis of the empirical evidence that follows. Indices tend to moderate a situation, that is, hide important differences that are revealed only at a more micro level.

Youth in the Greek labor market: Long run tendencies

The conceptualization of youth as a transitional social category directly implies the existence of an inherent instability in the relationship between youth and the employment structure. This has forced the ILO staff to propose seven distinct, though related, indices in order to anticipate and measure adequately the labor market involvement of young persons (ILO, 2003; ILO, 2001).

Youth unemployment is an important policy issue for many countries at all stages of development. For this purpose, the term "youth" covers persons aged 15–24, while "adults" are defined as persons aged 25 and over. Youth unemployment is presented in the following four ways: (1) the youth unemployment rate, (2) the ratio of the youth unemployment rate to the adult unemployment rate, (3) the youth share in total unemployment, and (4) youth unemployment as a proportion of the youth population (ILO, 2003; ILO, 2001).

The unemployment rate is probably the best-known measure of the labor market. Together with the labor force participation rate and employment-to-population ratio, it provides the broadest available indicator of economic activity and status in terms of labor markets for countries that regularly collect information on the labor force. The unemployment rate tells us the proportion of the labor force that does not have a job, is available to work, and is actively looking for work. It should not be misinterpreted as a measurement of economic hardship, although a correlation often exists (ILO, 2003; ILO, 2001). We have used all of the above indices together with the education ratio for young people. Thus, we hope to form a clear picture concerning the issue of youth unemployment. The key indicators of the labor market measures should be analyzed together; any of the seven, analyzed in isolation, could present a distorted image.

We have calculated these indices for Greece over the 1983–2013 period (all data are from the Labour Force Survey [LFS], Greek Statistical Service and refer to the second quarter of the year), in an attempt to establish long-term patterns and changes. We use three age groups, two belonging conventionally to the "youth population" and the third as a result of our estimations of the age in which this transition process reaches its end, that is, as a measure of employment "near maturity."

Where transition (roughly) ends?

In order to roughly define the age at which transition has almost come to an end, we have used the employment rate, that is the percentage of an age cohort in any form of employment in relation to the respective total population. There is a certain degree of ambiguity in choosing employment rate as an indication of the end of the transition process. However, our alternative estimations with persons in permanent full-time jobs did not change much of the conclusion, so for simplicity we have chosen to report the employment rate. Employment rates have been calculated with respect to gender and level of education for age cohorts 15–35 years in the year 2008. For simplicity, we have used three levels of education corresponding to elementary (level 1), secondary (level 2), and tertiary (level 3). The year 2008 was depicted as the last "normal" year, just before the beginning of the recent economic crisis.

Education levels may, under certain conditions, reflect the indirect effect of socioeconomic factors, whose influence has been well documented in theory and in some empirical work (parents' employment position, education level, etc.). LFS data do not provide such information, with the exception of youth staying with parents, which introduces a bias in estimation. We assume, therefore, that education exercises both a direct and an indirect effect on employment rates, as it also reflects indirectly unobserved factors of socioeconomic origin.

Figures 2 and 3 report the estimated rates of employment for males and females separately.

Figure 2: Employment rate by level of education and age – Males, 2008

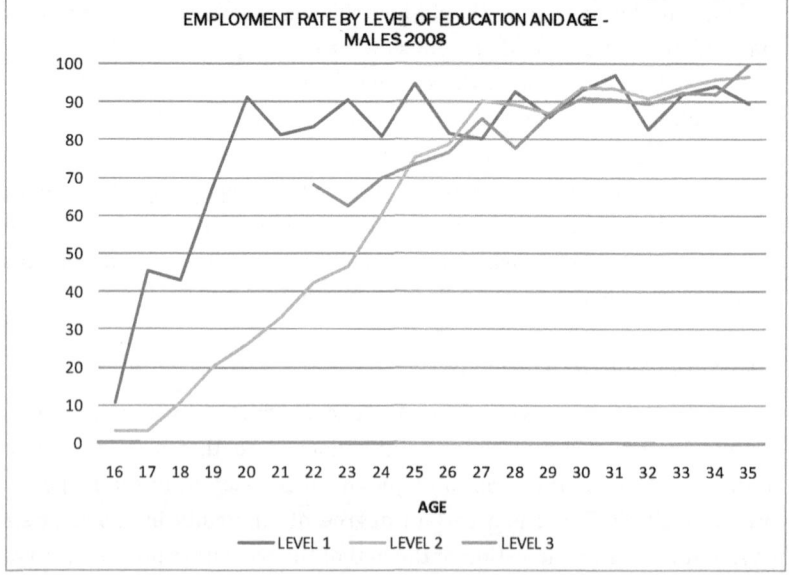

Figure 3: Employment rate by level of education and age – Females, 2008

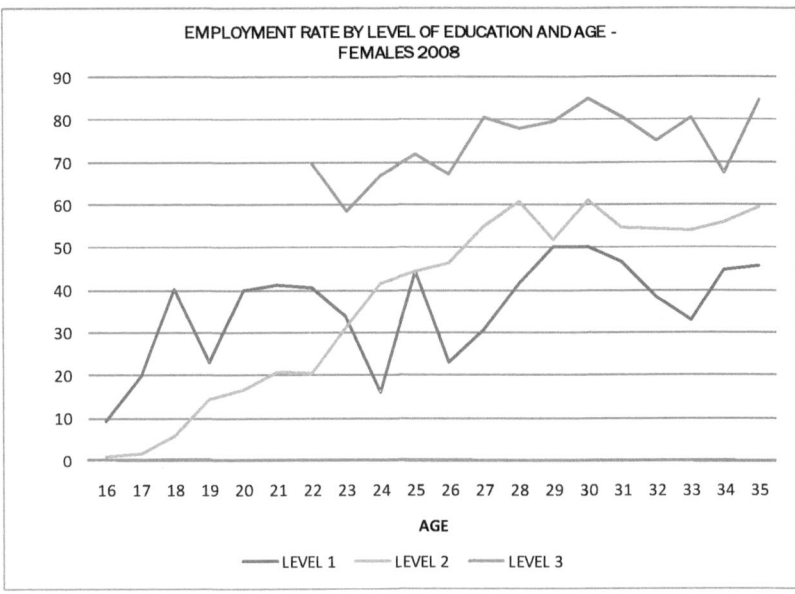

As expected, persons with an elementary education level enter employment earlier than those with higher levels of education. By age 20, young males of this category reach a peak in their employment rate (90%). The employment rate fluctuates randomly after that age with no clear tendency. For females of the same level of education, we observe two or three peaks at the age of 18, 25, and 29. Dropping out of school too early, does not simply determine early attempts to find a job but also forming a family and raising one child or more. This category of young females exhibits a most traditional pattern in their relation to the labor market and the structure of employment, the so-called "double reverse U." Employment relations are interrupted by marriage and child infancy. On the whole, their employment rate remains very low, lower than the other two educational categories—with the exception of the early 20s.

Both males and females with secondary education, exhibit a stable pattern of increase in their rate of employment until the age of 30. Male employment rates increase more rapidly until the age of 27 (90%) and then continue to rise at a much smaller pace, climbing to 96.3% at the age of 35. Female employment rate reaches its peak at the age of 28.

The employment rate of males with tertiary education does not show any difference in size after the age of 25 in relation to the other educational categories. One should note, however, two interesting indications: First, and contrary to theoretical predictions, males with tertiary education find a job earlier than those with a secondary education, but, second, the level of their employment rate remains marginally below the other two groups. Moreover, the age of 30 is also a good approximation for the age where the transition ends for this educational category.

The most interesting behavior is that of the employment rate of females with tertiary education. Firstly, the employment rate is much higher than the corresponding rates of the other two female groups, close to that of males with tertiary education at the age of 30, where it peaks (84.9%). This is a well-documented feature of the Greek labor market, with both the participation and the employment rates of females with tertiary education significantly exceeding corresponding rates of other females. In a sense, tertiary education has become a precondition for females to enter into an employment relationship. Secondly, employment rate exhibits a mild reverse U, a result of family creation and childbearing after the age of 30 years old.

Early dropouts apart, transition ends about age 30 (on average). However, marked differences exist in the behavior of the rate with respect to gender, education, and specific age.

The participation rate by gender: Long-run tendencies

Figure 4 indicates significant long-term differences in participation rates with respect to both gender and age. Though gender differences tend to be reduced, age differences have increased overtime. The evidence is summarized in Table 1.

Participation rates are falling rapidly over time for both genders in the age category of 15–19 years. The age category of 20–24 years shows a more complicated pattern. The participation rate of men tends to fall quite rapidly at the beginning of the period (1983–1992), stabilizes in the second sub-period (1993–2000), then falls rapidly (2000–2007), and stabilizes again after 2008 (the crisis period).

Figure 4: Participation rates, 1983-2013

Table 1: Participation Rates by Gender and Age Group 1983-2013

AGE GROUP	1983	2008	2013
MALE			
15-19	29.1	10.3	8.9
20-24	71.2	55.4	55.2
25-29	94.8	91.5	...
15-64	81.2	79.2	....
FEMALE			
15-19	20.3	7.2	6.1
20-24	49.1	45.2	46.0
25-29	48.2	76.4	81.6
15-64	39.0	55.1	58.7

One should note the divergence in the pattern of the participation rate of females in the 20-24 and 25-29 age brackets. For a rather long period, the two age groups tended to move together, but since 1999 they have moved in opposite directions. It is clear that the females aged 20-24 years postpone their participation in the labor force, as scholarization (schooling) rates for this population group have rapidly increased.

On the whole, participation rates for youth below 25 years old have been reduced significantly. This finding implies a postponement in the age of entering into the labor market, partly as the effect of extended participation in education. The severity of the employment crisis does not seem to have an effect on participation rates, that is the expected "additional laborer" effect has not been very strong.

The time period since 1983 is marked by the massive entrance of females into the labor force, with the female participation rate gaining 20 percentage points. It is clear that this phenomenon has been confined to females older than 25 years of age.

The employment rate by gender: Long-run tendencies

Figure 5 represents the long-run tendencies in the employment rate by gender and age group.

Figure 5: Employment rate, 1983-2013

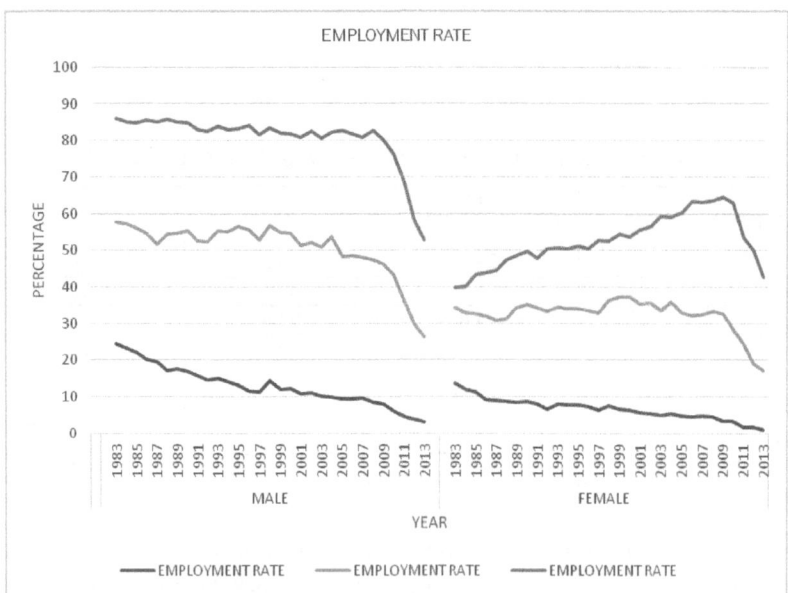

With respect to the employment rates, there are also gender and, to a lesser degree, age differences within genders. During the period 1983-2009, male employment rates fell steadily in all youth age groups, but this decline is not uniform. Female employment rates present a most varying pattern. In the age group of 15-19 years, there exists a steady and rapid decline. In the age group of 20-24 years, the employment rate, though fluctuating, remains relatively constant, while in the age group of 25–29 years, employment rates have rapidly risen.

Table 2 reports simple linear trends for participation and employment rates over the period 1983–2009, that is the period before the employment crisis of the Greek economy.

Table 2: Simple linear trends for participation and employment rates, 1983–2009

	MALE		FEMALE	
AGE GROUP	COEFFICIENT	R2	COEFFICIENT	R2
PARTICIPATION RATE				
15–19	0.584	0.912	0.405	0.745
20–24	0.480	0.557	0.017	0.001
25–29	0.109	0.334	1.109	0.964
EMPLOYMENT RATE				
15–19	0.559	0.911	0.285	0.876
20–24	0.303	0.564	0.045	0.044
25–29	0.179	0.728	0.873	0.965

The trend in employment rates is very strong and is a negative sign for persons of the 15–19 age group for both genders. It is also very strong but with a positive slope for females aged 25–29 years. It is less strong for males of the same age, but with a negative slope. There is no significant tendency for persons in the 20–24 age group, especially for females.

An examination of the relationship between the trends in participation and employment rates indicates the existence of common patterns. One might come to the conclusion that youth employment prospects are strongly determined by supply of labor factors. This would be a hasty conclusion. Demand factors, determining the availability of employment opportunities and the quality of the available positions, may influence participation rates as well as employment rates.

Employment in all age groups is rapidly reduced after 2009, as a result of the crisis in the Greek economy. Though participation rates are marginally altered, the probability of a person having a job, that is, the size of the employment rate, is significantly reduced, almost to half or even more for the 15–19 age group. Table 3 depicts this reduction in the historical probability of a person belonging to a specific age and gender group to be in employment. Employment rates are interpreted as the historical probability that a person belonging to a specific population group has a job.

Table 3: Probability of a person belonging to a specific age and gender group to be in employment

YEAR	MALE			FEMALE		
	15–19	20–24	25–29	15–19	20–24	25–29
1983	24.3	57.6	86.1	13.8	34.3	39.8
1993	15.1	55.4	83.9	8.1	34.5	50.6
2003	10.1	51.0	80.7	5.0	33.5	59.3
2008	8.4	47.4	82.8	4.6	33.3	63.5
2013	3.1	26.4	52.7	1.1	17.2	42.7

The unemployment rate and ratio by gender: Long-run tendencies

Needless to say, unemployment rates for youth went sky high during the years of the economic crisis. Youth unemployment rates have been relatively high for the whole 1983–2013 period, but it is its rapid increase over the past five years that created a dramatic and distressing situation. Figures 6 and 7 provide valuable information on the issue.

Figure 6: Unemployment rates, 1983–2013

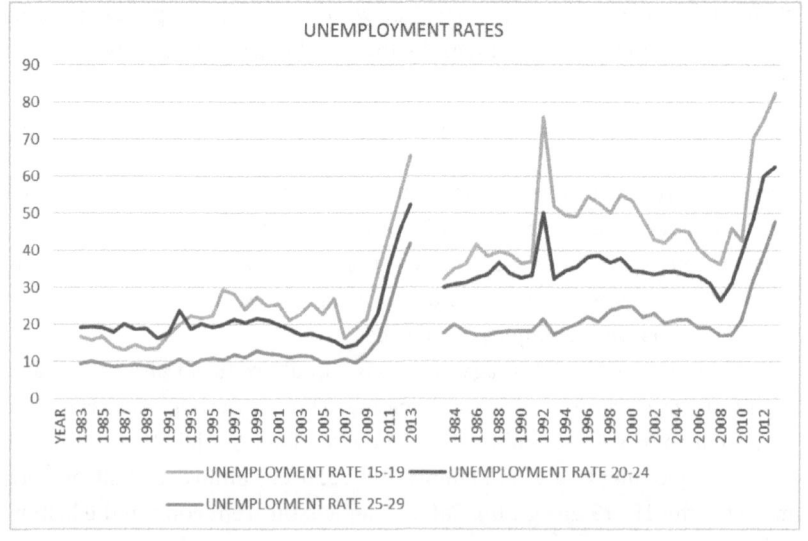

The picture does not change if we calculate the unemployment ratio, that is, the ratio of unemployment to the population, instead of the unemployment rate.

However, a significant difference exists between the two figures. If we look at Figure 6 we note that the unemployment rate of the 15–19 age group, in both genders, stands higher than the corresponding rates of the other two groups. However, Figure 7 reveals that the unemployment-population ratio of that age group during the period 1983–2013 remains well below the ratios of the other two groups.

This is an example of how the use of a single index—especially the unemployment rate—may lead to erroneous conclusions. Unemployment rate expresses the probability that a person belonging to a certain population group may face unemployment *under the condition that he/she already belongs to the labor force* (conditioned probability). This means that the unemployment rate expresses the burden of unemployment for those in the labor force, not the population of the group.

Figure 7: Unemployment ratio, 1983–2013

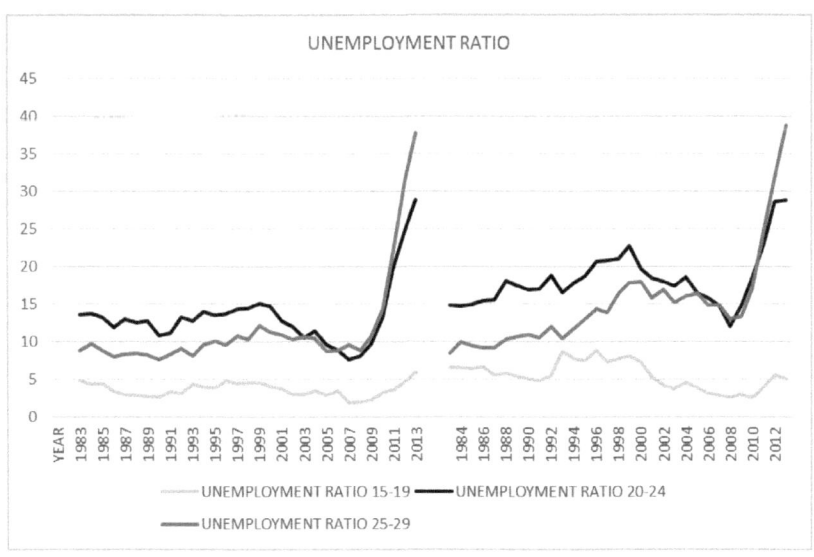

Econometric estimations by the authors (not reported in this chapter) indicate that participation rates of youth depend upon the mature persons' unemployment rate (current and lagged) plus a mild time trend.

Hence, up to a certain age, the decision to enter the labor force is affected by the state of the labor market.

The impact of unemployment on youth *population* is relatively larger for the 20–24 age group of both genders and, even more so for the 25–29-year-olds. The latter group is more severely hit during the crisis period.

Youth unemployment and the unemployment of adults

Figures 8 and 9 highlight the relation between youth unemployment and adult unemployment. Figure 8 depicts the share of youth unemployment in total unemployment, while Figure 9 indicates the ratio between the youth unemployment rate and the adult unemployment rate.

The sky-high levels of the youth unemployment rate tend to hide a more disturbing negative development of the Greek labor market, namely, the increasing burden of unemployment on the mature age groups.

Figure 8: Share of youth unemployment in total unemployment, 1983–2013

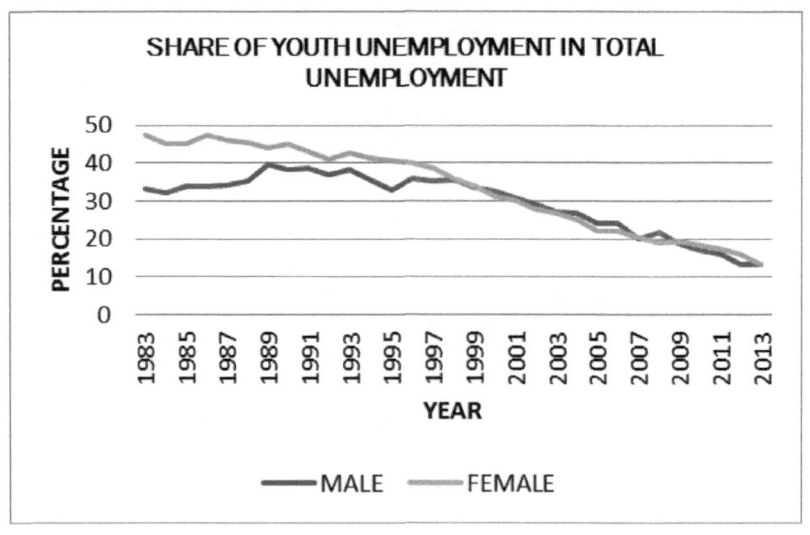

Figure 9: Youth unemployment rate to adult unemployment rate, 1983–2013

Figure 8 provides two kinds of information. First, it shows that, though the danger of being unemployed increases, the social burden of youth unemployment diminishes when compared to the social burden of adult unemployment. Second, though gender differences in unemployment rates continue to exist, youth unemployment shares converge. This implies the existence of a specific social mechanism discriminating against young females. Such a mechanism has lessened its impact since 1999, while the general employment discrimination against females irrespective of age is still functional.

The same conclusions seem to be reaffirmed when using the ratio of youth unemployment rate to adult (25–55 years old) unemployment rate. The ratio declines steadily since 1992, while young males are in a relatively worse position than young females, as compared to mature persons of the same gender.

A legitimate objection may be raised in this context: The falling share of youth unemployment in total unemployment may be attributed to demographic reasons, namely the decrease of the youth population. Using a shift-share analysis for the two genders and the three age groups, we decomposed changes in the level of unemployment for six consequent periods (1983–1988, 1988–1993, 1993–1998, 1998–2003, 2003–2008 and 2008–2013). Decomposition established the predominance of net cyclical (demand-side) effects over demographic factors in all cases with just a few exceptions. The graphs of the decomposition findings are included in Appendix II.

It is clear that the widely accepted view that the Greek unemployment problem has been caused by supply factors, that is by the low employability of youth and females, cannot be maintained. If that problem ever existed, it has long lost its significance, well before the eruption of the current crisis.

Participation in formal education

As indicated in Figure 10, schooling ratios have been rising steadily. Females have rapidly gained ground in participation in education, with education being almost a precondition for their participation in the labor market.

The fall in the schooling ratios for the 15–19 age group in 1999–2000 by 5 percentage points is due to a short-lived educational reform, which was reintroduced, but abandoned after the elections in January 2015.

Staying in the educational system has been a real option for young persons in their 20s. On the one hand, the opportunity cost for education is very low, given the situation in the labor market and on the other hand, education becomes a shelter against inactivity, as well as a private resource for migration opportunities. In fact, a large number of Greeks with university degrees have sought jobs in Germany, the Netherlands, and Sweden during the past few years. Yet, the rate of increase has been reduced during the crisis.

Figure 10: Schooling ratio, 1992-2013

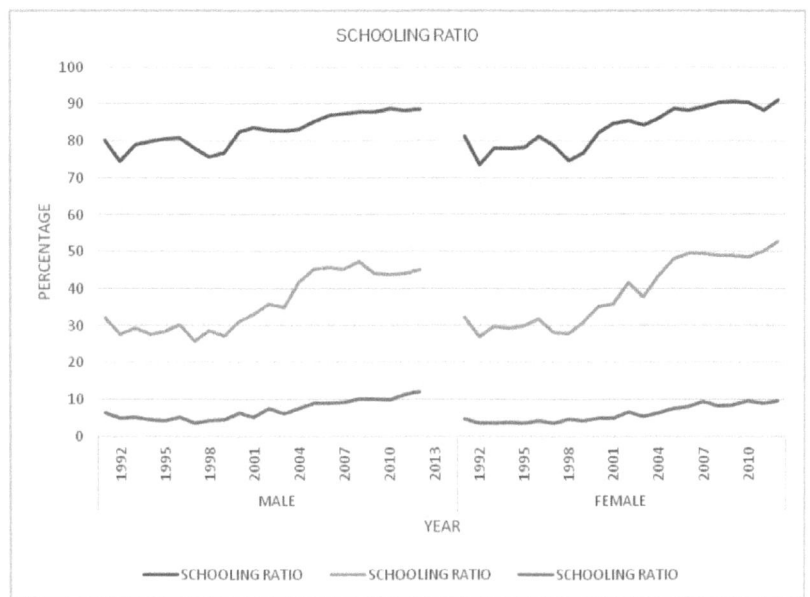

The effects of youth migration on population and the labor market magnitudes have not yet been reflected in official statistics, because of the sampling methods of the LFS. This creates an additional source of ambiguity in the aforementioned analysis.

Youth and the labor market: A quasi-cohort analysis

LFS data do not permit a formal longitudinal analysis to be attempted. Yet, we have tried a quasi-cohort analysis by observing changes in employment status, education, and household autonomy as the individuals belonging to a specified age cohort mature in age. The analysis is not an actual cohort analysis, in the sense that we do not observe exactly the same individuals through time, but individuals belonging to the same age. We have to assume that personal characteristics other than the ones we are checking are distributed with the same pattern in the consecutive samples of the LFS and we have not tried to adjust for changes in distribution.

We have chosen three distinct cohorts, that is, persons 15 years of age in 1999, 2004, and 2009. The choice was made in an attempt to estimate the effects of the economic crisis on youth. For each age cohort, we formed two sub-cohorts according to gender. The results are reported in the form of tables (see Appendix III).

Data (in the tables) are interpreted as consecutive historical probabilities of a person belonging to a specific cohort to be in a certain situation. Probabilities change as the person matures in age following specific patterns. As is shown, patterns are disrupted because of the crisis in the Greek economy.

The conclusions reached from the examination of the basic employment indices above are largely reaffirmed. The employment crisis has not affected participation in the labor market for either gender. The only indication to the contrary is the female 2009-15 cohort—at the age of 19, the participation rate is reduced by 8 percentage units in comparison to the 2004-15 cohort, but the schooling ratio has increased by 11 percentage units.

Employment rates have been significantly affected. A 19-year-old male in 2013 had an 8.5% probability of having a job in comparison to 22.7% of a 19-year-old in 2008, just before the crisis erupts. For females of the same age the probability, of having a job was close to zero, 2.2%, in comparison to 14.8% for those who were 19 years old in 2008.

The male cohort 2004-15 had an employment rate of 41.9 in 2013 (age 24 years old); one-third lower when compared to the rate of 63.5 of the older age cohort (1999-2015) at the same age. Within the same cohort (1999-2015) the employment rate is reduced by 7 percentage units (from 70.5 at the age of 25 to 63.7 at the age of 29. The same direction of change applies in the case of female cohorts.

Unemployment rates rapidly increased in all age and gender cohorts after 2008. From 13.4% at the age of 24, unemployment rate rises to 33.1% at the age of 29 for males of cohort 1999-2015. All other cohorts face a bleaker situation.

The comparison among the three age cohorts indicates that the crisis has increased schooling age for both genders, in accordance to theoretical predictions, but more for females than males. For females, getting a postsecondary education degree is considered a precondition for entering into the labor market and in employment structure. However, employment prospects seem rather bleak for both genders irrespective of their educational level.

The out-of-education/out-of-work fraction of the youth population, however, has been accelerating over the past five years, pointing to the reinforcement of social processes of exclusion, deprivation, and poverty. One has the feeling of a lost generation.

Figures 11 and 12 indicate the degree of educational and work exclusion of the age cohorts by gender. Though female cohorts participate more than their male counterparts in education, overall, they are more in danger of this "double exclusion." However, one should note the alarming steep increase of the ratio for the male 2009–15 age cohort at the age of 18 and after, that is, after finishing the secondary noncompulsory education.

It is clear that the danger of the double exclusion increases with age in each cohort. Postsecondary education provides temporary shelter during times of regular economic environment, but it fails during crisis. One may conclude that unemployment becomes a severe burden on youth as both crisis and age develop.

Figure 11: Out-of-work/out-of-education, male cohorts (%)

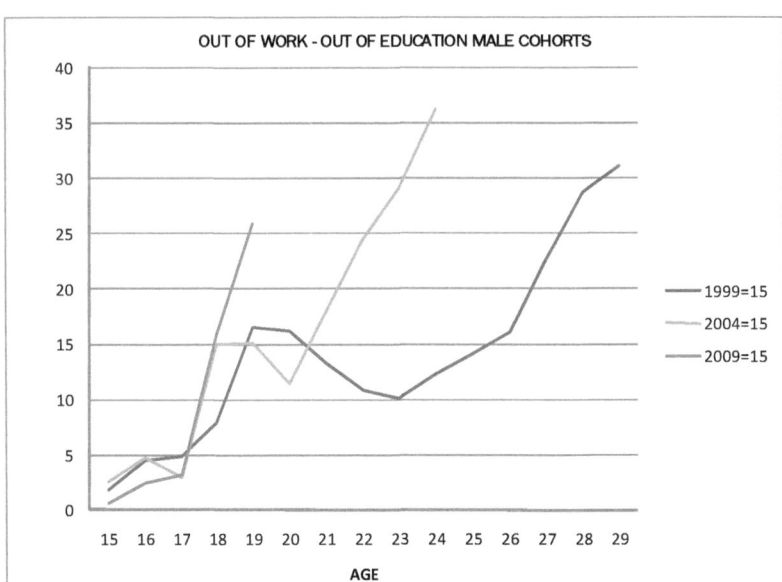

Figure 12: Out-of-work/out-of-education, female cohorts (%)

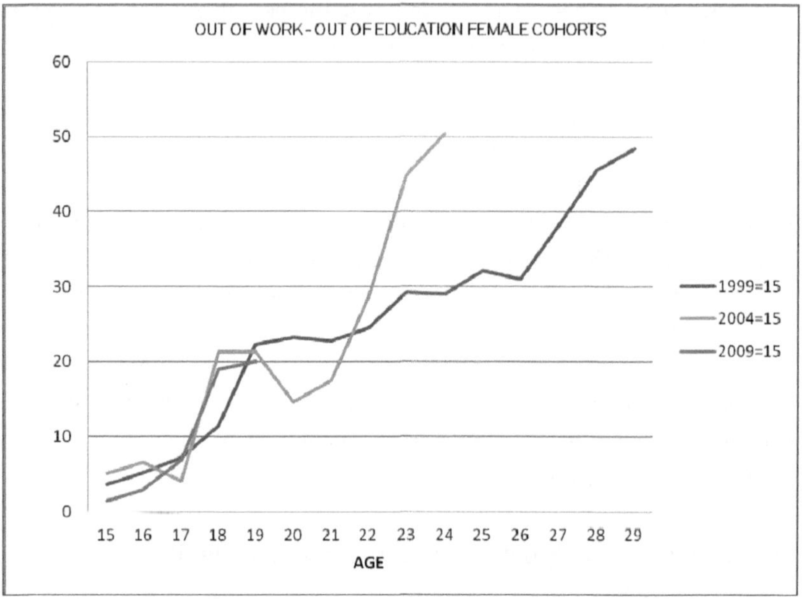

The impact of the employment crisis is best viewed by observing the sharp decline of autonomy from the parental household of the second cohort, that is, those of 15 years of age in 2004. Having reached a high degree of autonomy before the crisis (more than 50% for males and 60% of females) they tend to return to the parental family. Yet, the degree of achieving autonomy from parental family for the age cohort 1999-2015 supports fully our previous conclusion with respect to the age that the transition period ends.

Conclusions and policy Implications

Our analysis has reaffirmed some important conclusions concerning the youth employment problem.

First, it has indicated the close relation between youth and adult unemployment and their dependence on the growth rates. Unemployment will continue to be a persistent social and economic problem as long as recession continues, an obvious conclusion, which, however, has been overlooked in the formation and implementation of policies at hand.[2]

Second, in accordance with the theoretical predictions, the comparison between the three age groups showed that the crisis had increased the number of years youth remained in the education system. This is true for both genders, but more for women than for men. For women, getting a degree after secondary education is seen as a prerequisite for entry into the labor market and in the employment structure. However, prospects for employment looked rather bleak for both genders regardless of their level of education. Furthermore, the percentage of young peoples' autonomy has been reduced significantly. Young people face high unemployment, potential social exclusion, and reduction of their autonomy.

Third, the impact of the employment crisis is best observed in the sharp decline of autonomy from family homes of the second group, that is, those who were 15 years old in 2004. Having reached a high degree of autonomy before the crisis, more than 50% of men and 60% of women tend to return to the parental family during the crisis. However, the degree of achievement of autonomy from parental family for the age group 1999–2015 fully supports our previous conclusion with respect to the age that the transition period is completed.

The percentage of the "not in education—out of work" population (NEET), however, has accelerated during the past five years, which points to the strengthening of social processes of exclusion, deprivation, and poverty. Studying the degree of educational and labor exclusion, we note that although women's groups participate more than men in education, as a whole, they are more at risk of this double exclusion. It is clear that the risk of double exclusion increases as the age increases for each group. Higher education provides temporary shelter in times of "normal" economic environment, but it fails during economic crisis, postponing at best the phenomenon. One may conclude that unemployment becomes a serious burden at an increasing pace for the youth as crisis and age grow.

Based on our conclusions of long-term trends, the gender differences regarding participation and employment rates are very interesting and are a significant point of the empirical analysis. These differences are

---

[2] For the macroeconomic impact of the Memoranda structural adjustment programs in Greece, see Dedoussopoulos et al., 2013.

pronounced particularly for the 25–29 age bracket. More women stay longer in education and their participation exhibits a fast increase compared to men (for the 25–29-year-olds), thus there is a strong positive slope for women (in Table 1) for the period before the crisis. During the crisis, even though there is a convergence in unemployment risks between men and women, unemployment rates for women are still higher than for men (though there are variations with regard to male and female age brackets).

Though youth unemployment is a severe economic and social problem, the huge unemployment rates should not conceal the fact that its importance, relative to the unemployment of the mature population, is both limited and diminishing over time. Youth unemployment, especially female youth unemployment, remains a distinct problem that policy makers have to face.

On the other hand, youth unemployment has been a structural problem that predates the crisis (but it has been exacerbated by the crisis) and currently it is a relative rather than an absolute problem, as supported by the analysis. This brings into question the policies adopted before the crisis (2008), policies that continue to be applied in the times of crisis.

However, our main analytical conclusion is that "youth" is not a homogeneous social category. Sharp diversities exist even with respect to the three characteristics considered, that is, gender, age, and the level of education. Social structures result in inequalities that shape prospects, opportunities, and risks in the labor market. In this sense, this chapter provides a background work for the development of more detailed empirical research aiming at bringing into surface the functioning of salient social factors, most notably of social class.

With respect to policies aiming at combating youth unemployment, there have been three distinct areas of social policy activated: education, institutional arrangements and their implementation, and active labor market policies.

Very briefly, and putting aside the debate on educational reforms, institutional arrangements have tended to impose a further flexibilization on working conditions of youth—imposition of a youth minimum wage lower than the adult minimum wage, differential treatment toward new employees in social security contributions and benefits, no eligibility to unemployment benefits, relaxing preconditions for, and rates of, dismissal compensations plus extension of the initial "trial" period to one year, thus transforming all new contracts into temporary jobs. Undeclared work, part-time, and temporary jobs have flourished during the crisis. One may argue convincingly that policy has largely contributed in creating a precarious job nexus. Youth enter into a fully flexible and unprotected labor market. There are important questions raised concerning both short-term (mainly on productivity) and long-term impacts of these institutional changes. Long-term impacts relate to job stability, career prospects, low prospect jobs and poverty traps, and ability to secure a pension in the future.

The institutional creation of a flexible youth labor market is augmented by recent (2012) reforms in the minimum wage setting. Minimum wage is set by administrative decisions, annihilating collective bargaining and the role of social partners. With respect to youth up to the age of 25, minimum wages are set well below the set adult wage rate, irrespective of characteristics other than age. This policy seems to countervail gaps in productivity between youth and adult employees, according to neoclassical conceptions. Yet, one should note that the impact on youth employment has been very small, if any (Ghellab, 1998; Card and Krueger, 1995). This is not only due to the overall condition of the labor market, but is also in accordance with the third postulate of the Hicks–Marshall's elasticity of demand for labor theory. This rule implies that the larger the share of this labor in total cost, the larger the elasticity of demand for labor. The share of labor in total cost in manufacturing was 13% in 2007, meaning that a reduction by 30% of labor cost will result in a feeble 4% reduction of total cost. Given that youth employment cost is a small percentage of total labor cost, a failure of the policy in question had to be expected. In fact, youth employment has been stabilized in sectors where youth employment was relatively large, that is, in catering services. This is partially due to labor substitution between youth and mature age employees. The occurrence of such a substitution is confined in sectors or enterprises for which work experience is either not considered an asset or it is easily acquired.

Active labor market measures have promoted part-time and temporary jobs, stage work, and training schemes through vouchers. In all cases, youth eligible in participating in these measures have been treated mostly as an age category, overlooking other divisions. The Greek Manpower Organisation (OAED), responsible for designing and implementation of active labor market policies, remains ineffective. A recent study noted that OAED did not implement a thorough practice of individualized counseling (Dedoussopoulos, 2013). In fact, counseling has been totally abandoned during the crisis period. Furthermore, local job Centers never tried to contact local enterprises. As a result, measures are of a general character, unspecified and ignorant of both: the skill or other shortcomings of the unemployed and the skill needs of local enterprises.

Thus, a large-scale reorganization of OAED is badly required as a precondition of an effective active labor market policy to be implemented. Local job centers should be in constant contact with local enterprises and employers. At the same time effort should be made in trying to match young employee candidate needs to employers' needs, that is, individualized counseling must take effect.

Expansion of educational guidance and youth career consulting, as well as promoting general education (elimination of premature dropouts) is also needed. Targeted initiatives aimed at informing young people and their parents about current and expected labor market opportunities are vital initiatives that would, at the same time, require taking into account cultural backgrounds in the design. Policies are needed to ensure primary and secondary schooling, and to avoiding early school leaving. Policymakers should aim at providing basic skills for every young person and intensive personal support. This implies greater emphasis on personalized and customized support for young people at risk, educational guidance, and job search assistance.

We should note, however, that forecasting future labor market needs is a tricky project, due to the instability in consumer demand, technological and organizational changes, and changes in labor contracts and working conditions. The difficulties increases at times of crisis, because of the ability of employers to adjust at will the working times and duties.

Training policies up to now are based on the erroneous conception that specific to firm skills may be supplied by external to the firm skill providers (i.e. formal education, occupational training institutions). This conception is in accordance with the attempt by enterprises to externalize training costs, but in fact it has led to the creation of an industry of multiple training schemes of marginal, if any, real impact. We need to return to a simpler model, with formal education and occupational training institutions providing generic and social skills and leave the firm-specific skills provision to the enterprises themselves. Both schemes of stage jobs and of apprenticeships may become effective, provided that the employers are persuaded to invest in labor skills in anticipation of increased productivity.

References

Baethge, Martin 1989 *Individualization as hope and as a disaster: A socioeconomic perspective* (Berlin: de Gruyter).

Blanchflower, David G. 1999 "What can be done to reduce the high levels of youth joblessness in the world?" *ILO Report* (Geneva: ILO).

Blanchflower, David G. and Richard B., Freeman 2000 *Youth employment and joblessness in advanced countries* (Cambridge MA: National Bureau of Economic Research).

Blanchflower, David G. and Richard B., Freeman 1997 "The rising well-being of the young," *Working Paper 6102* (Cambridge, MA: National Bureau of Economic Research).

Brzinsky-Fay, Christian 2010 "The concept of transitional labour markets: A theoretical and methodological inventory," *Discussion Paper SP I 2010-507* (Berlin: Social Science Research Center, WZB).

Card, David and Krueger, Alan B. 1995 *"Myth and measurement: The new economics of the minimum wage"* (Princeton: Princeton University Press).

Dedoussopoulos, Apostolos (forthcoming) *Youth in the labour market.*

Dedoussopoulos, Apostolos 2013 *"Evaluation of the functions of the job centres: Employees, unemployed and enterprises"*, UI UDHR and OMAS (in Greek).

Dedoussopoulos, Apostolos, Aranitou, Valia, Koutenakis, Franciscos, and Maropoulou, Marina 2013 "Assessing the Impact of the Memoranda on Greek Labour Market and Labour Relations, 2013", ILO WP No 53 (Geneva: ILO).

Furlong, Andy, Cartmel, Fred, Andy, Biggart, Helen, Sweeting and Patrick, West 2003 *Youth transitions: Patterns of vulnerability and processes of social inclusion* (Glasgow: Scottish Executive Social Research).

Gaude, Jacques 1997 "L' insertion des Jeunes et les politiques d'emploi formation," *ILO Employment and Training Papers, no 1* (Geneva : ILO).

Ghellab, Youcef 1998 "Minimum wages and youth unemployment," *ILO Employment and Training Paper no 26* (Geneva: ILO).

Hurrelmann, Klaus and Engel, Uwe 1989 *"The Social World of Adolescents: International Perspectives"* (Berlin: de Gruyter).

ILO, 2001 *Key indicators of the labour market*, 2001-2002 (Geneva: International Labour Office).

ILO, 2003 *Key indicators of the labour market*, 3rd edition (Geneva: International Labour Office).

O' Higgins, Niall 1997 "The challenge of youth unemployment", *ILO, Employment and Training Papers no 7* (Geneva: ILO).

Rudd, Peter 1997 "From socialisation to postmodernity: A review of theoretical perspectives on the school-to-work transition," *Journal of Education and Work*, Vol. 10, No. 3, 257–279.

Vickerstaff, Sarah A. 2003 "Apprenticeship in the 'Golden Age': Were youth transitions really smooth and unproblematic back then?" *Work, Employment and Society*, Vol. 17, No. 2, 269–287.

APPENDIX I
MAIN THEORIES AND THEMES ON YOUTH EMPLOYMENT

	AREA OF FOCUS	MAIN CONCEPTS	MAIN FACTORS	FUNCTION	THEORETICAL FRAMEWORK	FAILURE
SOCIOLOGICAL THEORIES						
TRADITIONAL STRUCTURAL – FUNCTIONALIST THEORIES						
Durkheim	education	dual character of education	social institutions	consent (homogenisation) skills (differentiation)	social division of labour	anomy
Parsons	school class	role learning	teacher	differentiation of roles	occupation of positions	anomy
RADICAL STRUCTURAL – FUNCTIONALIST THEORIES						
Althusser	education	ideological state apparatuses	social class	dual reproduction of labour power	class positions	
Bourdieu	education	cultural capital - social capital	social class and race	differentiation	reproduction of inequality	educational failure
Bernstein	education	language codes	social class and race	differentiation	reproduction of inequality	educational failure

	AREA OF FOCUS	MAIN CONCEPTS	MAIN FACTORS	FUNCTION	THEORETICAL FRAMEWORK	FAILURE
INTERIM						
Willis	education - culture	conformity - rebellion - adaptability	structured individuality	differentiation		
INDIVIDUALISM						
Beck	education - labour market	individual management of opportunities and risks reflective modernity	individual	acquisition of skills	individual rationality	social exclusion
Transition	education - labour market	Paths, Trajectories, transitions rationalisation	individual	acquisition of skills	individual rationality	social exclusion
STRUCTURALISM – NON-FUNCTIONALISM						
Structured Transitions	education - labour market	transition	social factors, state policies		Structuralism – Non - Functionalism	structured inequality

	AREA OF FOCUS	MAIN CONCEPTS	MAIN FACTORS	FUNCTION	THEORETICAL FRAMEWORK	FAILURE
ECONOMIC THEORIES						
DEMOGRAPHIC	population	share of youth in total population	baby boom	through the supply of labour	neoclassical	unemployment
LOW PRODUCTIVITY THEORIES	Due to education or The lack of education	Labour Productivity	Direct relationship between level of education and individual productivity	Supply of Labour	Neoclassical – Theory of Human Capital	Wage inequality / unemployment spells
	education	Skill Mismatch - Employability	educational inflexibility- structural unemployment	supply of labour	neoclassical	unemployment
	Labour Market	segmentation	segmented educational system / segmented labour markets	Management / institutional	radical	trap to low prospect jobs
	education	signalling	differentiation through education	hidden discrimination	neoclassical	trap to low prospect jobs

AREA OF FOCUS	MAIN CONCEPTS	MAIN FACTORS	FUNCTION	THEORETICAL FRAMEWORK	FAILURE
LOW PRODUCTIVITY THEORIES (cont.)					
Lack of experience	wage discrimination	Productivity	hidden discrimination	neoclassical	temporary
Work instability	turnover ratio	Search / mobility	rationality	neoclassical	temporary
PORTS OF ENTRY					
economic sectors	first job providers	sectorial mobility / segmentation	skill demand	neoclassical	temporary or trap
LABOUR MARKET ORGANISATION					
Labour Management	occupational vs internal labour markets	segmentation	skill management / work place authority	radical/ neoclassical	inequality

APPENDIX II
UNEMPLOYMENT CHANGE DECOMPOSITION

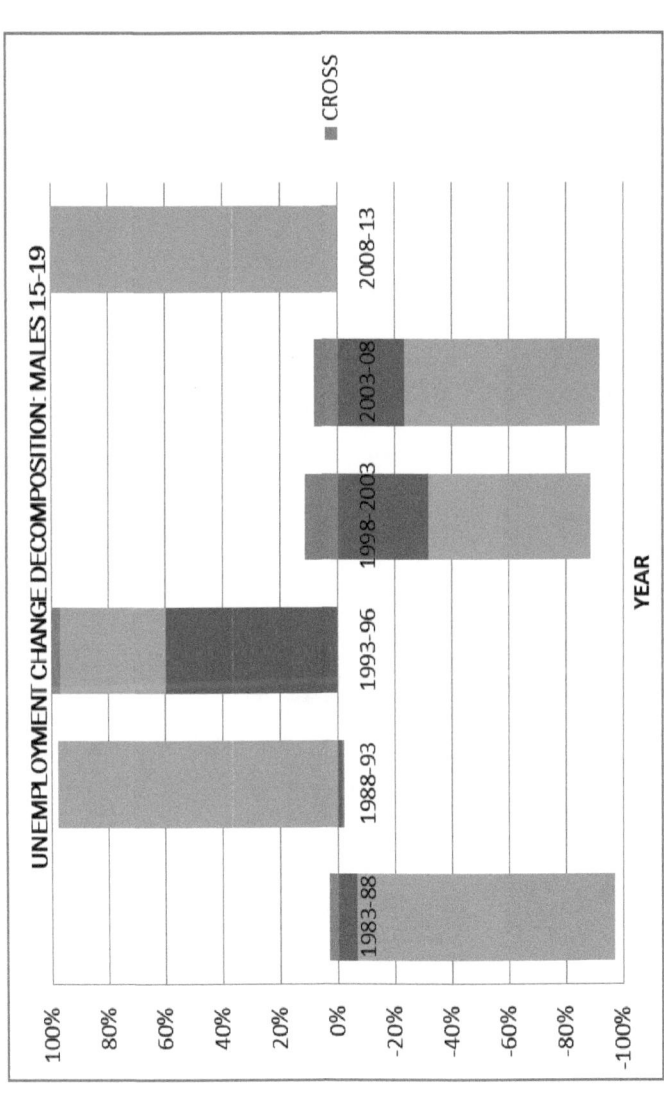

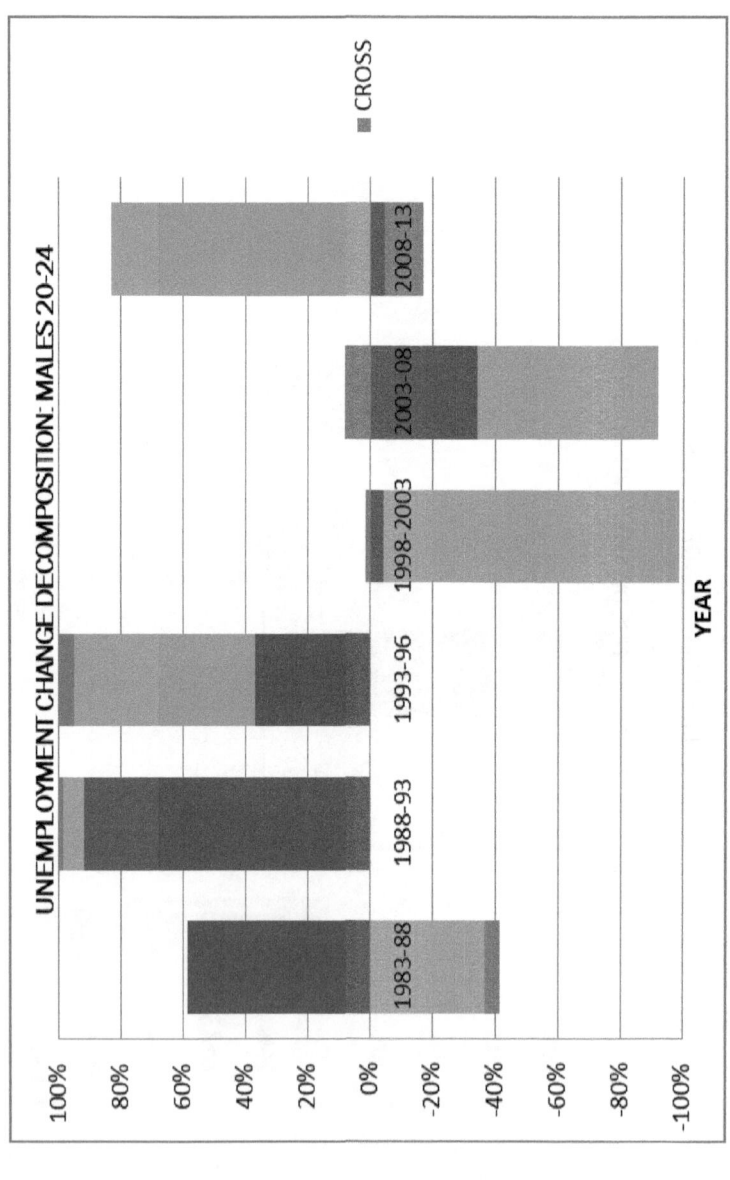

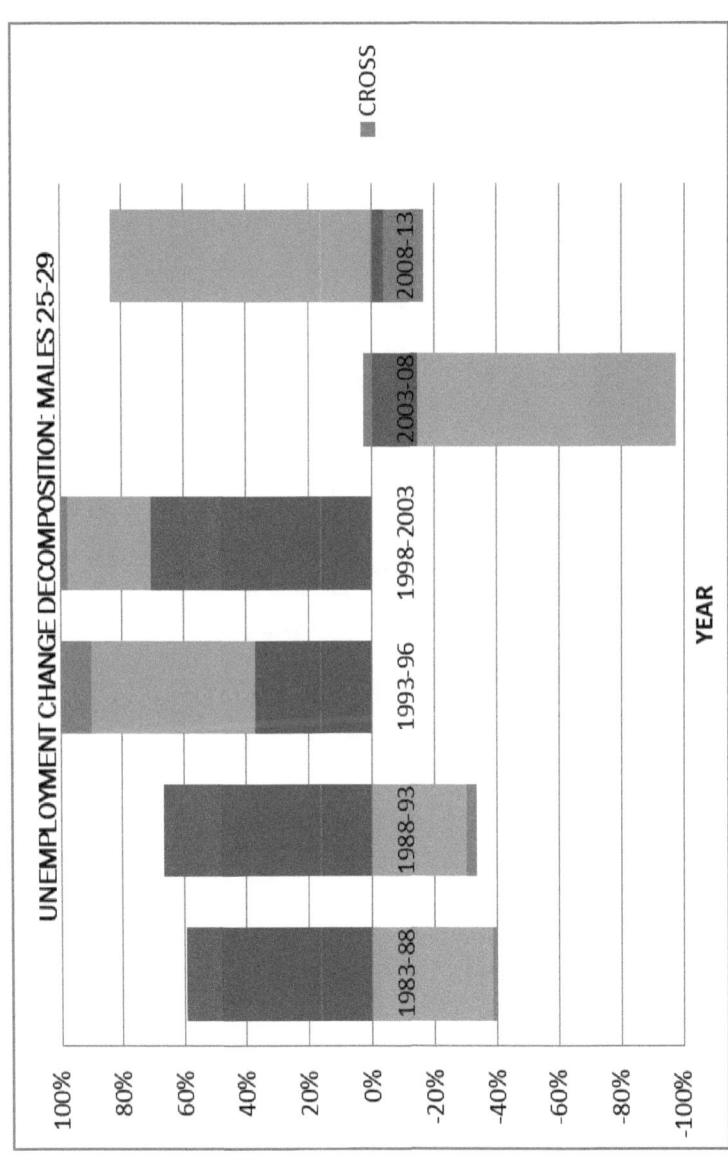

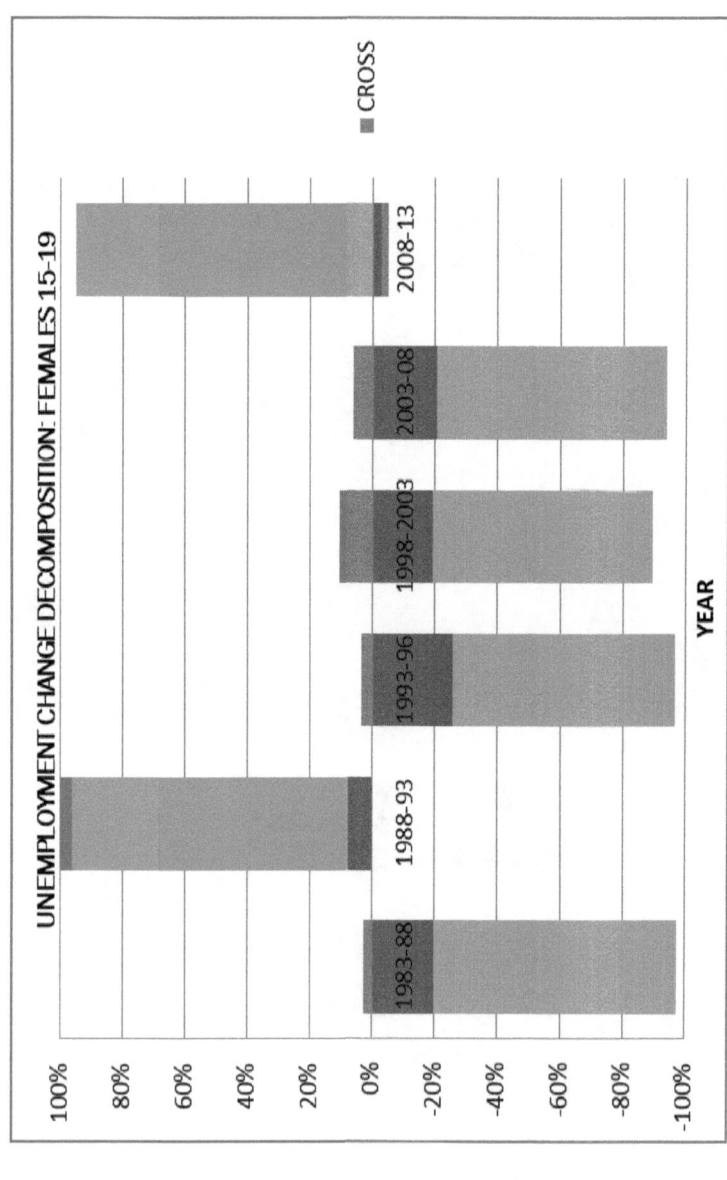

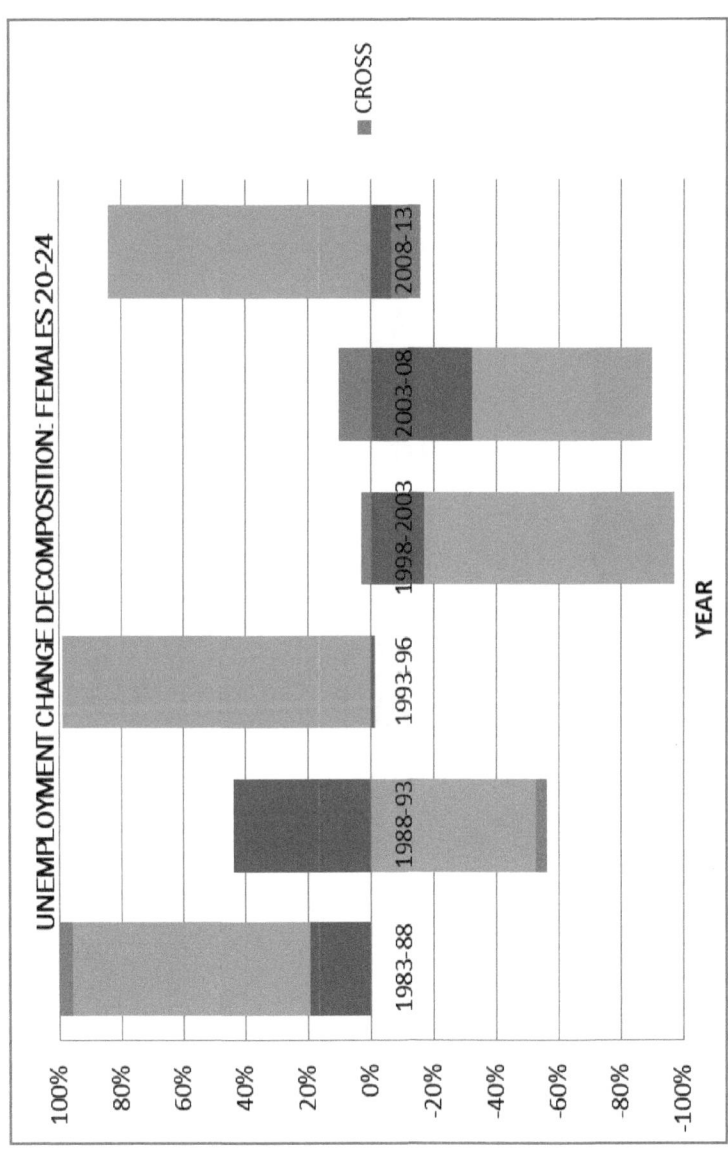

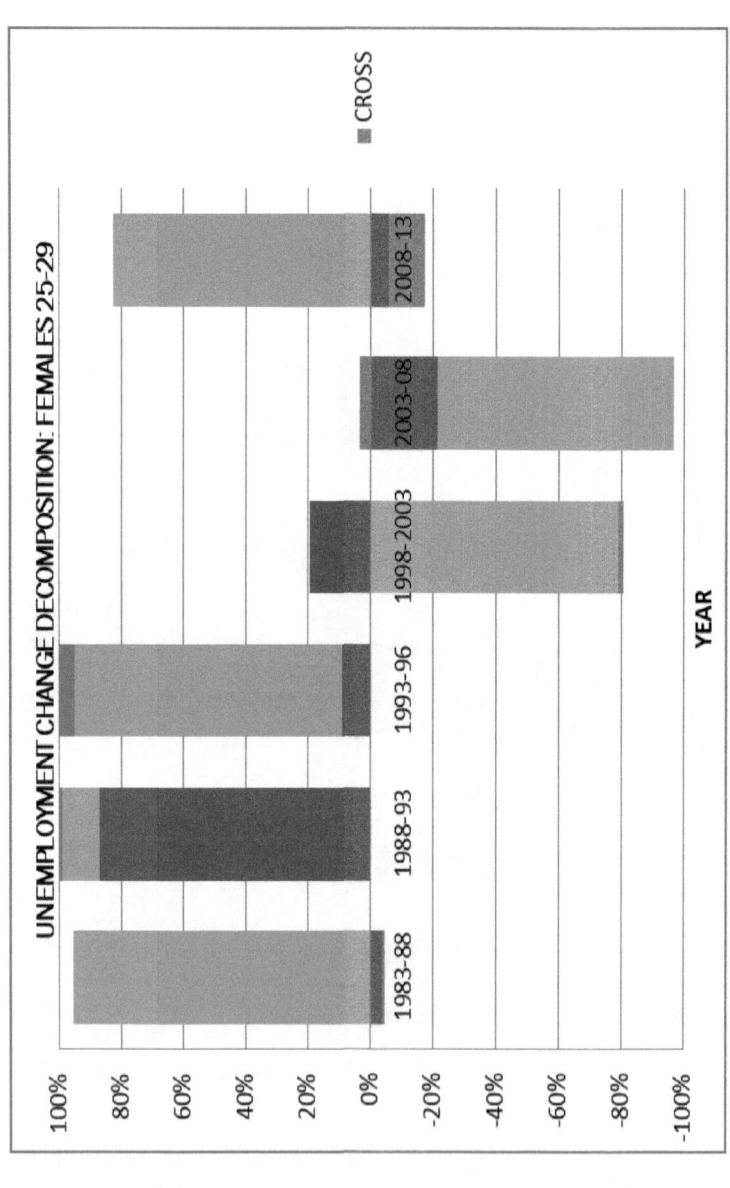

APPENDIX III
SEMI-COHORT TABLES

PARTICIPATION RATES

	MALE			FEMALE		
AGE	1999=15	2004=15	2009=15	1999=15	2004=15	2009=15
15	6.8	2.8	1.5	2.2	1.6	0.5
16	8.7	3.8	2.8	3.9	1.7	1.3
17	13.2	6.8	3.2	6.9	4.4	3.2
18	19.8	18.2	11.2	14.6	11.0	13.6
19	25.0	27.8	24.5	21.4	25.6	17.6
20	26.3	34.0		27.5	28.8	
21	47.9	45.0		39.6	38.2	
22	57.9	56.6		47.8	47.5	
23	64.1	62.9		59.4	61.8	
24	73.3	75.4		68.2	75.0	
25	81.7			75.3		
26	83.8			81.7		
27	91.0			85.5		
28	93.8			82.7		
29	95.2			84.9		

EMPLOYMENT RATES

	MALE			FEMALE		
AGE	1999=15	2004=15	2009=15	1999=15	2004=15	2009=15
15	5.5	2.1	0.9	1.6	0.8	0.5
16	5.9	3.0	2.2	2.5	1.3	1.3
17	10.5	5.4	1.7	4.0	3.4	0.7
18	16.4	14.6	4.4	7.7	7.6	3.8
19	19.4	22.7	8.5	11.8	14.8	2.2
20	18.3	25.4		13.9	16.2	
21	38.3	30.6		22.6	24.1	
22	49.0	36.3		29.4	25.7	
23	56.2	38.2		39.8	23.5	
24	63.5	41.9		51.6	28.6	
25	70.5			57.2		
26	69.9			61.2		
27	70.4			56.6		
28	63.8			50.2		
29	63.7			47.6		

UNEMPLOYMENT RATES

	MALE			FEMALE		
AGE	1999=15	2004=15	2009=15	1999=15	2004=15	2009=15
15	18.7	27.9	39.8	29.2	54.2	0.0
16	31.9	20.9	23.1	34.6	22.4	0.0
17	20.5	19.5	47.2	41.6	22.3	79.3
18	17.5	19.8	60.9	47.3	30.7	71.8
19	22.4	18.1	65.4	44.7	42.2	87.7
20	30.5	25.3		49.4	43.9	
21	20.1	32.0		42.9	36.9	
22	15.4	35.9		38.4	46.0	
23	12.3	39.2		32.9	62.0	
24	13.4	44.4		24.4	61.9	
25	13.7			24.1		
26	16.7			25.1		
27	22.7			33.9		
28	31.9			39.2		
29	33.1			43.9		

PART-TIME RATIOS

	MALE			FEMALE		
AGE	1999=15	2004=15	2009=15	1999=15	2004=15	2009=15
15	20.0	1.0	42.5	25.8	0.4	54.8
16	14.4	23.6	17.6	0.0	32.2	37.2
17	10.3	11.7	34.2	31.9	23.1	0.0
18	21.4	14.2	45.7	19.8	30.9	55.6
19	20.1	12.9	33.0	21.7	21.5	47.7
20	8.9	18.5		20.3	18.4	
21	7.4	16.4		20.8	22.7	
22	7.4	12.0		13.9	21.1	
23	6.7	15.7		15.9	12.9	
24	6.2	14.1		13.0	20.1	
25	6.1			17.7		
26	5.8			8.3		
27	7.5			11.4		
28	9.7			16.4		
29	7.7			11.4		

SCHOOLING RATIOS

	MALE			FEMALE		
AGE	1999=15	2004=15	2009=15	1999=15	2004=15	2009=15
15	93.2	95.9	98.9	95.3	94.4	98.3
16	90.8	93.4	95.8	92.2	92.1	96.6
17	87.1	92.7	96.3	89.4	93.6	93.0
18	79.4	72.6	81.3	81.6	74.2	78.7
19	68.7	65.5	67.6	68.1	66.5	77.8
20	67.6	67.2		64.9	73.0	
21	52.4	54.9		59.6	63.3	
22	43.0	43.1		49.5	50.0	
23	37.3	34.7		36.2	35.1	
24	28.7	25.2		22.9	24.1	
25	20.1			14.1		
26	15.0			10.8		
27	8.4			8.7		
28	8.4			5.7		
29	6.5			5.2		

OUT OF WORK – OUT OF SCHOOL

	MALE			FEMALE		
AGE	1999=15	2004=15	2009=15	1999=15	2004=15	2009=15
15	1.8	2.5	0.6	3.6	5.2	1.5
16	4.5	4.7	2.4	5.2	6.6	2.9
17	4.9	2.9	3.2	7.3	4.1	6.9
18	7.9	14.9	15.8	11.5	21.4	19.0
19	16.6	15.0	25.9	22.4	21.3	20.1
20	16.2	11.4		23.2	14.7	
21	13.2	18.0		22.8	17.5	
22	10.8	24.3		24.6	28.7	
23	10.1	29.1		29.3	44.8	
24	12.3	36.3		29.1	50.3	
25	14.1			32.2		
26	16.1			31.0		
27	22.6			38.1		
28	28.8			45.5		
29	31.2			48.4		

AUTONOMY FROM PARENTAL FAMILY RATIOS

	MALE			FEMALE		
AGE	1999=15	2004=15	2009=15	1999=15	2004=15	2009=15
15	0.0	0.3	0.0	0.0	0.2	0.0
16	0.4	0.2	0.0	0.8	0.7	0.4
17	2.1	0.3	0.0	2.2	1.1	0.3
18	12.3	4.0	7.4	13.3	8.0	7.3
19	11.7	14.4	14.8	15.2	25.0	22.8
20	21.2	28.5		27.1	33.3	
21	27.1	51.4		26.9	60.8	
22	21.7	48.2		31.1	59.3	
23	21.2	21.8		28.5	23.9	
24	22.6	19.3		28.4	26.2	
25	23.5			32.7		
26	22.2			35.0		
27	24.7			37.7		
28	27.1			44.6		
29	53.5			86.8		

SOCIAL ENTERPRISES, SOCIAL AND SOLIDARITY ECONOMY, AND YOUTH: What is the role for policy-making?

Sofia Adam

Social economy and social entrepreneurship are promoted as effective strategies against unemployment and social exclusion with particular reference to youth and vulnerable social groups both at the EU and national level.[1] What are the inherent attributes of these forms of economic activity that raise expectations for addressing such complex and worrying challenges as youth unemployment? To what extent are these expectations grounded on a sound theoretical base of social economy and social enterprises, on a close monitoring of what is happening in the field and on consistent policy formulation and implementation?

This chapter addresses the previous questions with regard to the reality of recent social enterprise development in Greece in comparison to the Latin American context. At the beginning, we define social economy and social enterprises through a review of the relevant literature placing emphasis on existing differences between the European and the Latin American context. Then we provide evidence on public policy the development of Social Cooperative Enterprises (SCEs) in Greece. With these preliminary results, we intend to highlight the discrepancy between policy expectations and reality as it unfolds in the field. This is followed by a brief description of the way solidarity economy is promoted in Latin America at the policy level. In the concluding section, we identify inconsistencies in policy-making and implementation and provide some insights for a reformulation of the relevant policies in Greece based on the insights provided by the Latin American context.

---

[1] Indicatively, one of the events conducted within the framework of the Greek presidency of the EU was an International Conference titled: "Social Entrepreneurship: A tool for addressing local development, youth unemployment and social needs" <http://www.esfhellas.gr/en/Pages/NewsFS.aspx?item=126> accessed September 10, 2014).

Social economy and social enterprises: Conflicting visions and expectations

The third sector consists of entities—such as cooperatives, nonprofit organizations, and mutual societies—that cannot be easily classified in the private or the public sector (Defourny, 2001). The term itself is widely accepted by a rich array of theoretical approaches (Moulaert and Ailenei, 2005) and emerges in many EU policy documents. In this respect, it seems plausible to use it as a starting point in order to delineate other concepts in use, namely solidarity economy, social economy, and the nonprofit sector.

Table 1: The terminological ambiguity of the third sector

TERM	Solidarity Economy	Social Economy	Nonprofit Sector
Definition	Includes all economic activities which aim at the economic democratization on the basis of citizen participation. They involve a dual perspective: • economic because they attempt to create economic relations based on reciprocity while making use of resources from the market and welfare state redistribution and • political because they attempt to create autonomous public spaces and open up discussion on both means and ends.	Includes all economic activities undertaken by enterprises, mainly cooperatives, associations, and mutual societies, which adhere to the following principles: • providing members or the community a service rather than generating profit • independent management • democratic decision-making, and • priority given to persons and work over capital in the distribution of income.	Include all nonprofit organizations with the following characteristics: • legal entities, institutionalized to some meaningful extent, • private, institutionally separate from government, • nonprofit-distributing, not returning profits generated to their owners or directors, • self-governing, equipped to control their own activities, • voluntary, i.e., involving some meaningful degree of voluntary participation.

Source: Adam and Papatheodorou (2010)

Table 1 describes the terminological pluralism that underlines diverse theoretical approaches and historical trajectories. The relevant concepts are presented intentionally from the left to the right in conjunction with their connotation in the literature. Schematically, the term *Solidarity Economy* is mostly associated with radical approaches that emerged in the framework of social movements mainly but not exclusively in Latin America. *Social Economy* is more francophone in its origin and clearly incorporates the experience of the European cooperative movement. The term *Non Profit Sector* follows the Anglo-American tradition of charities.

Having sketched the main terminological issues, it is important to proceed with a critical examination of the main theoretical approaches. The Anglo-American tradition has largely focused on the emergence of nonprofit organizations (NPOs) through the lenses of orthodox economic analysis (Weisbord, 1975; Ben Ner and van Hoomissen, 1991; Hansmann, 1987; Rose-Ackerman, 1996). As such, the third sector is analyzed as distinct from both state and market without any reference to its historical dynamics in specific social formations and is theorized as a response to state failures (provision of uniform services to diversified needs) and/or market failures (asymmetric information, transaction costs). In contrast, theoretical approaches of social and solidarity economy analyze the associated practices as hybrids within the intersection of state, market, and community practices and their respective underlying operating principles (redistribution, exchange, reciprocity). The social economy approach focuses more on the convivial nature of this interplay while the solidarity economy approach highlights the tensions inherent therein. It is useful to illustrate the main tenets of this heterodox approach with the use of Figure 1.

Figure 1: Positioning social and solidarity economy practices

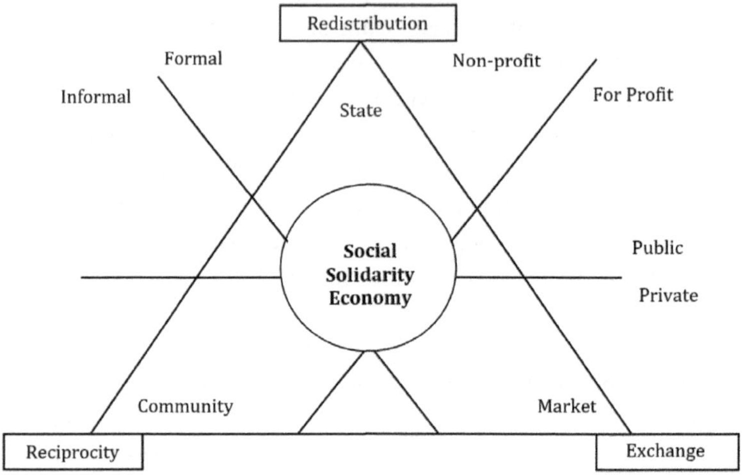

```
                    Redistribution
         Formal                    Non-profit
  Informal                                  For Profit
                      State

                    Social
                   Solidarity          Public
                    Economy            Private

         Community            Market
    Reciprocity                      Exchange
```

Source: Pestoff (2004)

Social enterprises express new dynamics within the third sector (Defourny and Nyssens, 2006). The aforementioned theoretical differences are reflected in alternative conceptualizations of social enterprises in the Anglo-American and European traditions.[2] The US-led approach defines social enterprises in a broader way (Kerlin, 2006; Kernot, 2009) placing them in a continuum of hybrid cases including NPOs trying to secure market income and for-profit enterprises developing socially responsible activities (Table 2). This positioning of social enterprises follows a number of underlying assumptions: (1) no collective ownership or decision-making is required, (2) market generating income is deemed the most important source of funding, and (3) the activity developed does not require the fulfillment of any specific criterion (i.e., social usefulness) as long as it generates income for a "good" purpose.

---

[2] It is important to note that this simplistic dichotomy between European and American approaches does not mean that there are not scholars in each region, reflecting alternative than the dominant views.

Table 2: Positioning social enterprises according to the US-led approach

Nonprofit with income generating activities	Social enterprise	Socially responsible business	Corporation practicing social responsibility

Source: Alter (2007)

The European tradition positions social enterprises within the universe of social economy practices as an intersection between two families of organizations: cooperatives and NPOs (Defourny and Nyssens, 2008). In particular, social enterprises resemble more worker cooperatives and NPOs with productive activities (Figure 2). On the one hand, they move closer to cooperatives, because they explicitly undertake a continuous economic activity. On the other hand, they move closer to NPOs because they do not serve only their members as traditional cooperatives did, but they often express the interests of different stakeholders formally (multi-stakeholder membership or management) or informally (open events, assemblies with the participation of community members). This approach is based on the following underlying assumptions: (1) social enterprises are collective initiatives, (2) they are democratically owned and/or operated, (3) they undertake activities with social usefulness, and (4) they involve the wider community in their operations.

Figure 2: Positioning social enterprises according to the European approach

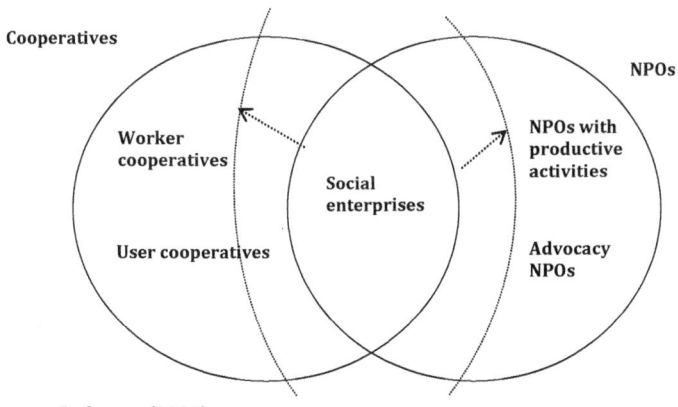

Source: Defourny (2001)

In sum, there are differing conceptualizations of social economy practices in general and social enterprises in particular. These alternative visions raise in turn different expectations. In a nutshell, social enterprises can be seen as market-driven solutions to social problems (neo-liberal discourse), as remedies for the correction of both market and state failures (third way thinking), as emancipatory projects for economic and social transformation (radical approach). Evidently, this ideal typology will not be found in a clear-cut form in the real world where the boundaries are often thin and elusive. However, it is important to bear in mind when we attempt to formulate policies to which we now turn.

Social economy in Greece: Policy and practice

Law 4019/2011 provided the legal framework for the development of social enterprises in Greece.[3] Three types of SCEs can be established in accordance with the principal goal pursued: (1) social inclusion with 40% of employees belonging to vulnerable social groups[4]; (2) social welfare for the provision of social care services to specific target groups[5]; and (3) general and/or productive purpose, which forms the broader category encompassing a multiplicity of goals and activities.[6]

The main requirements with regard to the start-up, operation and management of these enterprises are described in Table 3.

---

[3] The former law of 2716/1999 regarding social cooperatives of limited liability (KOISPE in Greek) addressed only the need for work integration social enterprises employing people with mental health problems.

[4] The category of vulnerable social groups includes: people with disability, former addicts or persons in treatment from addictions, HIV positive, ex-prisoners, and juvenile delinquents.

[5] These target groups refer to the elderly, children, people with disability or chronic illness.

[6] The indicated goals include local and collective benefit, employment creation, social cohesion, and regional development while the fields of activity include culture, environment, ecology, education, use of local products, and preservation of traditional activities and professions.

Table 3: Main requirements and provisions of Law 4019/2011

Field	Requirements and provisions
Membership	Physical or legal entities, 7 members for social inclusion, 5 members for social welfare and general purpose, public law entities are allowed to participate only in inclusion SCEs.
Start-up capital	No obligatory threshold, freely decided by members.
Shares	One obligatory and up to five supplementary shares.
Voting rights	One vote regardless of the number of shares.
Decision making	General assembly.
Management	Management committee (min. 3 persons, service 2–5 years).
Profit distribution	5% of profits obligatorily reserved, up to 35% distributed only to employees, minimum 60% reinvested at the enterprise for the fulfillment of objectives.
Liability	Limited for each member to the level of purchased shares.
Social insurance obligations	Membership does not create social insurance obligations. All workers sign dependent employment contracts and must be insured.
Reconciliation with other work status	Unemployed, employees in the private and public sectors and retirees are allowed to become members. Unemployed on benefits do not lose their social protection while members.

Source: Law 4019/2011, http://www.socialcooperatives.gr/page/30/110/greeklaws

Indicatively, the law on SCEs envisages the collective ownership and democratic decision-making of these entities without forcing excessive thresholds in terms of membership. In addition, limited profit distribution only to employees could deter opportunistic behavior on behalf of owners-members. Other factors, which increase the appeal of this legal form especially but not exclusively for young unemployed persons, are the lack of start-up capital thresholds, the noncompulsory social insurance of members, and the ability to reconcile membership with other work or nonwork status (i.e., insured unemployed with benefit).

The initiative for drafting and enforcing Law 4019/2011 as well as the registration of social enterprises lies within the Ministry of Labor, Social Security and Solidarity.[7] Law 4019/2011 was later followed by a Strategic Plan for the Development of the Social Entrepreneurship Sector in Greece (February 2013). According to the main tenets of this strategic plan, social economy is reduced to SCEs to the exclusion of other legal entities,

---

[7] At the time of the introduction of Law 4019/2011, the title was Ministry of Employment and Social Protection. There is a culture of renaming Ministries after each election round.

traditional actors of social economy (mainly but not exclusively other types of cooperatives). The underlying hypothesis is the inherent link between social economy, unemployment, and social inclusion with a sole focus on social enterprises. In this way, social enterprises are mainly seen as a tool for the (re-integration) into the labor market of those facing the strongest barriers.

In addition, the bundle of priority axes does not address the need for inter-ministerial coordination despite the fact that social economy entities fall under the supervision of at least four ministries in Greece (i.e., Ministry of Economy, Ministry of Agricultural Development, Ministry of Labor, Social Security and Solidarity, and Ministry of Health). Law 4019/2011 addresses the need for an inter-ministerial committee only for the preparation of guidelines regarding public procurement with social clauses.[8] This inter-ministerial committee has not materialized in practice so far. In turn, this fragmented institutionalization process is reflected in the field with the lack of a coherent representative network of social economy entities.

As a result of the policy framework and institutionalization process, the support measures envisaged mainly refer to grants and subsidies for the start-up and development of individual SCEs without a focus on more systemic approaches, which could potentially link social economy development with unmet social needs at the regional level (i.e., environmental sustainability, employment, and income generation) or more importantly with the untapped human capital of young unemployed persons (i.e., social economy enterprises in innovative sectors, such as IT, renewable energy, alternative tourism, culture, etc.).

However, even this short-sighted view of policy-making was not implemented in practice. All in all, SCEs developed thanks to the unassisted efforts of interested groups of people. From the introduction of the relevant law up to the end of September 2014, 632 entities have applied at the Social Economy Registry. From this data, we have an indication of the status of these entities according to the registration procedure. SCEs are divided

---

[8] In essence, it refers to guidelines that define the framework within which the wider public sector can include social criteria in the procurement of goods and services. One such criterion could be the preferential treatment under certain thresholds of work integration social enterprises.

into four categories (Figure 3): the ones with temporary certificate (mainly not having completed registration with the relevant tax authorities in order to start economic activity), the ones with permanent certificates (having completed all registration procedures), the ones with member certificate (having completed one year of operation), the deleted cases (mainly upon the request of the founding members themselves), and a few cases on unidentified status.

Figure 3: Number of SCEs according to registration status

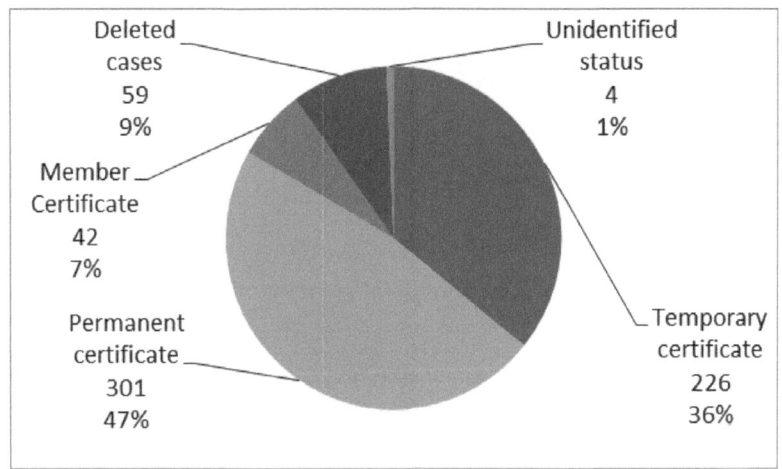

Source: Author's calculations based on data from the Registry of Social Economy, Ministry of Labor, Social Security and Solidarity

Figure 4 depicts the type of SCEs according to the main goal pursued. Contrary to the direct link expressed in dominant policies between social enterprises and social inclusion, the share of social inclusion[9] to total SCEs is relatively small with the vast majority falling under the general or productive purpose. This finding is of interest because it implies a tendency

---

[9] Social inclusion SCEs comprise two sub-groups according to the law: (1) new SCEs with at least 40% of employees from vulnerable social groups and (2) the established according to law 2716/1999 Social Cooperatives of Limited Liability with at least 35% of members from people with mental health problems applying for the new status of SCEs.

to resort to this business model in order to enact any type of economic activity albeit in a collective manner.

Figure 4: Number of SCEs by main goal pursued

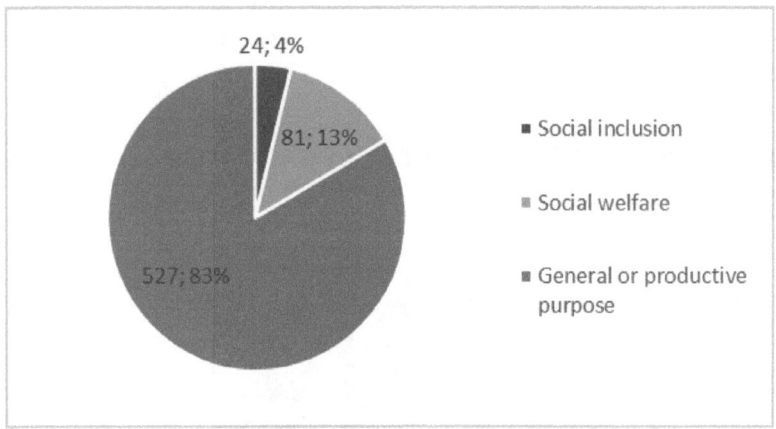

Source: Author's calculations based on data from the Registry of Social Economy, Ministry of Labor, Social Security and Welfare

Another interesting dimension involves the extent of collectivity as indicated by the number of founding members. In other words, do SCEs pursue a multi-membership approach or do they exhaust their membership to the required thresholds by the legal framework? Figure 5 sheds some light on the collective dimension of 330 newly formed SCEs in Greece, which have completed the registration procedure and for which data could be retrieved.[10] As indicated, half of SCEs (50.6%, or 167 SCEs) comprise the minimum threshold of foundation members, one-third of them (33,9%, or 112 SCEs) surpass the minimum threshold by five members, while numerous, in terms of membership, SCEs are clearly the exception. It is important to make two remarks at this point: (1) Membership is a constantly changing reality since members leave and new ones enter; and (2) a greater number of members does not entail more democratic decision-making of the respective SCE. However, membership conforming to minimum thresh-

---

[10] Excluding from 632 SCEs the deleted entities (59), the ones on temporary certificate (226), the ones on unidentified status (4), the social cooperatives of limited liability (6), and entities for which data could not be retrieved (7).

olds might conceal hidden family enterprises under the law for social enterprises.

Figure 5: Number of SCEs by number of founding members*

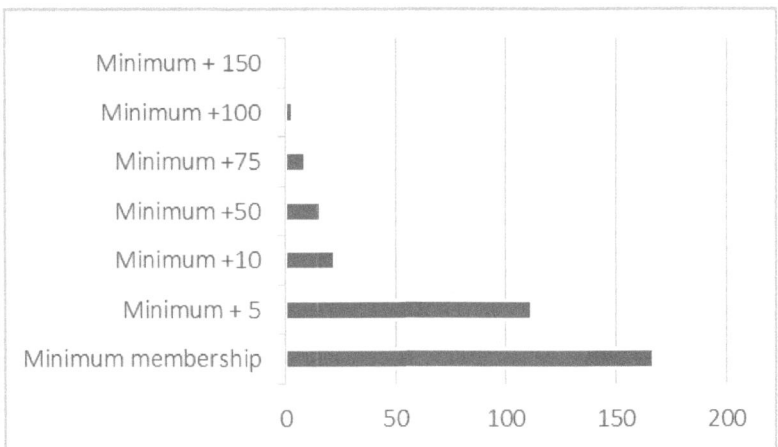

Source: Author's calculations based on data from the Registry of Social Economy, Ministry of Labor, Social Security and Solidarity
*By minimum number we refer to 7 members in the case of social inclusion SCEs and 5 members in the case of the other two categories (social welfare, general or productive purpose).

Figure 6 presents the age composition of the 2,895 SCEs members for which we were able to retrieve the date of birth in a total of 329 SCEs. Contrary to what might be expected, the biggest share of SCEs founding members belongs to the age group 45–64 years whereas the share of the age group of <25 years is the second from the bottom (191 persons, or 7% of all members). Even if we increase the age threshold to 29 years, the cumulative share amounts to 20.6% of total members. Another interesting finding is the significant for the specific age group participation of members above 64 years. These findings indicate that the development of SCEs in Greece has been mostly an elder age group development possibly reflecting the ability of such members to reconcile SCE membership with other work/retirement status. The rather significant participation of above 64 years members possibly reflects the tendency of retirees to participate in SCEs in order to assist younger family members and/or counterbalance reduced pensions.

Figure 6: Number of SCE members by age group

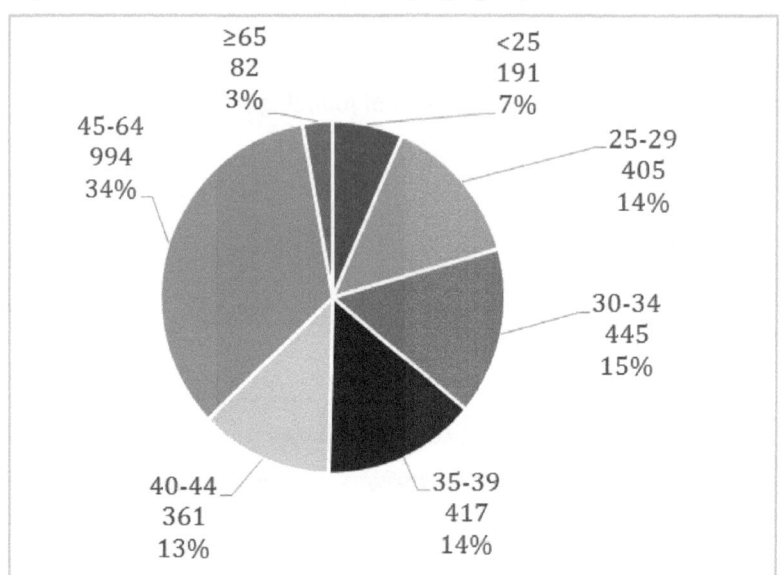

Source: Author's calculations based on data from the Registry of Social Economy, Ministry of Labor, Social Security and Solidarity

Finally, it is interesting to explore the median age of members per SCE in order to identify "youngsters" social enterprises (Figure 7). Only 8.5% of the 329 SCEs have a median age of membership below 29 years, while 32% have a median age of membership within the age group 45–64 years.

Figure 7: Number of SCEs by median age of founding members

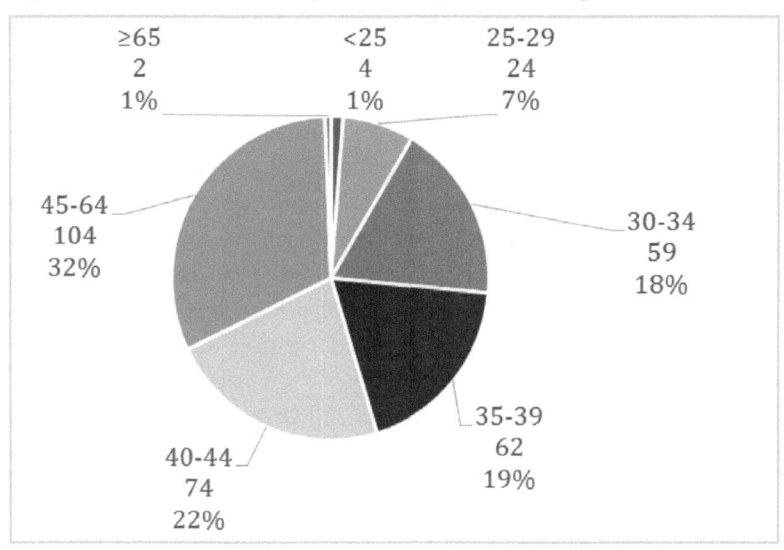

Source: Author's calculations based on data from the Registry of Social Economy, Ministry of Labor, Social Security and Solidarity

To sum up, the bulk of SCEs belongs to the third type of general or productive purpose, half of them involve members at the minimum legally enforced threshold and the age composition is skewed in favor of the 45–64 years age group. How can public policies for the promotion of social and solidarity economy affect the reality in the field? In particular, why expectations regarding the role of social enterprises for the confrontation of youth unemployment did not materialize in Greece? What are the missing links needed at the institutional levels in order to design, implement, monitor, and effect positive changes in the field?

Solidarity economy policies in Latin America

In order to draw some policy insights for the case of Greece, it is useful to explore policy-making for the solidarity economy in the Latin American context for a number of reasons: (1) The policy discourse adopted is oriented toward social transformation, which opens up the space for innovative policy-making much needed in a crisis-ridden country with endemic structural problems, such as Greece; (2) the significance attached to solidarity economy as a policy priority by the left-leaning governments that came to power in many Latin American countries during the past years is comparable with the policy discourse adopted by the newly left-leaning government in Greece; and (3) despite the geographical distance, there is an exchange of ideas and practices in the field with initiatives in Greece being inspired by the Latin American experiences.[11]

The theoretical foundation of solidarity economy as a social transformative project, as has been depicted in section 1, goes hand in hand with innovations at the policy-making level in many Latin American countries (Saguier and Brent, 2014). For comparative reasons, it is useful to briefly examine the way solidarity economy policies have been pursued there, even though there are socioeconomic and political differences between Latin American countries and Greece.

First of all, the priority given to solidarity economy in the Latin American context is crystallized in the development of specialized agencies at the governmental level with some countries going as far as to create a dedicated ministry in order to foster intergovernmental coordination (i.e., Ministry of Communal Economy in Venezuela). Table 4 displays the main locus of policies for the solidarity economy at the governmental level in selected Latin American countries.

---

[11] Indicatively: (1) The book by Andrés Ruggeri, activist-researcher-author, titled "Worker-recuperated enterprises in Argentina" was presented in the open discussions held in support of the occupied factory VIOME in Thessaloniki in February 2015. (2) Dario Azzelini, researcher-writer-documentary producer, was invited in Thessaloniki in March 2015 in order to inform on the practices and ideas of popular assemblies and solidarity economy initiatives in Chaves' Venezuela, (3) Euclides André Mance, member of the Popular Network for Solidarity Economy in Brazil (Solidarious) was invited in Athens in June 2015 by a number of initiatives (Solidarity4All, SynAllois—Cooperative of Solidarity Economy, Efimerida ton Syntakton—The Journalist's Newspaper, initiative for a public dialogue space on Solidarity Economy, Cooperators of Zografou, P2P Foundation, cooperative Sociality, portokaliradio.gr, cooperative grocery Sesoula) in order to exchange ideas and practices for a Solidarity Economy.

Table 4: National bodies in charge of solidarity economy in selected Latin American countries

Country	Ministry	Agency
Argentina	Social Development	National Institute of Associational Life and Social Economy
Bolivia	Productive Development and Plural Economy	Unit or Vice-Ministry for Solidarity Economy (to be created)
Brazil	Labor and Employment	National Secretary of the Solidarity Economy
Ecuador	Economic and Social Inclusion	National Institute of People's and Solidarity Economy
Venezuela	Communal Economy	–

Source: Adapted from Morais (2014)

Second, institutionalization reflects the interaction between public bodies and solidarity economy initiatives with the creation of national platforms and networks. The Bolivian governmental initiative for the creation of a vice-ministry or unit within the Ministry of Productive Development and Plural Economy could be seen as the outcome of a long process initiated by the Movement of Solidarity Economy and Fair Trade, while the creation of the National Secretary of the Solidarity Economy in Brazil is the outcome of a long struggle of the solidarity economy movement to instill changes and affect the public agenda (Morais, 2014). One of the most notable examples of the interaction between public bodies and solidarity economy initiatives is the Forum of Solidarity Economy in Brazil (FBES in Brazilian), acting as a platform that unites solidarity economy enterprises, support agencies, and public managers (representatives of local and state authorities) (FBES, 2006). FBES is active in seven intervention areas, namely: (1) social organization of the solidarity economy movement, (2) production, commercialization and consumption networks, (3) solidarity finances, (4) legal framework, (5) education, (6) communication, and (7) democratization of knowledge and technology. This example is also interesting in the way decision-making processes are formulated in order to represent the involved stakeholders. The supreme decision-making body is the National Coordination, which comprises 16 representatives of the national support and advisory organizations (NGOs and universities), plus three representatives at the state level,[12] two coming from the solidarity economy movement and one coming from local authorities.

Third, the significance attached to solidarity economy is manifested in the design and implementation of nation-wide multifaceted programs. The interesting structural aspects of these programs involve the combined use of policy tools, which defy clear-cut dichotomies between active and passive labor market policies and grant a dual role to the state both as a provider of support and as the recipient of goods and services.

In Argentina, the nation-wide program "Let's get to Work" (*Manos a la Obra* in Spanish) offers capacity building, technical assistance, and financial support to solidarity economy initiatives with a potential of sustainability (Morais, 2014). The Sustainable Integrated Agro-ecological Production Program (PAIS in Portuguese) in Brazil intends to create work and income for young people in rural areas with limited employment prospects by fostering agricultural production based on the so-called social technology. The latter involves the use of production methods that promote environmental preservation (i.e., no pesticides). In addition, technical assistance is provided in order to foster producers as well as marketing cooperatives and solidarity-based open-air markets. Part of the produce is purchased by municipal governments in order to provide healthy food at school canteens (Morais and Bacic, 2013). In Ecuador, the Ministry of Social and Economic Inclusion implements the "Agenda for the Revolution of the Popular and Solidarity Economy" (AREPS in Spanish) with programs in many sectors including construction, manufacturing, alimentation, tourism, services, and finance (Ruiz, 2012). For example, the program "Weaving Development" supports production of school uniforms from cooperatives and micro-enterprises through the facilitation of access to credit and the purchase of output from provincial public schools (Morais and Bacic, 2013). In Venezuela, the Ministry of Communal Economy (previously Ministry of Popular Economy) coordinated the support of cooperative production through the Mission "Changing Face"[13] (*Vuelvan Caras* in Spanish). The program offered training and financial support for the creation of worker cooperatives with members coming from poor and disadvantaged backgrounds (Azzelini, 2012). These cooperatives were granted access to credit

---

[12] Brazil has a federal government.
[13] By "changing face," it implies a change of direction in public policies. The program was later restructured and renamed as Che Guevara.

with preferential terms through the creation of specifically dedicated banks (i.e., Bank of Economic and Social Development). In the framework of the same program, the Ministry created endogenous development zones with the participation of state agencies and cooperatives in order to establish networks of cooperation that could promote a solidarity economy logic along a new development path.

All in all, these experiences with public policy-making imply the centrality given to solidarity economy as a social transformation project. The main tenets of this new approach involve an open view of solidarity economy as encompassing many types of entities and not only social enterprises, the creation of spaces for the interaction between solidarity economy movements and the state, the institutionalization of this process of interaction, the identification of unmet social needs to be addressed by solidarity economy initiatives, and the design and implementation of far-reaching multi-faceted fostering the intersection of solidarity economy with the public sector. Evidently, the trajectory of policy-making in the area of solidarity economy in these selected Latin American countries remains to be assessed. There are growing concerns over the efficacy of policies so as to avoid the replication of deficiencies that characterize this sector, namely the tendency of cooperatives to benefit members to the detriment of other broader social goals as well as the reproduction of corruption in the administration of public support to particular entities (Orhangazi, 2014). Nevertheless, policy efforts in this area denote an ambitious strategy for the incorporation of social and solidarity economy in the public agenda, which is of interest for the reformulation of the Greek public policy toward social and solidarity economy in at least four respects: (1) the adoption of a unified and broader view of the field which moves beyond social enterprises, (2) the enactment of interaction processes between initiatives in the field and the wider public sector, (3) the consolidation of inter-governmental coordination, and (4) the design of far-reaching multi-faceted programs.

Concluding remarks and policy implications

As mentioned earlier, social economy and social enterprises can be conceptualized as an intermediate area trying to rectify state/market failures or as a transformative strategy aiming at fostering an economy based on the principles of redistribution and reciprocity. The former constitutes a narrow approach that views social enterprises as a social inclusion tool for social groups unable to enter the labor market. The latter conceptualization allows for a broader view of social economy as a development pathway that aims to channel economic activities toward addressing unmet social needs in a collective and democratic way.

Despite the policy expectation of the narrow focus on social enterprises in Greek public policy agenda, the reality of recent social economy development in Greece shows that the bulk of these entities does not aim at social inclusion or social services provision but on collective start-up of general productive activities. Moreover, these entities are mainly created by elder persons even though a small percentage of founding members belongs to the age group below 25 years.

The trajectory of social enterprise development in Greece could be explained as a by-product of ill-conceived policy design and inconsistent policy implementation. In terms of policy design, the narrowing down of social economy as a social inclusion tool does not open up the space for innovative policies with far reaching transformational potential. In addition, the sole focus on social enterprises to the exclusion of other social economy entities hinders both inter-ministerial coordination and the consolidation of a collective identity in the field.

In terms of policy implementation, even this shortsighted view has not been implemented in full. On the contrary, people themselves followed the path of social economy unassisted both in terms of public support measures and collective representative social economy networks. That is, an instrumental view of social economy coupled with inconsistent policy implementation fell short even from addressing its narrow policy goals: namely, the integration into the labor market of the young and vulnerable social groups.

The broader vision of solidarity economy adopted in the public policy agenda of selected Latin American countries offers significant insights for policy reformulation in Greece even though concrete experiences cannot be replicated in different contexts. The main tenets of solidarity economy public policy in the Latin American context might indicate the direction of change in Greece along the following lines: (1) appeal to all social economy entities and not exclusively to social enterprises, after all the latter will thrive if the whole ecosystem of social economy thrives, (2) intense inter-ministerial coordination in order to enable the prioritization of social and solidarity economy in public policy-making, (3) identification of unmet social needs which could be better addressed by social economy entities instead of traditional for-profit enterprises or the public sector (i.e., innovative social and environmental services), (4) design and implementation of far-reaching programs targeting multiple goals, (5) special efforts to address the youth and other vulnerable social groups through intermediate support structures while acknowledging that social entrepreneurship is not suitable for everyone, (6) consolidation of social dialogue between state authorities and representative social economy networks, and (7) innovative policy-making for a fruitful interaction between the broader public sector and social economy entities (i.e., meals in school canteens by cooperatives and/or social enterprises).

The economic crisis presents enormous challenges especially for the young generation. It is of outmost importance to address social economic development. Otherwise, we risk missing another round of social economy development despite the dynamics displayed by the unassisted efforts of citizens themselves.

References

Adam, Sofia and Papatheodorou, Christos 2010 "The involvement of social economy organizations in the fight against social exclusion: a critical perspective" in *Studies* (Athens) Observatory of economic and social developments, Labour Institute, Greek General Confederation of Labour (available in Greek).

Alter, Kim 2007 "Social enterprise typology" in <http://rinovations.edublogs.org/files/2008/07/setypology.pdf> accessed 4 June 2012.

Azzelini, Dario 2012 "Economia solidaria en Venezuela: del apoyo ao cooperativismo tradicional a la construcción de ciclos comunales" in Lianza Sidney, Henriques, Flavio Chedid (eds.) *A economia solidária na América Latina: realidades nacionais e políticas públicas* (Rio de Janeiro) in <http://www.soltec.ufrj.br/images/PDFs/Livro_americalatina.pdf> accessed 15 May 2015.

Ben-Ner, Avner and van Hoomissen, Theresa 1991 "Nonprofit organizations in the mixed economy: A demand and supply analysis", *Annals of Public and Cooperative Economics* (New Jersey), Vol. 62, No 4, 519–550.

Defourny, Jacques 2001 "Introduction: from third sector to social enterprise" in Borzaga, Carlo and Defourny, Jacques (eds.) *The Emergence of Social Enterprise* (London and New York: Routledge).

Defourny, Jacques and Nyssens, Marthe 2006 "Social enterprise in Europe: recent trends and developments", *Social Enterprise Journal* (London), Vol. 4, No 3, 202–228.

FBES 2006 "Brazilian Forum of Solidarity Economy" in <http://www.fbes.org.br/biblioteca22/Brazilian_Solidarity_Economy_Movement.pdf> accessed 10 June 2015.

Hansmann, Henry B. 1987 "Economic theories of nonprofit organizations" in Powell, Walter W. (ed.) *The Nonprofit Sector* (New Haven: Yale University Press).

Kerlin, Janelle A. 2006 "Social enterprise in the United States and Europe: understanding and learning from the differences," *Voluntas: International Journal of Voluntary and Nonprofit Organizations* (New York), Vol. 17, No 3, 246–262.

Kernot, Cheryl 2009 "Social enterprise: A Powerful Path to Social Inclusion", The Centre for Social Impact in <http://www.csi.edu.au/assets/assetdoc/b1850e3801 86ee50/CSI%20Issues%20Paper%20No.%205%20%20Social%20Enterprise %20%20A%20Powerful%20Path.pdf> accessed 1 June 2012.

Morais, Leandro Pereira 2014 "Social and solidarity economy and south–south and triangular cooperation in Latin America and the Caribbean: contributions to Inclusive and Sustainable Development" in *Social and Solidarity Economy: Towards Inclusive and Sustainable Development* (Campinas) International Training Centre of the International Labour Organization in <http://www.ilo.org/wcmsp5/ groups/public/---ed_emp/---emp_ent/---coop/documents/publication/wcms_ 329359.pdf> accessed 12 May 2015.

Morais, Leandro Pereira and Bacic, Miguel 2013 "SSE, Social and Solidarity Economy, youth employment and the fight against poverty: the case of Public Works and Employment Programmes in Brazil" in <http://www.socioeco.org/bdf_fiche-document-3169_en.html> accessed 15 June 2015.

Moulaert, Frank and Ailenei, Oanna 2005 "Social economy, third sector and solidarity relations: A conceptual synthesis from history to present", *Urban Studies* (London and New York), Vol. 42, No 11.

Orhangazi, Ozgur 2014 "Contours of Alternative Policy Making in Venezuela", *Review of Radical Political Economics, Union for Radical Political Economics* (Amherst, MA) Vol. 46, No 2.

Pestoff, Victor 2004 "The development and future of the social economy in Sweden" in Evers, Adlabert and Laville, Jean-Louis (eds.) *The Third Sector in Europe* (Cheltenham, UK and Northampton, MA: Edward Elgar).

Rose-Ackerman, Susan 1996 "Altruism, nonprofits and economic theory", *Journal of Economic Literature* (Pittsburgh) Vol. 34, 701–728.

Ruiz Patricio, Andrade 2012 "La Economía Popular y Solidaria en la Construcción del Sumak Kawsay (Buen Vivir) en el Ecuador" in Lianza Sidney, Henriques, Flavio Chedid (eds.) *A economia solidária na América Latina: realidades nacionais e políticas públicas* (Rio de Janeiro) in <http://www.soltec.ufrj.br/images/PDFs/ Livro_americalatina.pdf> accessed 15 May 2015.

Saguier, Marcelo and Brent, Zoe 2014 "Regional Policy Frameworks of Social and Solidarity Economy in South America", UNRISD Occasional Paper (Geneva), Vol. 6.

Weisbrod, Burton A. 1975 "Toward a theory of the voluntary nonprofit sector in a three sector economy" in Phelps, Edmund S. (ed.) *Altruism, Morality, and Economic Theory* (New York: Russell Sage Foundation).

"GENERATION NOWHERE": The youth in South Africa's informal economy—the case of day laborers and waste pickers

Catherina J. Schenck, Phillip F. Blaauw, and Jacoba M.M. Viljoen

In his analysis of the value and meaning of work, Du Toit (2003) shares renowned psychologist Sigmund Freud's assertion, following a protracted study of the human condition, that work and love are the two essential ingredients of a healthy and well-adjusted personality. Work, according to Du Toit (2003), has the power to contribute to a person's well-being in many ways. First, having work implies that people receive an income as a reward for the effort expended in a productive endeavor, enabling them to sustain themselves and their families. Second, the work people do determines to a large extent where and how they live and socialize, and what their status is in society. Finally, work is a source of identity and can positively (or negatively) influence people's self-esteem and feelings of self-worth. Echoing these views, the economists Sen (1999) and Max-Neef (1991) regard the economic activities in which people are engaged as vital for their sense of well-being, their ability to function as humans and their collective freedoms (Sen, 1999) and critical for the satisfaction of multiple fundamental human needs (Max-Neef, 1991). Being unemployed, therefore, affects people's ability to function at multiple levels.

Youth unemployment has become an acute global concern, eating away at the productive core of many economies and weakening efforts to build stable societies for future generations (Du Toit, 2003; Marock, 2008;ILO, 2013; Yu, 2013). In fact, youth unemployment has reached an historical peak and is now three times higher than adult unemployment (ILO, 2013). Globally 74.5% of young people in the 15-24 age group were unemployed in 2013, which is 1 million more than in 2012. It is predicted that this upward trend will persist for the foreseeable future (ILO, 2013). In South Africa, young people certainly face poorer absorption prospects and higher unemployment rates than adults. Particularly worrying is the fact that the unemployment rate for young people in the 15-24 age bracket increased from 45.6% in 2008 to 51.3% in 2014, which is the largest increase among all age groups (StatsSA, 2015). This sets off alarm bells for the future of South Africa where nearly half the population is under the age of 25.

Jeffrey (2008) reveals that 85% of the world's youth (aged 16–30) live in Africa, Asia and Latin America. UNESCO (2013), in turn, reports that 89.7% of young people under the age of 30 live in the emerging economies and developing countries, with Africa and the Middle East being home to 70% of the world's youth population. Furthermore, present estimates suggest that more than 200 million people in Africa are between the ages of 15 and 24, with the median age being 18. This is no less than seven years younger than the median age in South Asia, which is the world's next youngest region (Fox, 2015).

According to the ILO (2013), only 35% of women and 59% of men aged 15–19 in the global South are engaged in paid employment. The rest are likely to be either unemployed or employed in low-skilled, low-paid informal work. "Productively employing Africa's 'youth bulge' is an urgent urban development problem" (Fox, 2015: 1). Fox views the discussion among urban leaders on this topic as focusing on the creation of more wage employment opportunities. Although this is undoubtedly important, most of the "youth bulge" aged 25 and under are not able to get any kind of wage or salaried employment, be it with a contract (indicating some sort of formality) or as casual labor (Fox, 2015).

As a result of the high rate of unemployment among young people, Jeffrey (2008) refers to the unemployed youth as the "Generation Nowhere." The World Economic Forum Global Risk Report (2014), in turn, refers to them as the "lost generation" while the ILO (2013) sees them as the "scarred" generation. At a conference on youth unemployment held at the University of Cape Town (UCT) in August 2014, the unemployed youth were referred to as the "waiting generation."

South Africa has the dubious reputation of having the third highest youth unemployment rate globally among the 15–24 age group (i.e., 50% if one excludes discouraged work seekers, or 63% if one considers both discouraged work seekers and the unemployed) (Rankin & Roberts, 2011; World Economic Forum Global Risk Report, 2014). Greece and Spain take the top two positions with 58% and 57%, respectively (World Bank, 2015). Furthermore, using the broader definition of youth (i.e., aged 15–34) as given in South Africa's National Youth Policy 2009–2014 (Office of the Presidency, 2009), youth unemployment in the country currently stands at over 36% (StatsSa, 2014). According to Banerjee et al. (2008), the main reasons for the high youth unemployment rate in the country are the structural changes that have been taking place in both the global and South African economies, generally low education levels, and a mismatch between what the education and training sectors deliver and what the labor market requires. Kingdon and Knight (2003) point to labor market rigidities as a major contributing factor to high and persistent unemployment. They suggest that for those who are not already accommodated in the formal economy, the informal economy, as an alternative, presents significant barriers to entry.

Ligthelm (2006) expresses the concern that unemployment tends to target the youth in South Africa, who generally have rudimentary skills and education, and have little to no experience of formal employment. What is particularly disturbing is that unemployment is regarded as the single biggest obstacle to poverty reduction in South Africa (Ligthelm, 2006). With the labor market in South Africa favoring more skilled workers, it is very difficult for unskilled individuals to find work (Banerjee et al., 2008).

Rankin and Roberts (2011) emphasize that youth unemployment matters because it impacts on the lifetime employment trajectory of the individual. Critical for the employability of the youth is that they possess technical skills but also that they are able to read and write, engage in basic arrhythmic and other fundamental activities such as problem solving, planning and decision making, and have the capacity for higher-order thinking skills, dependability, a positive attitude and other affective skills and traits. Without these attributes, a person will not be regarded as employable in the formal economy (Marock, 2008). It is for this reason that day laborers and waste pickers typically find themselves eking out an existence in the informal economy. As they tend to have few of the attributes and skills required to join formal businesses, they become marginalized and are forced into low-paying economic activities. Day laborers and waste pickers ostensibly operate on the fringes of society, where they tend to be seen and not heard. Yet they make an important contribution to the South African economy, offering useful services (albeit on a very small scale), reducing the obligation of the state to provide them with financial support (if they qualify) and often displaying an attitude that suggests they nurture a vision of better things to come.

The aim of this chapter is to summarize the results of the research that the authors have conducted over the past decade on the day laborer and waste picker communities in South Africa, of which the youth forms a major part. Given the complexities of the topic, the picture that is painted is not complete and the research is ongoing. Yet readers will acquire a new appreciation for this often-neglected group of people, their socioeconomic circumstances and how they view their lives.

The rest of the chapter describes the role of the informal economy in the broader South African economy and the attributes and contribution of day laborers and waste pickers, in particular.

South Africa's informal economy

The literature is yet to provide an unchallenged definition (Charmes, 2012; Valodia and Devey, 2012), and so for the purpose of this chapter the informal economy is viewed as a collection of "unorganised, unregulated and mostly legal, but unregistered economic activities that are individually or family owned and use simple, labour-intensive technology" (Barker, 2007: 59).

In the first quarter of 2014, there were 2.446 million people in South Africa (constituting 12.3% of the active labor force of around 20 million people) trying to make a living in the informal economy (excluding the agricultural sector) (StatsSA, 2014). Charmes (2012) estimates that 32.7% of South Africa's labor force works in the informal economy (including the agricultural sector). In terms of labor force absorption, South Africa's informal sector makes a small contribution compared to that of India (which absorbs 90%), the Democratic Republic of Congo (DRC) (which absorbs 77%), Cameroon (which absorbs 84%) and Mozambique (which absorbs 87.2%) (Harris-White, 2002; Charmes, 2012). Considering that South Africa has one of the highest unemployment rates (25.5% in 2015) and youth unemployment rates (50%) in the world, more people should theoretically be able to enter the informal economy. Yet between 2008 and 2014, the number of those employed in the informal sector essentially remained constant at 2.4 million (with a negligible increase of 13,000 jobs during the period in question; StatsSA, 2015).

Lund and Skinner (2004) are of the view that the informal economy in South Africa is still "underdeveloped," mainly due to a lack of education and skills, a negative mindset about the informal economy and its potential, and—importantly—a challenging policy environment (Valodia and Devey, 2012). Yu (2013) weighs in on this debate by asserting that some of the uneducated youth who struggle to find employment in the formal sector could survive in the informal sector, but that finding informal employment is hindered by various barriers to entry, ranging from unhelpful government policies and a lack of access to credit, to a dearth of training opportunities and susceptibility to crime. A concern expressed in the National Development Plan 2030, South Africa's overarching economic route map, is that those who make a living from informal activities will remain poorly paid and unable to build up savings, leaving them dependent on the state for health and social protection (NPC, 2012).

Two visible forms of informal worker in South Africa, apart from street traders, are the large numbers of day laborers who wait on the side of the road in anticipation of being picked up to do ad-hoc work, and street waste pickers who push their trolleys around the cities piled high with recyclable waste. Other waste pickers, who work on the landfill sites, are largely out of the public eye.

What is day laboring?

Day laboring is a national and international phenomenon that refers to people, mostly men, gathering at pick-up points (hiring sites) hoping to sell their labor for the day (or longer) to prospective employers in order to earn some income (Blaauw, 2010; Valenzuela et al., 2006). The number of day laborers appears to be growing steadily. In the United States, for example, the number of day laborers doubled between 1995 and 2004 to 117,000 (Louw, 2007; Valenzuela et al., 2006). In a study conducted by Harmse et al. (2009), it was estimated that every morning between 45,000 and 100,000 day laborers congregate at more than 1,000 hiring sites throughout South Africa (Blaauw, 2010).

A day laborer described his work as follows:

> Day labour work is the most feasible way of generating income. You don't need an identity document or certificates to get a job. In order to survive, you need to keep a low profile, stay away from the police, get a girlfriend who is a stay-in domestic worker for accommodation, and impress your employer the day

you get a chance to do a piece job. (Schenck, Xipu and Blaauw, 2012)

From this description of day laboring, it would appear that there are no concrete barriers to entry but a number of survival tactics are necessary.

What is waste picking?

Waste picking, particularly street waste picking, is a common phenomenon on the streets and landfill sites of South Africa. According to Samson (2010a, 2010b), waste pickers make a living by gathering waste from the streets and landfill sites and on selling it to entities operating within the recycling industry. While the waste pickers interact with the formal waste system, it seems that the structural gap between the formal and informal waste economy is significant (Samson, 2012; Schenck et al., 2012; Viljoen et al., 2012; Viljoen, 2014).

The recycling industry creates opportunities for people to earn an income by informally collecting and selling waste to the buy-back centers (BBCs), which in turn sell the waste to the bigger recycling companies. This process dovetails with the work of the municipal waste management departments, which collect waste and either dump it on the landfill sites or, if they have the capacity, recycle it to some extent and sell it to the recycling companies (Samson, 2012; Schenck et al., 2012; Huegel, 2013; Viljoen et al., 2012).

The World Bank estimates that there are around 15 million waste pickers across the globe. As is the case with day laborers, it would be practically impossible to determine the exact number and geographical spread of waste pickers in South Africa, as they are unregistered and unregulated. However, it is estimated that the country has between 35,000 and 70,000 waste pickers. Langenhoven and Dyssel (2007) cite the South African Yearbook 2000/2005, which proposes a number of 37,000 waste pickers operating in South Africa, while Schenck et al. (2012) suggest that 70,000 waste pickers is a good estimate. Waste picking is quite fluid, with pickers entering and leaving the field as their circumstances change. Some, for example, collect and sell waste only occasionally when they need additional income (Chvatal, 2010; Schenck & Blaauw, 2011a).

The following quote by a waste picker summed up the nature of his work:

> Waste picking is an unskilled profession that gives unskilled labourers the opportunity to enter the labour market. (Schenck and Blaauw 2011a; Schenck et al., 2012)

In further discussions with this particular waste picker, it emerged that, as with day laboring, waste picking has no direct barriers to entry, and any person—despite having little schooling and skills—who is physically fit can enter the profession (Schenck and Blaauw, 2011b; Schenck et al., 2012).

Research methodology

In studying day laborers and waste pickers, respectively, the authors adopted a case study research approach. In case study research, a unit of analysis is studied intensively (Welman et al., 2007; Du Plooy et al., 2014) so as to gain a comprehensive and detailed understanding of a particular phenomenon. It is used to answer "how" and "why" questions, while also attempting to give a voice to the powerless and the voiceless (Maree, 2007).

For their research on the day laboring and waste picking phenomena, the authors used a variety of data collection methods. Both studies are still underway. Up to the time of writing, the studies had unfolded as follows:

Day laborer studies

The authors' research on day laborers began as early as 2003 and has involved the following phases:

Study 1: (2003) Exploratory qualitative interviews conducted with day laborers at one hiring site in Pretoria (Schenck and Louw, 2005).
Study 2: (2004) Observation and reconnaissance in the broader Pretoria area, counting the day labor hiring sites and determining the prevalence of day laborers in Pretoria.

Study 3: (2004) Survey conducted in Pretoria with 242 respondents (using qualitative questions) (Blaauw et al., 2006, 2007; Louw, 2007).

Study 4: (2005/06) Observation and reconnaissance in various parts of South Africa to determine the geographical locations of hiring sites and to estimate the number of day laborers in South Africa (Harmse et al., 2009).

Study 5: (2007/08) National survey conducted with 3,830 respondents (Blaauw, 2010).

Study 6: (2008) Exploratory interviews with people affected by day laborers in Pretoria (Nell and Schenck, 2009).

Study 7: (2008) Observation of the activities and dynamics at day labor hiring sites (Schenck, Xipu and Blaauw, 2012).

Study 8: (2014) Pilot ethnographic study conducted on one-day labor site (report in progress).

Waste picker studies

The authors' research on waste pickers has followed a very similar pattern to that of the day laborer study.

Study 1: (2009) Exploratory interviews conducted with street waste pickers in Pretoria in order to understand their way of life (Schenck and Blaauw, 2011a, 2011b).

Study 2: (2010) Survey conducted in Pretoria with 142 respondents (Schenck and Blaauw, 2011a, 2011b).

Study 3: (2011) Observation and reconnaissance in the major cities of South Africa to determine the prevalence of BBCs and street waste pickers.

Study 4: (2012) National survey conducted with 910 street waste pickers and 68 BBCs in all the provincial capitals and major cities of South Africa (Viljoen et al., 2012; Viljoen, 2014).

Study 5: (2012) Survey conducted with 400 waste pickers on nine landfill sites in the Free State province of South Africa (Schenck et al., 2012).

The sampling process in both studies was challenging, as both the populations were unknown and mobile.

- In both the Pretoria and national day laborer surveys, cluster sampling was used. Cluster sampling is used when groups of sampling units occur (Louw, 2007; Blaauw, 2010) and the groups are informal and known only in their immediate environment (Blaauw, 2010). As day laborers start to assemble early, in time to be picked up from 06:00 onward, it was important for the fieldworkers to be at the hiring sites by no later than 06:00. At many sites, day laborers who had not managed to get a job by 10:00 started to leave.
- With regard to the waste pickers, snowball and availability sampling were used (Viljoen, 2014). As the street waste pickers were constantly on the move, the fieldworkers interviewed those waste pickers whom they could find either on the streets or at the BBCs. In contrast to the day laborer study, the best time to be at the BBCs was after the waste pickers had sold their recyclable materials and completed their tasks for the day.

Results

Profile of the day laborers and waste pickers

In a study conducted by Gonzo and Plattner (2003), it was found that 85% of the day laborers in Windhoek, Namibia were younger than 35. This number points to the fact that day laboring is more difficult for older people. One needs to be young and strong in order to do hard labor. However, street waste picking does not exclude older people, as evidenced in the fact that some of the individuals on the landfill sites were as old as 80.

Table 1: Profile of the day laborers and waste pickers

	Day laborers (national)	Street waste pickers (national)	Landfill waste pickers (Free State province)
Young day laborers	66% under 35 (Zimbabwe group: 77%)	42% under 35	42% under 35
Gender			
Male	96%	96%	52%
Female	4%	4%	48%
Total	**100%**	**100%**	**100%**
Race			
Black	92%	84.6%	98%
Colored	7.3%	14.6%	2%
Indian/Asian	0.4%	0.4%	0%
White	0.3%	0.4%	0%
Total	**100%**	**100%**	**100%**

Source: Research data

In terms of the gender split, a higher proportion of female waste pickers operated on the landfill sites (48%) than on the streets (only 4%). Moreover, females constituted only 4% of day laborers and 4% of street waste pickers. The trolleys are difficult to push over long distances, and the streets pose particular challenges for women given their vulnerability to harassment and crime.

Regarding race, black African people were the majority in both the day laborer and street waste picker groups, with colored (or mixed race) people making up the second largest group. The remaining 1% consisted of White and Indian people. The fact that Black people made up the significant majority of those working on the landfill sites in the Free State province should not be seen as representative of the whole country but rather as a reflection of the situation in that province only.

The profile of the day laborers in South Africa was very similar to that revealed in the study conducted in the United States. In the United States, the average age of day laborers was 34, while in South Africa it was 35. Similarly, 98% of the day laborers in the USA were males compared to 96% in South Africa (Theodore et al., 2015). Regarding the male dominance among day laborers, a fieldworker conducting the ethnographical study in

South Africa recalled a comment made by one of laborers: "This is a place where a man can still be a man." This suggests a masculine propensity to be seen to be the main wage earner and breadwinner.

The need to look after one's family was a recurring theme in a study by Makina (2013). Facing bleak prospects of getting into the job market in Zimbabwe, young Zimbabweans often travel to South Africa to look for work. This is widely seen as a "rite of passage" toward maturity where dependent families are living in poverty. Like many of the youth in South Africa, Zimbabweans often find themselves compelled to seek work in the informal sector, where neither waste picking nor day laboring has strict entry criteria.

Country of origin

In both groups the South Africans constituted the majority, with Zimbabweans making up less than 10%.[1] It is interesting that 15% of the street waste pickers and 9% of the landfill waste pickers were from Lesotho (a small independent country surrounded by South Africa). Less surprising, though, is the fact that very few waste pickers and day laborers came from Namibia and Botswana, both of which are politically and economically stable.

---

[1] In South Africa, the popular belief is that Zimbabweans are in the majority in the informal economy and are thus taking many of the job opportunities away from the South Africans. This belief has at times prompted xenophobic attacks. Preliminary results from a recent repeat of the nationwide survey among day laborers suggest that the picture reflected in Table 2 has changed dramatically, with the proportion of day laborers from Zimbabwe having more than doubled over the last eight years (Blaauw & Schenck, 2014).

Table 2: Country of origin of the day laborers and waste pickers

Country	Day laborers (national) (%)	Street waste pickers (national) (%)	Landfill waste pickers (Free State province) (%)
South Africa	85.2	72.3	89
Zimbabwe	9.5	8.3	1
Namibia	0.1	0.5	
Swaziland	0.2	0.3	
Mozambique	2.6	1.8	
Lesotho	1.4	15.7	9
Botswana	2	0	1
Other	0.9	1.1	
Total	**100**	**100**	**100**

Source: Research data

Whereas the majority of day laborers in South Africa were found to be South African citizens, the day laborers who featured in the USA study were predominantly (i.e., 93%) foreigners from Mexico, Central America, and South America. Only 7% were US-born workers (Theodore et al., 2015).

Education

Figure 1 is very revealing in a number of respects. Firstly, there was a significant difference between the level of education of the South African day laborers and the Zimbabwean day laborers. Fifty-one percent of the Zimbabwean day laborers surveyed had completed school and 12% had a post-school qualification. In contrast, 49% of the South African day laborers and 51% of the South African waste pickers had completed some secondary schooling, with those who had completed secondary school and obtained a postschool qualification being very much in the minority. For example, only 15% of the South African day laborers had completed school and 3% had a postschool qualification, while only 5% of the landfill waste pickers and 9% of the street waste pickers had completed school. In a country where people's level of schooling is closely aligned to their prospects of finding employment, it is not surprising that many people end up engaged in marginal activities in the informal economy.

Figure 1: Education of South African and Zimbabwean day laborers and South African waste pickers

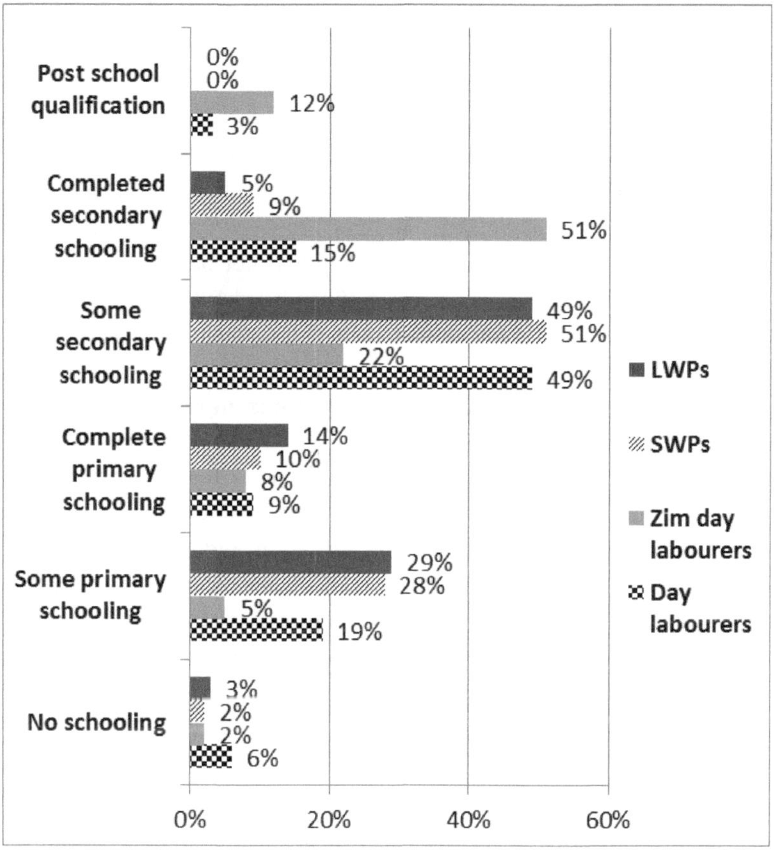

Category	LWPs	SWPs	Zim day labourers	Day labourers
Post school qualification	0%	0%	12%	3%
Completed secondary schooling	5%	9%	51%	15%
Some secondary schooling	49%	51%	22%	49%
Complete primary schooling	14%	10%	8%	9%
Some primary schooling	29%	28%	5%	19%
No schooling	3%	2%	2%	6%

Source: Research data

On closer questioning, it was revealed that many of the day laborers and waste pickers did not complete their schooling because they had failed their matric (i.e., Grade 12/the last year at secondary school) and had not returned to repeat the year. The most frequent reasons given for putting in a lackluster performance at school or not completing Grade 12 were related to poverty. The same unfortunate reality is echoed in Branson et al. (2013) and Green (2016), who indicate that, along with the inability to keep pace at school (academically), the three major reasons for dropping out of school are: pregnancy (even though schools are prohibited from expelling pregnant girls), an inability to continue their studies due to poverty, and the need to go out to work to support themselves and their families. According to the data, most of the participants in Green's study had tried (enduring multiple setbacks) to stay in school, but then one factor was the "final straw" that had pushed them out (Green, 2016: 1).

The plight of some of the day laborer and waste picker respondents in the respective studies was exacerbated by family problems, such as the illness or death of one or both parents, which reinforced their already poverty-stricken state. This left the rest of the family with no money to afford school, and the respondents had to go to work to support their parents and/or other family members. As they had not been able to extract themselves from their cycle of poverty (Chambers, 1983), their personal development had taken a knock and their employment prospects significantly dimmed.

Wilson et al. (2006) confirm that there is an undeniable link between poor education and an inability to find formal employment. This is supported by Nzeadibe et al. (2012), who found that most of the waste pickers whom they interviewed in Nigeria were unable to find jobs in the formal sector as a result of a lack of education and skills. The figures gleaned from the studies on day laborers and waste pickers in South Africa are supported by the last census of 2011 by StatsSA (2014), which indicated that 60% of the unemployed in South Africa had not completed their secondary schooling.

Income earned

In the South African studies, it was difficult to determine exactly what the day laborers and waste pickers earned as they did not get a fixed daily or monthly income. Based on the answers to the question: "What did you earn yesterday/last week/last month?" estimates were calculated.

Street waste pickers earned an average of ZAR 85 (USD 8) per day, while the landfill waste pickers in the Free State earned an average of ZAR 404 (USD 40) per day (Schenck et al., 2012).[2] Some landfill waste pickers said that they had chosen waste picking as they could earn more than if they were to work for the minimum wage, which is on average ZAR 80 (USD 8) per day for unskilled workers in South Africa. This income figure

---

[2] The US dollar values were determined from the prevailing nominal exchange rate at the time of the survey.

for the landfill waste pickers is confirmed by Reyneke (2012), who spoke about one of the waste pickers, Simon, on the landfill site in Pretoria:

> Simon earns more than R5000 a month working as a waste picker [.....] he further mentioned that he aimed at saving R10 000, because he wanted to buy a small motorcycle that he was going to use to increase his monthly income, transporting people and certain commodities he wanted to sell at the site. (Reyneke, 2012)

Over and above the opportunity of earning more than the minimum wage, other reasons given for being a day laborer or waste picker were: "I am my own boss," "I get sufficient income," and "I'm doing well enough." Some respondents, however, remarked that waste picking was "the only option" due to their having little education, few skills, and limited opportunities in the formal labor market.

Reverting to the issue of some South African day laborers harboring the xenophobic-induced belief that Zimbabwean day laborers were working for less than they were and therefore undermining their chances of getting work, the survey results were surprising. In a study by Schenck et al. (2012), one of the day laborers was quoted as saying:

> ...these Makwerekweres (derogatory term for foreigners) are spoiling the employers by charging R 20 (USD 2) per day when we charge R100. (USD 10) per day

The actual results, however, showed that the Zimbabwean day laborers earned from R 63–R 142 (USD 6–14) per day, while the South African day laborers earned from R 57–R 117 (USD 5–11) per day depending on how often they were employed on a particular day (Blaauw, 2010). It was also revealed that Zimbabwean day laborers were employed more often, probably because they were better qualified and more proficient in English (Blaauw, 2010).

As indicated earlier in this chapter, day laboring and waste picking have few barriers to entry in terms of qualifications and skills. However, it is to the workers' advantage if they have tools (day laborers) and a trolley (street waste pickers) and if they can speak English or Afrikaans in order to communicate with their prospective employers and understand their instructions (Blaauw, 2010; Viljoen, 2014). The data in the studies showed that those with postschool qualifications earned 18% more, and those day laborers whose language proficiency was good were hired more frequently than those who struggled to understand and negotiate in English or Afrikaans. Notes from the fieldworker in the ethnographic study attest to this:

> Frans (a day labourer) had been looking for work outside Builders Warehouse [...] He also had no tools of his own—a key component of finding work on a reliable basis. Frans, however, relied on his friendship with John, a man with his own set of tiling tools and who was something of a legend among the men looking for day work.

The fieldworker commented further on the circumstances of the day laborers, saying that they live complex economic lives and day laboring is but one of their economic activities. In addition to day labor:

> ... their economic activities stretch further—such as guarding cars (at motor shows or sports events or elsewhere) over weekends, gambling, cutting hair for other men outside Builders Warehouse, doing favors, selling drugs and offering cash loans.

An ethnographic study by Reyneke (2012) on a landfill site in Pretoria suggested that multiple economic activities, besides collecting and selling waste, were also being played out on landfill sites, such as producing useful or saleable items from the collected waste. These activities deserve further investigation.

Family obligations

A fieldworker in the day laborer study recalled how Frans, one of the respondents, had revealed rather poignantly how ashamed he felt when he did not have money to give his family what they wanted, and that a woman would not stay with a man who was not working.

In all the phases of the studies on day laborers and waste pickers, the results showed that each category of worker had to support an average of four people. Being mostly young and unemployed, they were not married but were, nevertheless, responsible for supporting their families. The question as to where they had slept the previous evening gave an indication of the type of family life the day laborers and waste pickers were leading while on the streets or landfill sites (Table 3).

Table 3: The place where the day laborers and waste pickers had slept the previous evening

Place or structure where they had slept	Day laborers (national) (%)	Street waste pickers (national) (%)	Landfill waste pickers (Free State province) (%)
Brick house	32	18	46
Shack	37	22	47
Elsewhere (construction site, street, open field, place of work, or with a domestic worker)	31	60	7
Total	100	100	100

Source: Research data

From a national perspective, 31% of the day laborers did not sleep at home at the time of the study, although the situation differed from towns to cities. In the rural towns, for example, day laborers were generally able to go home, while in the cities day laborers (and in particular migrants) might not have been able to afford to go home in the evenings if they were short of funds. It is significant that 60% of the street waste pickers slept elsewhere. It emerged that the street waste pickers could not leave their trolleys and their collected waste unattended, and so they slept with their trolleys on the streets, in empty buildings or in open fields. In contrast, only 7% of waste pickers on the landfill sites in the Free State province did not sleep at home. On all nine landfill sites, the waste pickers lived in close proximity to the sites and were able to go home each evening. Other studies, however, suggest that the situation on landfill sites in the big cities could be different. For example, Reyneke (2012) mentions that there are about 300–400 waste pickers working on the landfill site in Pretoria, yet not all these individuals live onsite. Only about 200 of the waste pickers own shacks on the landfill and the others commute back and forth on a daily basis. This means that around 50% of the waste pickers sleep on the landfill site.

Figure 2 shows that most street waste pickers in Pretoria were migrants from other provinces, which helps to explain why they sleep "elsewhere."

Figure 2: Provinces from which street South Africa's waste pickers migrated to Pretoria

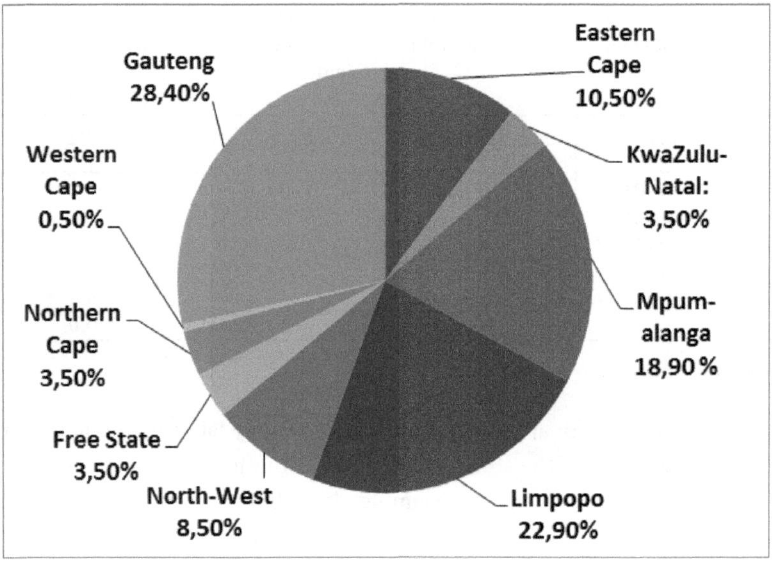

- Gauteng 28,40%
- Eastern Cape 10,50%
- Western Cape 0,50%
- KwaZulu-Natal: 3,50%
- Northern Cape 3,50%
- Mpumalanga 18,90%
- Free State 3,50%
- North-West 8,50%
- Limpopo 22,90%

Source: Viljoen (2014)

Only 28% of the South African street waste pickers found in Pretoria came from Gauteng province, where Pretoria is situated, meaning that 72% of the street waste pickers had migrated to Pretoria to look for or create employment opportunities.

The following comment from a fieldworker highlights the challenges faced by many day laborers and waste pickers in travelling to and from their places of work:

Frans (a day labourer) is a 33-year-old man from Polokwane (i.e. a migrant from another province)[...] he used to live in the public park up the road from Builders Warehouse. While living there, he found and saved materials until he eventually had enough to build the shack where he now lives in a relatively new part of Atteridgeville (a Black township on the outskirts of Pretoria). He travels up to five hours every day to and from Gezina (where he currently works), which is a 30-minute walk and a two-hour train trip from Atteridgeville.

As a migrant, Frans did not have a place to stay and therefore slept in the park. When he built a shack in the township, he had to leave home at around 04:00 in the morning in order to get to the hiring site by 06:00 or 06:30. He would probably visit his family in Polokwane no more than four times a year and send remittances possibly twice a year (Blaauw, 2010).

Food security

Food security is generally a major concern to day laborers and waste pickers as they do not always have access to proper food, particularly if they do not sleep at home and/or do not earn enough to buy good food. Table 4 shows that 32% of the street waste pickers surveyed indicated that they eat from the dustbins, with a typical refrain being: "You see somebody's supper from last night and you eat it."

Table 4: Access to food

	Dustbins (%)	Landfill sites	Other waste pickers (%)	Own/bring/buy (%)	Other (churches) (%)
Street waste pickers	32	–	15	40	32
Landfill waste pickers	–	31	15	83	15

Source: Research data

Thirty-one percent of the landfill waste pickers in the Free State province indicated that they acquired food that had been dumped on the landfill sites. Fieldworkers witnessed how landfill waste pickers dug out food from mounds of rubbish. Remarked one of the fieldworkers: "Some people hang meat in the sun and dry it until their next trip home." If they earned enough, waste pickers would buy food and often support each other by sharing. At times, pickers received food from churches and NGOs.

In the study on day laborers, 2,300 respondents (56%) indicated that they often did not have enough to eat. It was observed that at some of the more permanent or connected hiring sites, another type of informal economy had developed in the form of people selling food to the waiting day laborers, but not necessarily of the nutritious variety. At the one hiring site, the fieldworker had the following to say:

> Most food is bought from the two tuck shops on the road outside Builders Warehouse. The first tuck shop offers "magwinya" ("vetkoek" or bread dough deep fried in oil) for R 1.50 (US 0.15) and "spatlo" (polony and potato fries in half a loaf of bread) for R 10 (USD 1). They also sell fruit (apples and bananas) and packets of crisps, as well as coffee and tea for R 5 (USD 0.50) [....] The food goes together with the other parts of the business (cigarette sales, phone calls and cash loans).

Survival strategies

To be able to live under such harsh circumstances, survival strategies are needed (Blaauw, 2010; Viljoen, 2014). Du Toit (2003) indicates that there is a link between unemployment and psychosocial distress. The unemployed are often unstructured when it comes to time management, lack strong social contacts, are excluded from a collective societal purpose, and have no recognized social status or identity. To enter the informal sector is already an exercise in survival. To help stay the course, day laborers and waste pickers invoke various strategies, of which the two most prominent ones are networking and soliciting group support.

- **Networking (day laborers)**

    The fieldworkers in the studies found that day laborers often relied on the support of staff at, for example, hardware stores and other firms who would recommend them to clients who might be looking for workers. As one of the day laborers remarked to the fieldworker in the study by Schenck et al. (2012):

> ... when you befriend an edge trimmer and buy him "itakana" (liquor), you are set to become one of the regulars in the gardening service.

- **Soliciting social support**

In Schenck et al. (2012), a fieldworker shared his observation of what happened to those laborers who were not picked up for the day:

> ...if the day laborers do not manage to get a job by around 10:00 and have not already left the site, the mood changes from looking for work to socializing. They will share food and water and play "morabaraba" (a local "board" game which involves drawing a board on cardboard or in the sand, and playing with stones/marbles. (Schenck et al., 2012)

Blaauw (2010) explains that social support is very important for being able to cope with everyday hardships. Support can reduce the negative consequences of this type of existence and help maintain people's psychological and physical well-being (Gonzo and Plattner, 2003). According to Blaauw (2010) and Viljoen (2014), the day laborers and waste pickers participating in the studies tended to organize themselves into groups, which became support systems for identifying or accessing job opportunities, and providing food and regular accommodation or occasionally a place to sleep. Indeed, it was found that 73% of the day laborers viewed themselves as being part of a "support group." The waste pickers also indicated that they supported each other by providing food, looking out for other workers when they were ill, and even assisting in waste collection or in providing protection services (Schenck et al., 2012; Viljoen, 2014). Both day laborers and waste pickers revealed that if they slept on the streets or in a field, they would sleep in a group as a safeguard against gangsters and other criminals.

Despite the support they gave each other, it was clear that the day laborers and waste pickers (even those who were very young) had a strong sense of independence, that is, everyone worked for him/herself (Schenck and Blaauw, 2011a).

> I am my own boss; no one tells me [....] what to do, what, when and how....

> Your employer does not push you, even if you are not feeling well [....] He does not push you, he is not after you. You push yourself, your pay is determined by you.

> I am my own boss.

> I can say no [to a job].

Looking ahead

Day laboring and waste picking remain activities that provide significant economic benefits to a segment of the urban and rural unemployed youth, although it remains a survivalist existence (Nzeadibe et al., 2012). For as long as youth unemployment, or for that matter all unemployment, does not receive the necessary attention by policymakers, these two survivalist activities will continue. And that is not a bad thing, provided—in the opinion of the authors—efforts are made to improve the conditions under which day laborers and waste pickers are able to function so that they can earn a better (including more dignified) living.

Addressing the plight of (especially) young day laborers and waste pickers calls for a multidisciplinary and multisectoral approach because these groups of people are operating on the margins of many formal structures, policies, and economic sectors. The following framework, which is discussed in Schenck et al. (2016), offers useful guidelines for debating possible facilitating actions on the part of government, the private sector, and civil society.

Figure 3: Guidelines for facilitating actions for young day laborers and waste pickers

	Overarching theme: Recognition	
Theme 1: Policies and strategies	**Theme 2:** Operational challenges and enabling factors	**Theme 3:** Attitudinal enabling factors
Enabling policies and strategies at all levels of government (Voice)	Health, safety, protective clothing, access to jobs, educational and vocational skills and tools (Validity)	Officials, SAPD, Metro Police, business, public (Visibility)

Source: Authors' framework as adapted from Schenck et al. (2016)

Theme 1 (policies and strategies): According to South Africa's National Planning Commission (NPC, 2012), gaining entry into the labor market is not a smooth process for the youth, and so efforts should be made to streamline things with the adoption of more conducive policies. The NPC (2012) further emphasizes that these efforts are the responsibility of government at all levels (Banerjee et al., 2008). Theme 1 calls for existing policies and procedures to be scrutinized from the perspective of how they can facilitate greater access to work and economic reward for day laborers and waste pickers, respectively. Banerjee et al. (2008) suggest the introduction of policies that specifically assist the youth to look for work, develop skills in areas where they are needed, and address the mismatch between where the youth live and where the jobs are. All these collective actions should be taken by governments on national, provincial, and local levels, with the supporting policy framework being developed on the strengths of sound research results.

Theme 2 (operational challenges and enabling factors): Young day laborers and waste pickers need to be better supported so that they can overcome challenges and improve their job prospects and quality of life—from gaining access to affordable education, vocational training, and health services, to acquiring the equipment that will help them ply their trade (such as protective clothing and tools). Responsibility for this should be appropriately apportioned among government departments, NGOs, civil society, faith-based organizations, and businesses (NPC, 2012).

Theme 3 (attitudinal enabling factors): Day laborers and waste pickers deserve to be brought in from the fringes of society and afforded more recognition for the work that they do and afforded more security in their places of work. Supportive attitudes from the South African Police Service, the Metro Police, businesses, and ordinary citizens with whom day laborers and waste pickers interact could make a world of difference to their state of mind and level of productivity, while also providing the springboard for additional, more lucrative business opportunities.

Conclusions

High levels of poverty and unemployment have been evident in South Africa for many years, and government and business leaders have long been wrestling with the twin challenges of creating a lean and competitive economy, while also fueling economic opportunities for millions of people whose educational and social backgrounds have left them ill prepared for mainstream economy activity. With youth unemployment rising at an alarming rate, however, South Africa is looking at a future in which the mainstream economy, which has helped to position the country regionally and globally, will be hollowed out in the face of dwindling human capital.

All over the world, the informal economy offers an outlet for people to take up a trade, polish their skills, provide for their families, and acquire a sense of purpose and pride. It has been empirically shown that people can even be better off working in the informal economy than in the formal economy with its sometimes stern performance criteria and other workplace rigidities (Ligthelm, 2006). The existence of a large and sprawling informal economy in South Africa is acknowledged and tentatively welcomed, but it is not well understood. Assorted initiatives have been launched in an attempt to stimulate informal economic activity, but these seldom gain traction, and large numbers of people remain marginalized. A contributing factor is that the prevailing economic mindset and government policy framework focus on stimulating economic growth but give insufficient attention to how to build an inclusive and sustainable society. An antidote to this is to put entrepreneurship at the center of the country's development plans.

Day laboring and waste picking are excellent examples of entrepreneurship in action, as they have become established features of big cities in South Africa and elsewhere, despite the odds often being stacked against them. Day laboring and waste picking typically attract the youth as they demand a fair level of stamina and mental agility, particularly in the need to be constantly on the lookout for ways to make money and steer clear of danger. As revealed in the authors' studies on these two groups in South Africa, day laborers and waste pickers also often display an air of independence that is characteristic of an entrepreneur.

Taking a serious look at the barriers that make it difficult for the day laborer and waste picker communities to ply their trade and earn decent wages, while also providing more practical support to these informal operators, will signal South Africa's willingness to tackle the country's growing unemployment crisis. At the same time it will also start to address the worrying "youth bulge" which, if left unattended, could eventually manifest as an older population that is increasingly reliant on the state's dwindling reserves. If successful, the strategic model applied to day laborers and waste pickers could be adapted for other parts of the informal economy as well.

The youth represent South Africa's future and the country can ill afford at this juncture to turn a blind eye to the needs and potential of those who are trying to make ends meet in informal settings across the country. Young workers have age, energy, and sometimes hope on their side, and these attributes need to be harnessed by an empathetic government and responsive community before youthful enthusiasm morphs into the type of anger that cannot be quelled.

References

Banerjee, Abhijit, Galiani, Sebastian, Levinsohn, Jim, McLaren, Zoë and Woolard, Ingrid 2008 "Why has unemployment risen in the New South Africa?" *Economics of Transition, Vol.* 16, No. 4, 715–740.

Barker, Frans 2007 *The South African labour market*, 5th ed. (Pretoria: Van Schaik).

Blaauw, Phillip Frederick and Schenck, Rinie 2014 "I am a slave in boots. I am myself in sneakers. A portrait of day labourers in South Africa" (Johannesburg: University of Johannesburg, Department of Finance & Investment Management) Colloquia – 27 October 2014.

Blaauw, Phillip Frederick 2010 "The socio-economic aspects of day labouring in South Africa", *DCom thesis* (Johannesburg: University of Johannesburg).

Blaauw, Phillip Frederick, Pretorius, Anna Maria, Louw, Huma and Schenck, Catherina Johanna 2007 "The socio economic reality of being a day labourer in Pretoria," *Social Work/Maatskaplike Werk* (Stellenbosch), Vol. 43, No.3, 224–233.

Branson, Nicola, Hofmeyr, Clare and Lam, David 2013 "Progress through school and the determinants of school dropout in South Africa", *A Southern Africa Labour and Development Research Unit Working Paper Number 100* (Cape Town: SALDRU, University of Cape Town).

Chambers, Robert 1983 *Rural development: Putting the last first* (London: Longman).

Charmes, Jacques 2012 "The informal economy worldwide: Trends and Characteristics," *Margin: The Journal of Applied Economic Research* (Los Angeles), Vol. 6, No. 2, 103–132.

Chvatal, Jessica 2010 "A study of waste management policy implications for landfill waste salvagers in the Western Cape," *Unpublished master's dissertation* (Cape Town: University of Cape Town).

Du Plooy-Cilliers, Franzel, Davis, Corné and Bezuidenhout, Rose-Marié 2014 *Research matters* (Pretoria: Juta).

Du Toit, Renette 2003 "Unemployed youth in South Africa: The distressed generation," *Paper presented at the Minnesota International Counseling Institute* 27 July–1 August (Minneapolis: University of Minnesota).

Fox, Louise 2015 "The informal sector in Africa is here to stay. Are city governments ready for this challenge?" In <http://www.thebrokeronline.eu/Blogs/Inclusive-Economy-Africa/The-informal-sector-in-Africa-is-here-to-stay.-Are-city-governments-ready-for-thischallenge?utm_source=The+Broker&utm_campaign=ad71924e90-2015_11&utm_medium=email&utm_term=0_ce1057f088-ad71924e90-318278045#> accessed 12 February 2016.

Gonzo, Webster and Plattner, Ilse Elizabeth 2003 *Unemployment in an African country: A psychological perspective* (Windhoek: University of Namibia Press).

Green, Pippa 2016 "The Forgotten Half: What about the students who didn't make it to matric?" Daily Maverick in <http://www.dailymaverick.co.za/article/2016-02-09-the-forgotten-half-what-about-the-students-who-didnt-make-it-to-matric/#.Vr4D73p4que> accessed 12 February 2016.

Harris-White, Barbara 2002 "India's informal economy – facing the 21st century", *Paper delivered at the Indian Economy Conference*, 19–20 April 2002, Cornell University, Cornell, USA.

Huegel, Christopher 2013 "Skarreling for Scrap: A case study of informal waste recycling at the coastal park landfill in Cape Town," *Master of Arts in the Department of Political Studies* (Cape Town: University of the Western Cape).

Harmse, Alet Catharina, Blaauw, Phillip Frederick and Schenck, Rinie 2009 "Day labourers, unemployment and socio economic development in South Africa" in *Urban Forum* (Dordrecht) 20: 363–377 DOI 10.1007/s12132-0099067-8

International Labour Organization (ILO) 2013 "Global employment trends for the youth 2013: A generation at risk" in < http://www.ilo.org/wcmsp5/groups/public/---

dgreports/---dcomm/documents/publication/wcms_212423.pdf> accessed 10 October 2014.

Jeffrey, Craig 2008 "'Generation nowhere': Rethinking youth through the lens of unemployed young men," *Progress in Human Geography* (Los Angerels), Vol. 32, No. 6, 739-758.

Kingdon, Geeta and Knight, John 2003 "Unemployment in South Africa: The nature of the beast," *World Development* (Amsterdam), Vol. 32, No. 3, 391-408.

Langenhoven, Belinda and Dyssel, Michael 2007 "The recycling industry and subsistence waste collectors: A case study of Mitchell's Plain," *Urban Forum* (Dordrecht), Vol. 18, No. 1, 114-132.

Ligthelm, André 2006 "An evaluation of the role and potential of the informal economy for employment creation in South Africa," *South African Journal of Labour Relations,* Vol. 30, No. 1, 30-50.

Louw, Humarita 2007 "Men at the margins: day labourers at informal hiring sites in Tshwane." *Unpublished doctoral thesis* (Pretoria: University of South Africa).

Lund, Francie and Skinner, Caroline 2004 "Integrating the formal economy in urban planning and governance. A case study of the process of policy development in Durban, South Africa," *International Development Planning Review* (Liverpool), Vol. 26, No. 4, 431-456.

Makina, Daniel 2013 "Migration and characteristics of remittance senders in South Africa," *International Migration* (Oxford), Vol. 51, No. 1, 148-158.

Maree, Kobus (ed.) 2007 *First steps in research* (Pretoria: Van Schaik).

Marock, Carmel 2008 "Grappling with youth employability in South Africa", *HSRC employment growth and development initiative* (Pretoria: HSRC).

Max-Neef, Mannfred 1991 *Human scale development: conception, application and further reflections* (New York: Apex).

National Planning Commission (NPC) 2012 "National Development Plan 2030. Our future – make it work" (Cape Town: National Planning Commission).

Nell, Dehlia and Schenck, Catherina Johanna 2009 "Too close for comfort: perceptions and experiences of people affected by day labourers at three hiring sites in Tshwane, South Africa," *The Social Work Practitioner-Researcher* (Pretoria), Vol. 21, No.1, 98-112.

Nzeabide, Thasseus Chidi, Anyadike, Raymond and Njoku-Tony, Roseline 2012 "A mixed methods approach to vulnerability and quality of life assessment of waste picking in urban Nigeria," *Applied Research in Quality of Life* (Dordrecht), Vol. 7, No. 4, 351-370.

Rankin, Neil and Roberts, Gareth 2011 "Youth unemployment, firm size and reservation wages in South Africa," *South African Journal of Economics,* Vol. 79, No. 2, 128-145.

Reyneke, Pierre 2012 "Garstkloof Landfill: The micro-organisation of waste pickers," *Unpublished Honours research report* (Pretoria: University of Pretoria).

Samson, Melanie 2012 "Wasting value and valuing waste: Insights into the global crisis and production of value reclaimed from a Soweto Garbage Dump," *D.Phil. Thesis,* University of York, Toronto, Canada.

Samson, Melanie 2010a *Reclaiming livelihoods* (Pietermaritzburg: Groundwork). In <http://www.groundwork.org.za/Publications/Reclaiming%20Livelihoods.pdf> accessed 15 July 2013.

Samson, Melanie 2010b "Reclaiming reusable and recyclable materials in Africa", *Women in informal economy globalising and organising* (Cambridge, MA: WIEGO). In <http://wiego.org/informal-economy/occupational-groups/waste-pickers> accessed 14 July 2013.

Schenck, Catherina Johanna, Blaauw, Phillip Frederick and Viljoen, Kotie 2016 "Enabling factors for the existence of waste pickers in South Africa's informal economy: A systematic review of evidence" in *Social Work/Maatskaplike Werk*, Vol. 52, No. 1, 35–53.

Schenck, Catherina, Blaauw, Derick and Viljoen, Kotie 2012 "Unrecognized waste management experts: Challenges and opportunities for small business development and decent job creation in the waste sector in the Free State", *Research Report for a Study Completed for the South African SME Observatory*, hosted by the Department of Economic Development, Tourism and Environmental Affairs of the Free State Province (DETEA) and the International Labour Organisation (ILO), December 2012 (Free State Province, South Africa and Geneva: DETEA and ILO). In <http://www.ilo.org/wcmsp5/groups/public/---ed_emp/---emp_ent/documents/publication/wcms_195724.pdf> accessed 12 February 2016.

Schenck, Rinie, Xipu, Lawrence and Blaauw, Derick 2012 "What happens during those long hours next to the road? An exploratory study of three informal day-labour hiring sites in Tshwane," *Social Work/Maatskaplike Werk* (Stellenbosch), Vol. 48, No. 1, 35–46.

Schenck, Catherina Johanna and Blaauw, Phillip Frederick 2011a "Living on what others throw away: An exploration of the socio economic circumstances of people collecting and selling recyclable waste," *Social Work Practitioner – Researcher* (Pretoria), Vol. 23, No. 2, 135–151.

Schenck, Rinie and Blaauw, Phillip Frederick 2011b "The work and lives of street waste pickers in Pretoria – a case study of recycling in South Africa's urban informal economy," *Urban Forum* (Dordrecht), Vol. 2, No. 4, 411–430.

Schenck, Catherina Johanna and Louw, Huma 2005 "An exploratory study on day labourers in Elardus Park, Pretoria," *Social Work/Maatskaplike Werk, Vol.* 41, No. 1, 1–9.

Sen, Amartya 1999 *Development as freedom* (New York: Knopf).

Statistics South Africa (StatsSA) 2015 "Labour market dynamics in South Africa, 2014 report", Press statement, April 2015. In <http://www.statssa.gov.za/?p=4445> accessed 10 February 2016.

Statistics South Africa (StatsSA) 2014 *Quarterly Labour Force Survey, 4th Quarter 2013* (Pretoria: Government Printers).

The Office of the Presidency 2009 *National Youth Policy 2009-2014* in <http://www.thepresidency.gov.za/MediaLib/Downloads/Home/Publications/YouthPublications/NationalYouthPolicyPDF/NYP.pdf> accessed 14 November 2014.

Theodore, Nik, Blaauw, Derick, Schenck, Catherina, Valenzuela, Abel, Schoeman, Christie and Melendez, Edwin 2015 "Day labor, informality and vulnerability in South Africa and the United States," *International Journal of Manpower*, Vol. 36, No. 6, 807–823.

UNESCO 2013 *The World Radio* (Geneva) in <http://www.unesco.org/new/en/unesco/events/prizes-and-celebrations/celebrations/international-days/world-radio-day-2013/statistics-on-youth/> accessed 11 April 2015.

Valenzuela, Abel, Theodore, Nik, Melendez, Edwin and Gonzales, AnaLuz 2006 *On the corner: Day labour in the United States* (Los Angeles: UCLA).

Valodia Imraan and Devey Richard 2012 "The informal economy in South Africa: Debates, issues and policies", *Margin – The Journal of Applied Economic Research* (New Delhi), Vol. 6, No. 2, 133–157.

Viljoen, Jacoba Maria Magdalena 2014 "Economic and social aspects of street waste pickers in South Africa," PhD in Economics, University of Johannesburg, South Africa.

Viljoen, Jacoba Maria Magdalena, Schenck, Catherina Johanna and Blaauw, Phillip Frederick 2012 "The role and linkages of buy-back centres in the recycling industry: Pretoria and Bloemfontein", *Acta Commercii* (Bloemfontein), Vol. 12, 1–12.

Welman, Chris, Kruger, Fanie and Mitchell, Bruce 2007 *Research methodology*, 3rd ed. (Cape Town: Oxford University Press).

Wilson, David, Velis, Costas and Cheeseman, Chris 2006 "The role of informal sector recycling in waste management in developing countries," *Habitat International* (Philadelphia), Vol. 30, No. 4, 797–808.

World Bank 2015 *Unemployment, youth total (% of labor force ages 15-24) Modeled ILO estimate* in <http://data.worldbank.org/indicator/SL.UEM.1524.ZS > accessed 15 February 2016.

World Economic Forum 2014 *Global risk report* in <http://www.weforum.org/reports/global-risks-2014-report> accessed 14 February 2016.

Yu, Derek 2013 "Youth Unemployment in South Africa since 2000 revisited", *Stellenbosch Economic Working papers 04/13*. A working paper of the Department of Economics and Bureau for Economic Research (BER) (Stellenbosch: University of Stellenbosch).

"INDEPENDENT, YET NOT GROWN UP": Young migrant workers' journeys in post-Mao China

I-Chieh Fang

This chapter is based on research conducted among young people from the Chinese countryside who migrate away from home to work in urban factories. These young people are sometimes referred to as "new generation migrant workers." They are generally thought to have some different characteristics and behavior patterns from previous generations of migrant workers (Wang, 2001).

There are two types of question that can be said to preoccupy young migrant workers in China today. On the one hand, they ask themselves, "What are my dreams?" On the other, they also ask, "How can I possibly achieve these dreams when the real world is so tough?" As they start out in life, they need a strategy for reconciling their dreams and desires with a reality that is often difficult and disappointing.

Through examining the cases of young people, I hope to shed light on the process of rural-to-urban migration in today's China. More specifically, in this chapter, migration from the viewpoint of young people from the countryside is examined. I choose *progression through the life course* as my primary focus in this chapter, since young people perceive the strong constraints imposed by markets and social structures precisely when they must move through it as they mature, that is, in the flow of time. I deal primarily with the stage of adolescence and postadolescence, since a number of key life decisions must be made in these stages. Here the struggles, negotiations, and compromises of young people with the inconsistencies of the structure around them are sharply revealed.

A key point is that migration, for young people, is not a purely economic activity. It is now an essential rite of passage for them, a fundamental part of the process through which they gain full membership in their communities and the wider society. In this sense, migration functions as a mechanism for modifying social statuses and constructing new subjectivities, or for establishing a "valuable self" in the market economy. For the young people who go through it, uncertainty, fluidity, and ambiguity—including in relation to "who they are"—have become the norm. By studying migration as it unfolds during the life course, we can therefore shed light not only on this particular case but also on more general questions of human agency and resistance. This chapter argues that migration in the Chinese context is an incomplete "rite of passage" for many contemporary rural youths.

Most migrant workers of the younger generation inevitably have to experience separation, multi-locality, and the informalization of their jobs. This, largely, alters the way in which they perceive social norms and relationships between themselves and others. Leaving home to become factory workers makes them "independent" from rural society, from which they are keen to leave in order to rid themselves of the stigma of being "backward," and of "low quality." However, they soon learn that it is hard to "achieve adulthood" in the destination coastal city due to the restraints imposed on them by the *hukou* (household registration) system.

Being "independent, yet not grown up" leaves their rite of passage incomplete and hanging. They are held between two societies (rural village and city) and two statuses (child and adult), never achieving full membership in Chinese society. The dual characteristics of the adolescent play a role here: On the one hand, the childhood of workers is prolonged. Workers are told to obey, in the interest of human resources and management. On the other hand, their adulthood arrives earlier, when factory and party-state ask them to handle their own disadvantage and be responsible for themselves. These characteristics thus rationalize the paradoxical phenomenon of migrant workers' drift to the margins while remaining highly dependent on paternalism and the support of natal family and rural community. This chapter will suggest changing this situation by removing the barrier imposed by the *hukou* system to allow migrant workers to fully integrate in their new urban location, enjoy state-supported rights, and become full citizens.

Literature review and discussion: Youth and problematized transition to adulthood

According to the existing literature, the experience of young Chinese migrant workers reflects the general situations young people encounter under globalization, such as the extension of adolescence, the rupture with parents' experience, and becoming constantly stuck in precarious work. All these could be deep reasons behind youth poverty. Apart from globalization and the global market, the case of young Chinese migrant workers also reminds us of the crucial role of state policy influencing youth poverty. We should take into account the role of the state in urbanization, labor regulation, and the welfare system. Previous research has already pointed out that the rural–urban dichotomy, implemented through the *hukou* system, has led to peasants from countryside, especially the youth, paying the cost of Chinese economic transition and its rapid development (Anagnost, 2004; Pun, 2005; Lee and Kofman, 2012).

Adulthood does not come naturally by reaching a certain age. It is a prolonged process, which may never be complete (Blatterer, 2007). For anthropologists, adulthood is never judged by age. Adulthood is marked by a ritual of "transition to adulthood," like initiation. Through initiation, a child is transformed into an adult. It is marked by completing the shift of social status attached to a person. Anthropologists have paid attention to youth and see adolescence as an important transitional stage in the life course (Mead 1928, 1970, 1975). Growing up means becoming an independent, recognized member of society with corresponding social responsibilities, power, and duties. The stage of youth is situated in between childhood and adulthood, which reproduces the original social structure but meanwhile also resists and undermines it. Thus, anthropologists have conducted research on initiation, that is, the ritual that marks the transition to adulthood in various cultures, and tried to find out what criteria are applied in particular cultures to measure the achievement of adulthood.

In the global era, both the content and progress of the "transition to adulthood" have already been transformed (Cole and Durham, 2008; Durham, 2008). Some scholars call for a fresh and systematic understanding of adulthood, which has been taken for granted and used in various ways for so long (Blatterer, 2007). In this chapter, two notable characteristics with reference to youth under globalization are particularly considered. First, young people, especially migrant youth, suffer from the rupture with their parents' experience and the strain on family relationships. Second, the youth are facing the transformation of work, from regular to precarious.

Several pieces of research emphasize that the period of transition to adulthood is prolonged (Blatterer, 2007; Cole and Durham, 2008). Both the timing and the sequencing of events in the transition to adulthood are supposed to have been subject to changes. During the era of globalization, motion and migration have become the norm. Migration to the city, for migrants, is not only motivated by the desire to pursue modernity but has become the central part of adolescent life (Osella and Gardner 2003). The youth, during their transition, are facing different contexts from their parents, whose experiences are hardly helpful to pass on to the next generation. When parents still feel they are shouldering the responsibility of giving some guidance to their children, the conflicting and inconsistent instructions might make the transition to adulthood even more complicated, confusing, and experimental (Fong, 2007; Anagnost, 2008). This can be called "rupture."

The rupture has occurred not only with parents' experiences and guidance, but also in the social context. When migrant youth are transiting to adulthood, they are mostly in new social settings, separated from family members and familiar social relationships. They need to handle the ruptures and manage to achieve adulthood without the effective support of their parents. This calls for a new arrangement in the sphere of reproduction. The kinship relationship, which people normally take as a strategy to count on when social institutions collapse, is fragmented and shaky. Reproduction (i.e., growing up, marriage, rearing children, retirement, etc.) changes its meaning and content in terms of practice due to the rapidly changing social context. For example, intimate relationships shift from reproduction to companionship, from companionship to recreation (Bernstein, 2007: 6). Consequently, it is hard to pass on the customary practice to the next generation. In the face of a new social context, without their parents' support, young people must respond to their world and find a way to cope with great creativity and flexibility. They might reinvent traditions, hybridize globalization and localization, or adopt brand new ideas exploiting new technologies. Meanwhile, the nation-state has largely withdrawn from the private sphere. Social contracts are being revised (Cole and Durham, 2008). In short, a new arrangement is called for in terms of social reproduction, and the youth under globalization are obliged to respond.

Globalization, precarious work, and informal workers

Second, there has been a surge in work with high flexibility and informality in the global markets (Standing, 2009; Kuruvilla et al., 2011; Standing, 2011; Standing, 2014), which has created insecurity in both economic and social realms. In the era of precarious work, young people inevitably have to learn to deal with the new workplace arrangement. Arne Kalleberg claimed that neoliberal globalization brought in the era of precarious work in the USA since 1970 (Kalleberg, 2009: 2). Law, policy, and workflow are adjusted to spur globalization. Consequently, the employers seek the most flexible employment relationship in order to cope with changes at the macro level. Kalleberg argues that "it is important to understand the new workplace arrangements that generate precarious work and worker insecurity . . . [E]mployment relations form[s] the foundation of theories of the institutions and structures that generate precarious work and the cultural and individual factors that influence people's responses to uncertainty" (Kalleberg, 2009: 10). Precarious work firstly leads to economic insecurity and instability, then makes the household unstable too. Standing (2011) calls the precariat "a new dangerous class." Who are the most likely to become the precariat? This is affected by education, age, family responsibilities, type of occupation and industry, and the degree of welfare and labor market protections in the society (Kalleberg, 2009: 10). Some people are more fragile than others, such as members of ethnic minority groups. Quite surprisingly, well-educated young people easily become the victims of precarious jobs (Jeffrey, 2008).

    The life course, that is, childhood, adolescence, adulthood, and retirement, which is defined from a labor-centric viewpoint, seems no longer workable. Informality and flexibility is corresponded to the adolescent stage. Since the economic recession and economic crisis of the 1980s and 1990s it has been common to see young people who are NEET (not in education, employment, or training). This makes adulthood even harder to achieve (Cole and Durham, 2008). Under such conditions, the question arises of whether prolonged adolescence plays an important mechanism to justify the changing arrangement of work characterized by informality and flexibility, by saying it offers young workers a sense of freedom. What if public discourse tries to justify the workplace rearrangement and the poverty it creates under the era of global neoliberalism by saying precarity is affordable for young people?

    The experiences of young migrant workers in contemporary China reflects this situation. First, the unique household registration (*hukou*) system forces them to move back and forth between countryside and cities. Migrant workers are constantly separated from their families, only experiencing short reunions during Chinese New Year. This "multilocality" forces them to find a flexible and creative arrangement to handle their lives. Second, the *hukou* system also causes them to face the high informality of work when working in the cities. Without urban registration, they can only sign short working contracts with lower wages. What is worse, this informality of work can last a very long time, even become a norm.

This chapter asks how these two unavoidable situations affect young migrant workers in contemporary China in their process of growing up. What kind of future awaits young migrant workers, growing up in conditions of multilocality and informality?

Young peasants in marketized socialist China: Who pays the cost of development?

When we use the two approaches outlined earlier to understand young migrant workers in China, we should of course not leave out the crucial fact of China's version of socialism. Only by taking it into account are we able to contextualize the in-between predicament of Chinese rural youth. Under the current economic policy and household registration system, they are forced to live with a broken family, in between constant moves and precarious jobs, and with a future prospect which might never be realized. If we look into their "transition to adulthood," we shall see they are the group bearing the cost and expense of China's rapid development, which echoes the conclusions of other research on migrant workers.

The regime in contemporary China is officially called a "socialist market society with Chinese characteristics" (Brandtstädter, 2009: 142). That is, China has implemented economic reforms based on market principles but retains its "socialist" political form, that is, this is a world of party-led marketization, involving its own pattern of national development rather than following the Western route. Leonard, for example, states that the Chinese party-state is not willing to allow so-called "Western ideology" to dominate China—even if it emerges naturally from the market economy— even more so after China gained in confidence following its economic miracle (Leonard, 2008: 14–16). This shows that "socialism with Chinese characteristics" can function better than Western neoliberalism. In pursuing economic growth, the Chinese party-state embraces neoliberal values selectively. As a socialist regime, its aim is to provide the world with another set of values and ideologies that can compete against the "universalization of Western liberal democracy" (Leonard, 2008: 117).

Since the Chinese party-state has its own agenda vis-à-vis development, Chinese youth are growing up under "socialism with Chinese characteristics." One consequence is that there are considerable tensions and contradictions between the official ideology that children learn in school and the practices and ideology they experience in everyday life (Kwong, 1994). Individualism is encouraged (Yan, 2010) but only the kind that will fulfill China's need for competitive, self-responsible individuals who can help fuel national economic growth (Rofel, 2007; Yan, 2010). Chinese youth are expected "to be individualistic in some aspects (entrepreneurial and competitive) but not others (self-expression and empowerment)" (Weber, 2002: 347), although self-expression is picked out as associated with neoliberal values in some ways. They therefore grow up in a highly ambiguous situation.

This issue can be traced back to the historical root of individualism in China. Modern notions of individualism have been coming to China since the Qing dynasty in the 17th century. However, this was not the Western model. As promoted by intellectuals, who asked citizens to be independent, autonomous, and responsible for themselves, the intention was that people should fundamentally serve the "big self" (i.e., the nation or society as a whole) (see Liu, 1993; Yan, 2010). As an ideology, individualism was conceived not as an end in itself but as the means to collective goals (nationalism) and the remedy to cure a weak nation. Such "individualism with Chinese characteristics" is thus intrinsically intertwined with collectivism (and long before the socialist era). Correspondingly, it is less about free choice, the development of individuality and individual autonomy than it is about taking on individual responsibility for achieving collective goals.

In this sense, as part of growing up, Chinese youth have to "feel their way towards a functional coexistence of individualistic and collectivist value systems" (Weber, 2002: 347). The rapid pace of marketization in China makes the process of growing up for contemporary Chinese youth somewhat experimental. Because being a "desiring subject" is a relatively new status for Chinese adults, the processes of "learning how to express various longings, needs and aspirations" and "struggling over how to display and embody the correct class subjectivity toward diffuse lessons on how to become cosmopolitan desiring subjects" are still unfolding (Rofel, 2007: 11). There are no firm norms, rules, and role models for Chinese youth to follow. This opens a space within which Chinese (urban or neo-urban) youths can negotiate between grassroots values and neoliberal values (Kwong, 1994; Yan, 2010) and "push the parameter of acceptable behavior" (Weber, 2001; Weber, 2002). Kwong thus argues that Chinese youth are experiencing an ideological crisis under the Party's continued rule (Kwong, 1994). This leaves young people in the position of having to figure out almost for themselves "the definition of self and relation to society" which is the crucial content of youth stage (Gold, 1991: 597). They must achieve adulthood but their own parents are not able to provide them with viable role models and guide them through the rapidly changing realities that confront them (Fong, 2007).

This leads to a significant consequence for the new generation of rural migrants. The contest of values between marketized China and socialist (and pre-socialist) China often happens in between urban and rural settings. In Fujian, according to Brandtstädter (2009: 153), rural villagers actively contest the "official narrative of improving their quality": instead, they insist they want to be *pusu* (simple and plain). Distinguishing *bendiren* (local persons) and *waidiren* (outsiders), they reinforce local solidarity and readopt gift exchange as a way of re-building social relationships. They reject consumerism in the name of a "politics of sincerity" redeploying "class politics" to uncover fake goods (Brandtstädter, 2009: 143, 153–54). According to Brandtstädter's study, from rural people's perspective, the values of the market, which to a large extent are equal to "money talk" values, are seen as intrinsically selfish and opposed to the collective good (Brandtstädter, 2009: 150). Far from agreeing that they are "backward," peasants criticize richer households as "money-minded, greedy and without *renqingwei* (moral standards and human feelings)" (Brandtstädter, 2009: 150). They use Maoist language and traditional *renqing* (moral standard of human feeling) to criticize corruption and consumerism and have "developed an attitude of general doubt against any official narrative or statement" and were "always searching for the 'real thing' behind the surface appearance" (Brandtstädter, 2009: 149). To give another example, rural villagers in Shandong apparently reject the role of individualized peasant-citizen, preferring to remain altruistic peasants (Keane, 2001). This leads to a question that this chapter attempts to answer: How do young migrant workers decide what kind of self to become as they try to fit into contemporary, marketized, socialist China?

Fieldwork and data collection

I spent twelve months conducting fieldwork in China (October 2007–October 2008), primarily in an electronics factory in Shenzhen's Special Economic Zone (SEZ). I refer to this factory as THS. I also collected material in three other factories (KS1, KS2, and KS3) in Kunshan, near Shanghai. My most important informants were the young migrant workers of THS. My roommate in the factory dormitory, Silk, was particularly important as she was especially willing to tell me her story and bring me into her social circle. She also took me to her home town in Hubei province for three weeks during the Chinese New Year. I therefore met her natal family, some of her relatives, and some of her classmates. I visited the homes of her uncles, aunts, and grandparents during my stay and visited the nearby town several times with Silk and her *laoxiang* (friends from the same native place). These opportunities to understand her story and her situation in detail gave me insights into the position of (especially female) migrant workers that were confirmed by my interactions, formal and informal, with others.

In order to understand which "valuable self" young migrant workers judged to be most useful for fulfilling what they wanted, I sought to collect data about: (1) how young migrant workers negotiated their marriage and career goals; (2) how they made sense of these goals and their own sense of where their migration and the factory system have helped or failed them; and (3) what influenced the choices they made.

I was interested in the possibilities and constraints that shape individual choice in this context. I therefore paid attention, for example, to managerial strategies in the workplace and the ways in which migrant workers reacted to them. I listened to conversations when young migrant workers talked about their future dreams and decisions. Since they never understood what an "anthropologist" was and often confused me with a psychologist, they would come to me to talk about their *xinshi* (worry, frustration, angry, negative feeling). For me, although I was quite embarrassed in failing to answer questions, like "If I cannot sleep, what should I do?," this was an ideal opportunity to understand their feelings, thoughts, and reasoning. Luckily, they were also willing to share their happy moments with me, chatting about things they found interesting and exciting. During the Beijing Olympic Games, we watched the matches in the dormitory or the common room and shared information about our favorite sports.

Background of the workers

As might be expected, the young migrants came from different provinces across China. There are 1,545 workers in total at the KS2 factory in Kunshan. The largest proportion is from relatively nearby, in Jiangsu province (24.6%, 380 workers). Second and third places are taken by Shandong (17.73%, 274) and Anhui (13.85%, 214) provinces, while Henan (10.49%, 162) is fourth. At the THS factory in Shenzhen, the largest number of workers was from Henan province (21%, 25), the second largest from Hubei (16%, 19), and the third largest from Guangdong (13.4%, 16). There were also workers from Guangxi (11.8%, 14), Jiangxi (9.2%, 11), and Hunan (7.6%, 9). However, these proportions have changed over time. For example, older workers at THS say that migrants from Hubei formerly outnumbered migrants from Henan; today the situation has reversed. This has come about, they said, as a result of conflict between the Hubei and Henan groups. Indeed, I noticed soon after I started my research that "local knowledge" about the backgrounds of different groups of people—and especially about their places of origin—was a regular topic of conversation among the migrant workers (and also among local people outside the factories). In an environment consisting of many unknowns, this was a way of trying to gauge their colleagues, who might be from very different cultural backgrounds, speak different languages, eat different food, and make different moral judgments from themselves. Workers need to find ways, however crude, to interact in everyday life.

However, even though migrant workers come from different provinces, their family background tends to be rather similar. They generally grew up in rural villages. Their parents are mostly farmers—or at least officially classified as such. The young migrants themselves are registered in the *hukou* system as *nongmin*, that is as farmers/peasants (Knight and Song, 2005). The government has allocated the majority of them land to farm. However, at least half of them do not know how to farm and have almost no agricultural skills, knowledge or experience (Yu and Pan, 2008; Chen, 2010). Some of them do not have land allocated under their names, that is because their birth violated China's birth control policy or because their families were affected in other ways by government land policy (Gao, 2010: 10).

Starting with or before their parents' generation, rural people began to crowd into nearby towns or cities farther away on a large scale to *dagong* (work for a salary). Consequently, about half the migrants I met grew up as *liushou ertong* ("children left behind") (Ye and Pan, 2011) and were taken care of by their grandparents or uncles and aunts, seeing their parents only during the Chinese New Year period.

These young people are part of what is generally known in the literature as "new generation migrant workers" (*xinshengdai nongmingong*). This expression is used by some scholars specifically to describe migrant workers born after 1980 (Li, 2009; Chen, 2010; Gao, 2010) in order to distinguish them from the first generation of migrant workers, those born before 1970, and the second generation, who were born between 1970 and 1979 (Wu and Xie, 2006). According to a survey conducted in 2009 by the National Bureau of Statistics, more than 120 million migrant workers in China today were born after 1980, which means that this group constitutes about 60% of the total migrant workforce (Bian et al., 2010; Chen, 2010: 79–80; Gao, 2010: 9). One quarter of young people (aged 16–30) in today's China are "new generation migrant workers" (Chen, 2010: 80).

Unlike first-generation migrants (who for the most part had already married before migrating, had children in their home towns, and shifted back and forth between their urban and rural bases) and second-generation migrants (who also tended to marry before leaving home but typically stayed longer in the city and lived separately from their spouse and children), most of the new generations have still not married (Wu and Xie, 2006; Yu and Pan, 2008; Fu and Huang, 2009: 28; Chen, 2010). In a society where marriage remains a defining feature of full adulthood, this is a crucial fact, as discussed next.

The circumstances of these young migrants have attracted much scholarly and political attention in recent years, especially after the State Council of the PRC issued a call for "resolving the issues of new generation migrant workers" in its Central Number One Document (*zhongyang yihao wenjian*) in January 2010 (Chen, 2010; Gao, 2010). Corresponding to the official stance, much of the current discussion treats new migrants as a problem—an obstacle to the satisfactory urbanization and modernization of China. International attention was recently focused on migrant workers when 14 suicides occurred at Foxconn, Apple's biggest original equipment manufacturer (OEM) factory in China. They were all migrant workers aged 18–25 (Chen, 2010). Even the doubling of salaries seemed to leave the problem of worker disaffection unresolved: The suicides continued. This led people to ask, "Who are these young workers, how do they think and what exactly do they want?" China (and perhaps the world) began to realize that these new generation migrant workers might not be the stereotypical submissive, hardship-bearing "producing subjects"; new research on this generation of migrant workers began to flourish. However, as will be explored in the next section, much of the existing research is hampered in answering these questions by assumptions about the homogeneity of the migrant workforce rather than paying attention to the diversity behind the collective term "migrant workers" (*nongmingong*) (Fu and Huang, 2009: 24).

The desire to be a proper person

Even if these young migrants wanted to stay in the countryside, a high proportion of them cannot actually make a living there. Most young workers do not know how to farm. Only 30% of them said they had previously done farm work. Even so, when asked to say something about farming methods, some of them could not elaborate because their experience of farming was simply assisting their parents, following their parents' instructions without any reflective or abstract knowledge of the work. Those were the ones who claimed to have some knowledge of farming. The other 70% of those I interviewed said they knew nothing about farming, even though their households were registered as farmers and they themselves were born with the class status of farmers. In her ethnographic account, Pun also describes her surprise at learning that the migrant workers she met did not even know the size of their household's landholding or even roughly what the annual farm income was (Pun, 2005: 55). This seems a widespread phenomenon among rural migrant youth today.

Even if they wanted to learn to farm, some of them would encounter another problem: They have no land (Gao, 2010: 10). Only 60% of the households of workers in my sample were still engaged in farm work. Their own parents had also left home to be migrant workers or to engage in petty business in nearby country towns. They rent out their household's land to relatives (close or distant) or to professional farming teams. Such teams have grown up as part of a new business model that has emerged, in which companies rent the farmland of migrant workers. By joining up the small, fragmented lands from each household and combining them into a larger whole, such companies can farm the land professionally and make a higher profit than the sum of the households who previously farmed the land. The relationship between peasants and land in China, as Fei (1992) describes, had already significantly changed before the current generation of migrant workers.

Although lack of farming knowledge and access to land to farm are practical reasons that may lead to the migration decision, the more influential reason is the moral discourse among villagers about "what an ideal youth should do." Although born in rural villages, it seems that no one seriously expects them to become farmers or stay in their place of birth. For villagers, the synonym for "staying in one's home town" is "not engaged in decent work" (*buzuo zhengjing shi*). When I went with Silk to her home town in Hubei, I found many middle-aged villagers in the town who could hardly explain what they did for a living. They did all kinds of different jobs to earn money, taking advantage of whatever was available. For example, they would do farm work; help neighbors who were building houses; go fishing in the river in order to sell the fish; or engage in some small-scale business. It is hard to give this kind of "career" a name; while they can earn some money through this kind of casual work, neither their relatives nor they themselves feel proud of their occupations.

Correspondingly, it appears that the "ideal typical" understanding of "youth as a stage in the life course" has changed from its meanings for previous generations (Gold, 1991). Today, a young person who chooses to stay home to farm will inevitably be subject to the negative moral judgments of those around them (Fu and Tang, 2009). There was a consensus among the villagers that young, healthy, and decent people are supposed to work outside their hometown doing a "decent job" (*zhengjing gongzuo*) rather than stay at home doing this kind of casual work. These temporary and ad-hoc jobs in the village are viewed as having "no future" and "no promotion prospects," as "not promising" and "not an opportunity for something bigger." In short, to stay in a rural village means that the opportunities provided for social mobility by *dagong* will be lost (Fu and Huang, 2009). In comparison to middle-aged villagers, young people are expected to show greater concern for the future and, in effect, to try harder. If they do not leave home for work, their rural network will deem them "conservative," lacking a "sense of progress" and "incapable" (Fu and Tang, 2009: 47). It will be said of such a young person that this is someone who is *meichuxi* (has no future): without a serious purpose in life—as shown by migrating for *dagong*—they are useless and will never amount to anything.

Interestingly, this builds on a dichotomy that emerged during the migration of previous generations: The idea that one goes out of the village in order to work and one stays at home in order to engage in leisure activities such as gambling, attending banquets, visiting friends, and so on. Exhausted migrant workers often opted to go home in order to rest and "play" (*wan*) for a while. Therefore, today a young person staying home after graduating would be judged as *lan* (lazy). They should go out to "work," not stay at home to "play" (*zai jia wan*).

Older villagers have other reasons to push young people to leave (Fu and Tang, 2009). Thanks to financial remittances from migrant workers, new houses have been built, and modern furniture has been bought (Murphy, 2002). Although it has been argued that the comparison between households that benefit from *dagong* income and those that do not is often not obvious (Murphy, 2002; Zhou et al., 2008), one important potential impact is on marriage decisions. A young girl and her family will judge if a household is worth marrying into on the basis of its material conditions (Yan, 2003; Yan, 2006). If a young man or woman does not follow their neighbors in migrating out for *dagong*, their household is likely to experience "downward mobility" in their village (Zhou et al., 2008).

What Murphy has termed "social remittances" (Murphy, 2002: 11) also plays a part in this pressure to migrate. Villagers look forward to the information, skills, and new ideas brought back by young migrants. For example, Silk's parents expect her to integrate into the modern world and bring new knowledge of modernity back to them. This desire to have updated information about the developments in the city is part of what young workers hope to gain for themselves from "seeing the world" (*jianshimian*)—but it also reflects the fear of the rural villagers that they might be left out of modernized China. Therefore, to have some members migrate out will, in theory, benefit collective welfare. No matter how slim the chances of success, villagers take the potential for success into account and expect their young people to at least try, not only for themselves alone but as an obligation or responsibility to "the bigger self." It is also important to note that, especially in respect to expectations of "social" remittances, it is young people's success not only as workers, but as consuming subjects that their fellow villagers, parents, and relatives expect (Yu and Pan, 2008).

Thus in both practical ways and through the huge pressure of moral discourse, new generation migrant workers are virtually forced to participate in the competitive milieu of marketized China as part of their process of "growing up." While their parents at the outset still had some choice as to whether to farm or migrate for work, there is almost no alternative for today's rural youth. In order to be an adult, they must make the step of going to the city for work. In this sense, it is legitimate to speak of a "crisis" in their life course. Once they leave, they feel they cannot go home with nothing to show for it (Murphy, 2002; Fu and Tang, 2009). Therefore, they rarely give up trying, on the basis that "if they must die, they would rather die in the city" (*si yeyao sizai chengshili*)—that is, die trying to succeed. To be migrant workers is related to their future identity, whether in the hope of being successful urbanites or decent rural adults.

When the young migrant workers at the KS2 and THS factories are asked why they had left home, they do not say "because we want consumer goods," nor do they say "because we are victims of the Chinese government's rural policies." During interviews with these workers, nearly everyone said that the reason they left home was because they hoped to do two things: to "grow up" (*chengzhang*) and to "become independent" (*duli*). This answer seems to fit strongly with the impression that they are like children in many respects—but they are on their way to becoming adults. Typically, they leave home when they are 17 or 18 years old, although some leave earlier and some later. They have just graduated from school and are supposed to find a job and get married. In this period, they are between being children and adults. So what exactly do "growing up" and "becoming independent" mean, in this context?

The changing meaning of "growing up" and its difficulties

For them, "growing up" (*chengzhang*) means to learn something new and to change in ways that will enable them to see, fit into, and then take part in "modern China," which is taken to be very different from their rural home towns. The hope to take part in the society of the modern city is often described by young migrants as the desire to *kanshijie* or *jianshimian* (literally "to see the world," meaning "to become worldly/sophisticated").

Given the various "push" factors leading young people to leave their villages, and their education and skill levels, the jobs they can easily get are in factories that require low-skilled workers. As a result of the economic boom, there are such factories all over China. Quite a few are very close to their home towns, where they can work in a Township–Village Enterprise (TVE); indeed their parents may already work in these factories. In other words, if they wanted, they could just find a job in a factory near to their home town rather than traveling thousands of miles to Shenzhen or Kunshan. When young workers are asked why they had chosen to go to the big cities along China's east coast, they answer that it was because they wanted to *jian yixia shimian* (see a bit of the world). These youths from rural areas have neither the money nor the time to do a "grand tour" in the classic European style. Factory work far from home becomes the best option for them to see modern China, which they have heard a lot about. Their first month's wage from the factory is neither sent back home nor is it used to buy things they want. It is usually used to pay for the debt they have incurred just in traveling to the city.

Delicate, a factory worker at THS factory, explained how important *dagong*—waged labor, almost always undertaken away from home—is for young people from the countryside today:

> No matter what you do in the future, if you have had the experience of *dagong*, then people will consider you to be a person who has *jianguo shimian* [seen the world]. If you always stay at home, people will think that you know nothing and you are just like an idiot.

The desire to *jian shimian* could in turn be interpreted as resting on a more general desire: To change one's identity. A rural youth will be recognized as no longer being only a rural youth if s/he has had the experience of working in the big city. The identities associated with the place of destination lead rural youth not to want to stay near their home towns. Moreover, migrant workers have a very hierarchical judgment of various cities in China. Because the city where a migrant worker goes implies different levels of the "modernity" that they can see and experience, this is closely related to their identity.

For example, Silk is from Hubei. She left her home for Shanghai when she was 14, and then later moved to Shenzhen. But Shanghai is considered more modern than Shenzhen. Having worked for five years in Shanghai, Silk feels she is superior to her colleagues in Shenzhen. She left

Shanghai for the Shenzhen factory on 5 March 2004 (she still remembers the exact date) very reluctantly and considered the move a "down-grade." She left only because she had no other choice: Her cousin Ling, who took care of Silk for several years in Shanghai and at whose house Silk stayed, had now been relocated to Shenzhen. She asked Silk to come and help her. Silk felt she could not say no. Yet, intriguingly, Silk also said that she actually hated Shanghai people because they "abused their power and bullied people from other places" (*zhangshiqiren, paiwai*). She was looked down upon while she was in Shanghai—just as she now looks down upon Shenzhen and her colleagues there. Her feelings of superiority were also because the factory where she had worked in Shanghai was owned by a Japanese businessman (rather than a Taiwanese or mainlander). Because she attached her identity to the city where she had migrated for *dagong*, she reckoned herself to be a person who had "seen the world," just like a Shanghai local or even a Shenzhen local.

But *chengzhang*—growing up—is not only about seeing the modern world; it is also about the endeavor to fit into it. In this sense, *chengzhang* is strongly related to learning, specifically getting some knowledge that will be "useful" (*youyong*) in the neoliberal economic environment they actually have to cope with. In interviews, young people mentioned a highly varied list of things that they thought might be worthwhile. For example, it is useful to gain knowledge of electronics and computers. It is good to have the skill of recognizing "quality" in goods (whether you are making them or consuming them). It is good to be able to cook, drive, do hairdressing, and manage other people. It is good to have social skills appropriate to an urban environment (and in particular communication skills, coordination skills, and tactics for surviving in the factory, for achieving promotion, for avoiding scams and conflict, for seeking and seizing opportunities, etc.). Interestingly, they do not normally consider it useful to learn English, which is useless for their current stage of upward mobility.

Many of the skills they are most interested in relate, in some way, to their working lives. For them to succeed in their working lives is clearly one of the most important aspects of "growing up"—as is getting married and forming a family. Many of the informants gave a simple and firm answer to what would make them adults: "getting married and forming a family (*chengjia*) and establishing oneself in a career (*liye*)."

What these young people are actually yearning for is a change of status—from child to adult and from a rural villager to a sophisticated urbanite. However, change of this kind is not only an individual desire. Friends and relatives in the migrants" home village also expect to see such effects in someone who has had the chance to "see the world." If a young worker fails to display "changes" after they have stayed in the city for several years, they will be judged as failures. In this sense, the desire for young people to change and grow up is collective. There is an expectation on the part of the individual and also the collective that a change in identity (e.g., an improvement in their "quality," *suzhi*) is a desirable outcome of migration. An individual's hope for change thus reflects the wider social attitude.

What kind of change would count as the *chengzhang* (growing up) that a migrant worker is expected to achieve and to demonstrate to others? Some clues are provided by the case of Phoenix, a young woman. She worked at a big hotel for businessmen near THS. She had formerly worked for three and half years at FXK, an electronics factory with 800,000 workers. Just as the cities are ranked by migrant workers, so too are the factories. Because FXK is big and famous, working there is the kind of job that nearly every young worker dreams of getting in the early period of migration. To work there would definitely be to "see the world." When migrant workers talked about someone getting a job offer from FXK, their tone of voice suggested she had got an offer from Harvard University. People would assume s/he must be outstanding because the recruitment process of FXK is stricter than other smaller factories. But, Phoenix had decided to quit her job at FXK a few months earlier. The reason was that, when she went home during Chinese New Year, her relatives and friends all laughed at her and said:

> You left for the city several years ago. Tell us why your dresses still look like those of a country bumpkin. Your disposition is still so stupid and uncouth. Didn't you learn anything from dagong? You've come back from the big city. You shouldn't still look the same. Look at your classmates; they worked in a hotel in Shanghai. See how beautiful they are!

Therefore, she quit the factory job and "job hopped" to the hotel, where she gives massages to businessmen. Compared to the routine job in the factory, she thought the hotel job offered a better chance for her to become an articulate, fashionable young woman, like the ideal youth of her relatives' expectations.

When discussing this topic with a group of factory workers, they agreed that the "change" they are seeking and expecting via migration for work should include the following: First, young workers should become more articulate (*hui shuohua*) than before. Second, they should know a good deal about "fashion" (*hui daban*) and other "modern things." Third, they should be smarter, more poised, and confident (*jingming nenggan*). Where do these expectations come from? In part, they come from the city life rural people see depicted in television dramas, which are the basis for many urban expectations, imaginations, and fantasies. When they set off from the countryside, they were looking forward to this kind of life.

However, they soon discover that life in factories is not as "colorful" as rural people collectively assume. The working schedule is always the same, day after day. The only people you meet and talk to are your fellow workers. Most often, the people who become friends in the factory are those who share similar backgrounds. In addition, the working hours are extremely long, leaving limited leisure time, which they usually spend in big supermarkets or food stalls at night markets nearby (which are still part of the SEZ). In fact, the real city, Shenzhen city, is about an hour by bus away from the factory. Coming out of the factory after working for hours, all migrant workers can see are endless factories, and other young people from very similar rural backgrounds wearing the uniforms from their various factories on the streets.

Although factory life is disappointing in some ways, the yearning for change is not abandoned. This results in an interesting attitude among the young migrants: They are willing to learn and welcome new things, no matter what. They are highly open to new values and discourses and appear to easily accept, at least superficially, the new morality that the factory inculcates. Fly, a 19-year-old man from Hubei, told me that, from his perspective, life in rural villages was actually freer. There he could sleep as long as he wanted and decide how to use his own time. In the factory, he has to work on the shop floor 12 hours a day, 6 days a week. The strict daily schedule of the factory means that he has almost no personal time. Despite all that, he thought this change was good and he felt happy about it. He said that life in rural villages was too lazy and comfortable. Now he has turned into a useful young man. Not long afterward, I heard similar words spoken by the factory director at the monthly assembly of workers. The young workers seemed to absorb what he said like a sponge.

Why was Fly seemingly prepared to embrace this system wholeheartedly, rather than resisting, even though it arguably exploits him? His acceptance probably comes from his hope for a bright future, that is, the anticipated change of status and identity. Migrant workers come for better life opportunities—a sense of unknown chances—which are generally presumed to be unavailable in their rural hometowns. They hear many inspiring stories from their neighbors, friends, and mass media about how people changed their lives overnight. Most of them want to "give it a shot." It could be said that they come here as a gamble.

Becoming independent by declaring independence

The term *duli*, "independent," is often heard in the factory. In the talk of young migrant workers the phrase *rang ziji duli* (so that I will be independent) comes up again and again. At one level, this probably reflects the way that the whole society is embracing a modernization process in which talk of "individualism" and "being independent" is politically correct—even though the Chinese version of individualism does not entirely copy the Western model. At a more personal level, the desire to be independent is partly grounded in migrants' hope to say goodbye to their rural family backgrounds.

Again, Silk's case offers a fascinating example. She does not like going back to her home town during the Chinese New Year holiday. When she took me to Hubei for the Chinese New Year holiday, she apologized to me many times before we set off. As she saw it, for me to go home with her in winter was to *chiku* (literally, "eat bitterness," in this context meaning to endure a poor quality of life), and she worried that, "You won't be able to endure it" (*shou bu liao*). When we arrived, she kept on telling me, "I am just like you. I'm not used to it" (*bu xiguan*, not used to village life). Later, I realized that this was Silk's way of telling me that she was not a country girl any more. She is modern and civilized.

Silk spent most of her free time while at home hanging around with *laoxiang* (friends from her home town or home province). As a young migrant worker, she has a relatively wide network of friends in the city. When we arrived in the countryside, a new house for Silk's family had just been completed. She told me that she had organized borrowing the money for the new house building through her *guanxi* (network, connections) among the factory leaders and her friends in Shenzhen. She saw it, therefore, as her responsibility to pay back the debt. (Although her parents did share some responsibility for the debt, it was mostly on Silk's shoulders.) She told me that she had chosen to take on this burden entirely of her own free will. Her parents had not forced her or put any pressure on her. She had taken it on because she "had more [rich] friends than them." Here, we can see newly established social relationships, that is, those created by Silk in the course of migration and work, interacting with her given kinship relationships and changing her bargaining power within her family. Thus, overall, the bargaining power of the daughter in the household has increased because of her newly established knowledge and relationships. This, at least to some extent, gives Silk a new identity within the household.

On the first day of the Chinese New Year, Silk and I woke up very early. Silk shouted at her brothers and sisters to get them out of bed. She led us all out of the house to visit every household in the village to make the traditional New Year calls, offering New Year greetings, *gongxi facai* (congratulations and become rich). As we visited, Silk would sit for a while with some families in their homes, asking the host how everything was going, inquiring after the health of their elder members, teasing the children, and praising children as cute in front of their mother. She seemed to know well the courtesy expected of her, and how to talk gracefully on such occasions. Silk, like the other young migrant workers, is basically the public representative of her natal family.

Walking along the street and greeting people on the way, we saw many other young people in groups led by their eldest siblings. They were all doing the same thing: visiting relatives and neighbors, making New Year calls. Silk explained to me that when they were small children the family visits were led by their parents, but now the children have grown up, their parents stay at home and rest. Only the children now go out to *bainian* (pay New Year calls). Once they have reached a certain age, the eldest child, whether male or female, substitutes for the parents and acts as the representative of the household.

They too were migrant workers just returned home for the Chinese New Year. When they met on the snowy, winding path, one of the first questions they asked each other was, "When will you go back to the city?"

Their connection to the city was emphasized; returning to the city is taken for granted. No one assumes these young people will stay in their home towns after the Chinese New Year. They constantly declare their independence: from their parents, and from their hometown.

Silk is using a very strong method in order to "declare" that she is different now. She is different from her past, and will become an adult who is very different to her parents. In other words, she is independent, detached, and separated from her previous connections. She uses the rude, crude, and most obvious way to show her independence, which implies not only that she no longer depends on her parents but also that she has a superior status to them.

Separation from parents and their kind of adulthood

Young migrant workers generally do not pay much heed to their parents' suggestions because they feel that the experiences their parents went through when growing up are not applicable or relevant to their own lives. As first- or second-generation migrant workers, parents were generally married before migrating out, as noted earlier. They went out mainly in order to earn money and support their families, who still lived in rural areas. But for new generation migrant workers, the problems they need to deal with during their migrant journey are mainly about sorting out their future, a situation that their parents have never encountered and thus have no experience to share. In addition, given that the world is changing so quickly, most parents of new generation migrant workers, even though they are migrant workers too, know almost nothing about their situation in the cities. This means that the new generation workers have to "figure out the future" for themselves from the vantage point of places like Shenzhen or Kunshan.

Indeed, parents frequently have to learn things from their children, a phenomenon known as "cultural feedback" (Zhou, 1999). The parents of young migrants, typically rural peasants, lack the confidence to insist that their children obey their instructions, not least because they rely to a great extent on their children's knowledge of the modern world. Although parents still shoulder the responsibility of guiding their children as they grow up and become independent, and although the children are still supposed to show respect and filial piety to their parents, the situation of these parents implicitly pushes the young peasants to seek other role models to follow. Considering their parents' experiences to be mostly irrelevant to their lives, young migrant workers have to grow up, to some extent, without effective guidance from their parents.

In sum, then, "growing up" and "becoming independent" can be seen as a two complementary goals that migrant workers are keen to achieve. *Duli*, independence, represents their hope of separation (from their old, past village context, including their parents) and—to use the terminology of Victor Turner (1967) in characterizing rites of passage—the creation of "anti-structure," that is, the breaking down of pre-existing social relationships. By embracing this hope, they come to the factory in the SEZ. *Chengzhang* (growing up) represents the process of entering a new world (the neoliberal world in this case) and gaining a new social status. It is a process that makes young migrant workers integrate into the social structure again but a different social structure from that of the villages they hope to have left behind. Their *duli* (independence) follows from their denial of the past and the breaking down of their former relationship with their parents, while their hope of *chengzhang* (growing up) follows from their embrace of an (imagined) "modern world."

Thus, it should be emphasized that these young people from the countryside have a quite different relationship with their parents from the one described in Vanessa Fong's research (2007), which was carried out in the large city of Dalian. These young people did not seem to take their parents' words that seriously or try to internalize their parents' views into their own way of seeing things. If migrant workers, like urban singletons, feel confused about the society around them, this is not likely—as Fong suggests of her urban informants—to arise from the complexities of cultural transmission (Fong, 2007). On the contrary, young migrant workers from the countryside are keen to detach themselves from their relationship with their parents. Consequently, they make themselves responsible for becoming adults.

"Independent, yet not grown up": Separation without integration

To return to the notion of rites of passage: The period when migrant workers stay in the factory can be understood as a period of liminality associated with the change from one status to another; they have separated from the world of the countryside but not yet re-integrated into the world. Although the factory might be the easiest way available to them to gain access to "modern China," it does not really provide the appropriate conditions for them to (re-)integrate into "society." In the factory, they struggle to form a stable identity against the background of the alienated/impersonal and differentiated environment (Carrier, 1992) produced by industrialized capitalist society. Young migrant workers in the factory can thus be seen in terms of liminality, a stage of "betwixt and between" characterized by "ambiguity, openness and indeterminacy," in Turner's terms, "a period of transition where normal limits to thought, self-understanding, and behavior are relaxed—a situation which can lead to new perspectives" (Turner, 1967).

From this point of view, a job in a factory in the SEZ is not the ultimate destination that the young migrant workers are seeking, unless it is accompanied by a transformation of social status. In fact, as we have seen, for this generation of young workers the change of social status from child to adult is equated with a change from being a "traditional" rural person to a member of "modern" China. A job is therefore just the starting point, the opportunity to create something new and make the desired transformation possible: getting married and establishing a working life that is different from that of their parents. Migration separates the young people from their fixed position and kinship ties in their villages and gives them a certain freedom to negotiate their identity. They have temporarily left their position in the fixed social structure. At the point where they enter the factory, they are just leaving their identity as rural people and are "negotiating" their state of being. Their sense of freedom may be seen not so much as a reflection of the new world itself—which in the case of the factory is in fact highly constrained—but, rather, as associated with the state of liminality, which Turner characterizes as a "realm of primitive hypothesis, where there is a certain freedom to juggle with the factors of existence" (1967: 106).

The reality is that the modern city does not welcome these young rural migrants, as has been extensively noted by other authors. For example, Jacka (2006) describes in her ethnography how urbanites discriminate against migrant workers and view them as dirty and uncivil. Pun describes an occasion when a group of female migrant workers go to a cafe to buy a drink and are treated scornfully by the waiters and local guests, who look down on them, saying they have "dirty hands" (Pun, 1999; Pun, 2005). It could be argued that it is their ambiguous and incomplete transformation, the fact that they are "in between" social statuses, that causes them to become a scapegoat for social problems (see Douglas, 1991). To integrate into modern China is harder than to separate from a rural village. They have, in effect, announced their separation from their parents and the past. Yet, in the factory, the transformation that young migrant workers desire does not seems to come naturally. To put it simply, they get stuck in the liminal phase.

The search for a process of "growing up" and "being independent" leaves young migrant workers in a predicament: They have renounced their rural identity but they do not yet have a new one. Achieving a new identity as a "player" in modern China turns out to be much harder in reality than in their expectations—not only in the social milieu of the city, but in the factory itself. Indeed, all young people in today's China face a far more complex social world than the type of social situation that Turner focused on, stable stratified societies. What has been said of urban youth in China (Weber, 2002; Fong, 2007), also applies—perhaps even more strongly—to these young rural migrants: They are confronted with many different value systems, which sometimes contradict each other. Just like urban Chinese children (Fong, 2007), these new generation young migrant workers can be said to be "confused" with respect to cultural models possibly without being aware of it, but in very different ways. So how do young migrant workers handle this situation?

Kwong's research (1994) suggests that Chinese youngsters sometimes reject certain of these values and adopt the relatively attractive ones from among those on offer. The migrants also select particular values—especially in order to legitimize their behavior when the context allows them to do so. For example, they might quote their cousins' or colleagues' words in response to lectures from their parents—but sometimes they would quote their parents' words or traditional values if they felt it would benefit them in other contexts. For some, who realize that there may be no future for them in either the rural village or the city, profound depression and despair may follow.

Conclusions

The argument suggested here is that migrating for work is the crucial process through which new generation migrant workers gain their adulthood—and that this was not the case for previous generations of migrant workers. Previous generations had effectively finished their rite of passage and become adults before the experience of outside work. To put it simply, the structure of the older generation's rite of passage would be: separation phase (in home town), liminal phase (short, in or near home town), and reintegration (home town). The structure of the new generation's rite of passage would be: separation (from home town), liminal phase (in urban factory), and (attempted) reintegration (in urban setting). This different structure of the rite of passage is the fundamental difference between new generations and the old ones. Through paying attention to migration as a rite of passage, we thus can see clearly that the difference between these generations is deeper and more profound than some have suggested—it is not just that they are "spoiled" children.

Today, adulthood does not come "naturally" for young people, that is, via marriages arranged by their families or via state policies offering them land. For rural youth, this leads them to face an awkward, challenging situation. Rural home towns are almost empty after mass emigration and social relationships there are often fragmented. It is impossible for them to gain adulthood there and, in fact, no one in the village expects them to do so. They have little choice but to go out to the city to earn their adulthood and become a recognized member of society.

The factory may look like the destination of their migration but actually it is only a start, the beginning of their search for adulthood and self-responsibility. Young migrant workers are keen to *chengzhang* (grow up) and hope to integrate into neoliberal, modern China. Equally, they are keen to announce/declare their *duli* (independence), hoping to say goodbye to their parents, their village backgrounds, and the "backward" peasant world of the countryside. Their boldness in announcing their separation to their parents to some extent reflects the fact that their parents are incapable of providing useful guidance and support as they move toward (self-responsible) adulthood. However, their endeavor to grow up and become independent arguably leads them to have little sense of their class situation in the factory, and it also leaves them in a liminal situation. Because of their wish to integrate into modern China and become an adult, they are willing to absorb and embrace change, new things, values, and ideas that the factory feeds them. Driven by the wish to be independent and separate/detach from their home town and natal family, that they get trapped in a liminal situation. It is actually hard for them to integrate into urban life because of the alienated/impersonal environment of the factory, which they face every day, and the hostile social milieu. Yet they have limited access to the state-supported rights of the *hukou* system and so cannot simply "return" to a rural way of life.

References

Anagnost, A. 2004 "The corporeal politics of quality (suzhi)", *Public Culture* Vol. 16, No. 2, 189–208.

Anagnost, A. 2008 "Imagining global futures in China: the child as a sign of value" in Cole, J. and Durham, D. (eds.) *Figuring the future: globalization and the temporalities of children and youth* (Santa Fe, N.M: School for Advanced Research Press).

Bernstein, E. 2007 *Temporarily yours: Intimacy, Authenticity, and the Commerce of Sex* (Chicago: University Of Chicago Press).

Bian, G., Zhang, Z. and Jiao, J. 2010 "The subject consciousness of new generation migrant workers", *Theory Probe* (Beijing)Vol. 3, 95–97.

Blatterer, H. 2007 *Coming of age in times of unvertainty* (New York and Oxford: Berghahn Books).

Brandtstädter, S. 2009 "Fakes: Fraud, value-anxiety, and the politics of sincerity" in Sykes, K. M. (ed.) *Ethnographies of moral reasoning: Living paradoxes of a global age* (New York: Palgrave Macmillan).

Carrier, J. G. 1992 "Emerging alienation in production: A Maussian history", *Man, New Series* Vol. 27, No. 3, 539–558.

Chen, R. 2010 "The sociological reflection on suicide events of 'after 80s, after 90s' new generation migrant workers—start with Foxconn series suicide events,", *The Journal of Youth Research*, Vol. 6, 79–85.

Cole, J. and Durham, D. 2008 "Introduction: Globalization and the temporality" in Cole, J. and Durham, D. (eds.) *Figuring the future: globalization and the temporalities of children and youth* (Santa Fe, NM: School for Advanced Research Press).

Douglas, Mary 1991 *Purity and danger: An analysis of the concepts of pollution and taboo* (London: Routledge).

Durham, D. 2008 "New Horizons: Youth at the millennium," *Anthropological Quarterly*, Vol. 81, No. 4, 945–957.

Fei, H. 1992 *From the soil, the foundations of Chinese society: A translation of Fei Xiaotong's Xiangtu Zhongguo* (Berkeley: University of California Press).

Fong, V. L. 2007 "Parent-Child communication problems and the perceived inadequacies of chinese only-children," *Ethos*, Vol. 35, No. 1, 85–127.

Fu, P. and Huang, S. S. 2009 "Between dream and reality: Research on the relation of the post-80s generation of migrant workers and their 'Four Worlds'," *Youth Studies*, Vol. 4, 24–33.

Fu, Ping, and Tang, Youcai (2009) "Inverted U-shaped trajectory and the social mobility of new generation peasant workers," *Zhejiang Social Sciences*, Vol. 12, 41–47.

Gao, R. 2010 "Focusing on the issues of 'new generation migrant workers'," *Rural Economy*, Vol. 12, 9–12.

Gold, T. 1991 "Youth and the state,", *The China Quarterly*, Vol. 127, 594–612.

Jacka, Tamara 2006 *Rural women in urban China: Gender, migration and social change* (Armonk, NY: ME Sharpe).

Jeffrey, Craig 2008 "'Generation Nowhere': Rethinking youth through the lens of unemployed young men," *Progress in Human Geography*, Vol. 32, No. 6, 739–758.

Kalleberg, Arne L 2009 "Precarious work, insecure workers: employment relations in transition," *American Sociological Review*, Vol. 74, No., 1–22.

Keane, M. 2001 "Redefining Chinese citizenship," *Economy and Society*, Vol. 30, No. 1, 1–17.

Knight, J. and Song, L. 2005 *Towards a labour market in China* (Oxford and New York: Oxford University Press).

Kuruvilla, S., Lee, C. K. and Gallagher, M. E. 2011 "Introduction and argument" in Kuruvilla, S., Lee, C. K. and Gallagher, M. E. (eds.) *From iron rice bowl to informalization: Markets, workers, and the state in a changing China* (Ithaca: Cornell University Press).

Kwong, J. 1994 "Ideological Crisis among China's Youths: Values and Official Ideology," *The British Journal of Sociology*, Vol. 45, No. 2, 247–264.

Lee, C. K. and Kofman, Y. 2012 "The politics of precarity: Views beyond the United States," *Work and Occupations*, Vol. 39, No. 4, 388–408.

Leonard, M. 2008 *What does China think?* (London: Harper Collins).

Li, Wei-dong 2009 "The study of adaptation of new generation migrant workers," *Social Science of Beijing* (Beijing), Vol. 4, 29–33.

Liu, Lydia H. 1993 "Translingual Practice: The discourse of individualism between China and the West," *Positions*, Vol. 1, No. 1, 160–193.

Mead, M. 1928 *Coming of age in Samoa: A psychological study of primitive youth for Western civilisation* (New York: William Morrow).

Mead, M. 1970 *Culture and Commitment: A study of the generation gap* (Garden City, NY: Natural History Press).

Mead, M. 1975 (1930) *Growing up in New Guinea* (London: Penguin).

Murphy, R. 2002 *How migrant labor is changing rural China* (Cambridge: Cambridge University Press)..

Osella, F. and Gardner, K. 2003 "Migration, Modernity and Social Transformation in South Asia," *Contributions to Indian Sociology (n.s.)*, Vol. 37, No. 1-2, v–xxviii.

Pun, Ngai. 1999 "Becoming dagongmei (working girls): The politics of identity and difference in reform China," *The China Journal*(Canberra), Vol. 42, 1–18.

Pun, N. 2005 *Made in China: Women factory workers in a global workplace* (Durham: Duke University Press).

Rofel, L. 2007 *Desiring China: Experiments in neoliberalism, sexuality, and public culture* (Durham: Duke University Press).

Standing, G. 2009 *Work after Globalization: Building Occupational Citizenship* (Cheltenham: Elgar).

Standing, G. 2011 *The Precariat—The New Dangerous Class* (London: Bloomsbury).

Standing, G. 2014 *A Precariat Charter: From denizens to citizens* (London: Bloomsbury)

Turner, V. 1967 *The forest of symbols: Aspects of Ndembu ritual* (Ithaca: Cornell University).

Wang, C. 2001 "Xinshengdai nongcun liudong renkou de shehui rengtong yu chengxiang ronghe de guanxi [Social identity and social integration of the new generation of rural-urban migrants]," *Shehuixue yanjiu [Sociological studies]*, Vol. 3, 63–76.

Weber, I. 2001 "Shanghai youth's strategic mobilization of individualistic values: Constructing cultural identity in the age of spiritual civilization," *Intercultural Communication Studies*, Vol. 10, No. 2, 23–46.

Weber, I. 2002 "Shanghai Baby: Negotiating youth self-identity in urban China," *Social Identities*, Vol. 8, No. 2, 347–368.

Wu, Hong-yu and Xie, Guo-qiang 2006 "The characteristics, interests claims and role-changing of workers of new generation from the rural: A survey in Tangxia Town, Dongguan," *South China Population*, Vol. 2, No. 21, 21–31.

Yan, Y. 2003 *Private life under socialism: Love, intimacy, and family change in a Chinese village, 1949-1999* (Stanford, Calif.: Stanford University Press).

Yan, Y. 2006 "Girl power: Young women and the waning of patriarchy in rural North China," *Ethnology*, Vol. 45, No. 2, 105–123.

Yan, Y. 2010 "The Chinese path to individualization," *The British Journal of Sociology*, Vol. 61, No. 3, 489–511.

Ye, J. and Pan, L. 2011 "Differentiated childhoods: impacts of rural labor migration on left-behind children in China," *Journal of Peasant Studies*, Vol. 38, No. 2, 355–377.

Yu, X. and Pan, Y. 2008 "Consumer Society and remaking the subjectivities of 'new generation of Dagongmei'," *Sociological Studies*, Vol. 3, 143–171.

Zhou, Xiao-Hong 1999 "Cultural feedback: Cultural transition between parents and their children in changing society," *Yingyong xinli yanjiu (Applied Psychology Research)*, Vol. 4, 29–56.

Zhou, Yingying, Han, Hua and Harrell, Stevan 2008 "From labour to capital: Intra-village inequality in rural China, 1988-2006," *The China Quarterly*, Vol. 195, 515–534.

CONCLUSION

Aldrie Henry-Lee, Christos Papatheodorou, Maria Petmesidou, and Enrique Delamónica

> Poverty anywhere is a danger to prosperity everywhere. (Declaration concerning the aims and purposes of the International Labour Organization [DECLARATION OF PHILADELPHIA], p. 1)

As nations turn their attention to the fulfillment of the Sustainable Development Goals (SDGs), this book underscores the urgent need to focus and specifically target some of the most disadvantaged groups in our societies: poor children and unemployed youth. While there has been some progress in the global reduction of monetary and multidimensional poverty in the last three decades, there are still billions of children and youngsters materially deprived, struggling to survive with insufficient income to purchase a minimum amount of food, and lacking opportunities to become fully productive citizens. The recent global economic crisis has reversed any hope for sustained poverty and unemployment reduction. It has been made evident that these phenomena are embedded in modern societies. It has also been revealed that the relevant policy responses at local, national, and supranational level have failed to produce promising results in alleviating poverty and promote full employment and sustainable development. Even many developed countries have experienced an alarming increase of child poverty and youth unemployment in recent years. The African Youth Decade 2009-2018 Plan of action, the Europe 2020 Agenda, the Japan-Asian Plan of Action and the Strategic Plan for the Caribbean Community 2015, and the 2014 Baku Commitment to Youth Policies will fail miserably if the global community does not increase its focus on the younger members of their societies. Investment in children and youth is key to the fulfillment of the SDGs. The full participation and engagement of children and youth are critical for the development of national economies and societies. By providing empirical and theoretical analyses in Europe, Latin America and the Caribbean, Africa, and Asia, this book assesses the structural causes of child poverty and youth unemployment and their short-and long-term effects on individuals and societies. Furthermore, it discusses key policy interventions aiming at alleviating child poverty, youth unemployment, and employment precariousness. It reminds us that we need to harness the productive capabilities of children and youth to secure safe and economically viable societies. One striking point of this book is the consensus among authors from varied disciplines on the urgency of the problems of child poverty, youth unemployment, and social exclusion. Focusing on various aspects of child and youth poverty and labor force participation in different countries and regions, the chapters of this book expose the multidimensional nature of these phenomena. Also, the variety and plethora of complex issues associated with these phenomena manifest the need to expand and adjust our theoretical and methodological tools.

The contributions to this volume engage and critique the current definitions, concepts, and theories of child and youth poverty, unemployment, and social exclusion. They provide new and different ways of examining these complex phenomena. For example, Dedoussopoulos and Papachristopoulou argue that youth is not a homogeneous social category since sharp diversities exist as far as gender, age, and level of education are concerned. Thus they go beyond the standard single index of unemployment rate to include youth participation, employment and unemployment rates, the ratio of youth unemployment rate to mature (30–55 years old) unemployment rate; the share of youth unemployment to total unemployment; the rate of youth unemployment to youth population; the scholarization index, that is, the rate of youngsters in formal education to the youth population; and the out-of-work-out-of-school index. This more thorough examination of youth unemployment lays the basis for more gendered, detailed, and focused empirical research. The theoretical contribution is further enhanced by the development of vulnerability indexes to grapple with definitions of poverty. Minujin, Born, Lombardía, and Delamónica, found the category NEET (not in education, employment, and training) that dominates the contemporary public and academic debate, restricting and misleading in analyzing and exposing the nexus between education and employment for adolescents and youngsters (A&Y). They develop an alternative measurement of vulnerability in education and employment among A&Y, the VEL (Vulnerability in Education and Labor), which incorporates educational achievements and type of employment (formal/informal employment, unemployment). Utilizing this new measure they reveal that in

Latin America and the Caribbean the proportion of A&Y with vulnerability in education and labor is almost 30%, which is twice as high as the relative NEETs figure. Moreover, Garrido, Gutiérrez, and Guillén introduce the concept of "biographical dualism" to describe youth employment in Spain, which emphasizes two outstanding traits: On the one hand, the low quality of school-to-work transitions and, on the other, the high intensity of the insider-outsider dualism in the labor market. Biographical dualism is a major trait that links the temporary pattern of incorporation into the labor market with the dimension of age. One conclusion from this book is that child poverty and youth unemployment cannot be examined without a multidimensional and multifaceted analysis of the phenomena.

This book also underscores that the analysis of poverty and unemployment, and consequently the definitions and methodology employed, must reflect the objective and subjective nature and effects of poverty, unemployment, and social exclusion. Bastos cautions that in spite of the importance of the family in the child's everyday life, even the integration of family's conditions in the analysis should be carried out through indicators that could measure the impact of these conditions on children. Focusing on the EU countries, she stresses the limitations put by the broadly used measures (such as income based) in analyzing and understanding child poverty, and consequently in designing effective social policies to alleviate this issue. She further states that child poverty assessments should avoid the inclusion of data that is not directly related to children's material deprivation. Even more, appraisal of child poverty should take into consideration children's specific needs and vulnerabilities. Thus, apart from the income-based and multidimensional approaches, she also reviews the holistic and the child's rights approaches that go beyond the access to material and market goods, where qualitative and quantitative data are combined for assessing children's well-being. Finally, in order to overcome the limitations of the child poverty approaches that are broadly used in analyzing and assessing child poverty, Bastos suggests methodological guidelines concerning the unit of analysis, the multidimensionality, the type of variables, and the data employed.

The contributions in this book have shown that problems and challenges facing children and youth are a global phenomenon. From the Caribbean to Europe to Africa to Asia, the authors examine the structural causes of poverty, based on both quantitative and qualitative research. The authors reveal that child and youth deprivation pose serious social and economic problems that affect both developed and developing countries. Using available data for the EU countries, Papanastasiou, Papatheodorou, and Petmesidou enhance the literature by providing empirical estimates on child monetary poverty and its intensity, poverty spell duration, and the probability of exit from or reentry into poverty. They combine these elements to assess the magnitude of intergenerational poverty transmission and the impact of social protection system on mitigating the influence of the family of origin on children's future outcomes. The analyses embrace association statistics, correlation structures, and log-linear models.

Schenk, Blaauw, and Viljoen examine youth in the informal economy in South Africa utilizing longitudinal data for a period of 10 years and employing a variety of quantitative (surveys) and qualitative data collection methods, such as observations, ethnography, and individual interviews. Whether through qualitative or quantitative data analysis the authors examine the causes of the increased participation of youth in informal economy (waste picking and day laboring) as survivalist activities. Special attention is given to the barriers of entry into formal economy of these groups of young unemployed.

Utilizing sound empirical data, this book reveals that large numbers of children and youth are subjected to cumulative disadvantages, which have deleterious effects on their adulthood. Some of these detrimental effects include: social exclusion, marginalization, homelessness, and improper transition from adolescence to adulthood. The authors discuss the long-term effects of youth unemployment, informality, and labor precariousness. There is enough evidence in this book to show that quality of life and contribution of adults to their societies depend on what assets they had access to when they were younger and the enabling environment that was created for them as they grew up. From the streets of South Africa to post-Mao China, the effects of lack of effective investment in the early years are discussed using novel empirical evidence and analytical tools.

Poverty in the 21st century is complicated by issues of social exclusion, denial of rights, security, and migration, increased individual and household vulnerabilities in a context of trade liberalization, globalization, and global conflict. While there are negative effects of poverty and unemployment on individuals and households, increased social instability may ensue if the marginalization and social exclusion of children and youth are not addressed immediately. The adverse effects of child poverty and youth unemployment are not confined to one country or a continent and it is imperative that these issues be given immediate global attention.

The contributions to this volume critically raise the question of what policy strategies can break the vicious cycle of intergenerational transmission of poverty and social exclusion. There are proposals made at global, national, local, and micro level (individual and household). At the global level, the Millennium Development Goal Number 8 (Target Number 8 C) did call for special attention to be given to the special needs of land-locked developing countries and Small Island Developing States (SIDS), an issue that remains relevant and is included in the SDGs. Henry-Lee laments the low achievement of the goals set in the Programme of Action for Sustainable Development of SIDS since its adoption in 1994. In the pursuit of global partnerships, particular attention must be paid to the special conditions of the less-developed nations, which remain heavily dependent on external markets and sometimes, unfavorable trade rules. Small island developing states are also very susceptible to climate change and natural disasters. They need some specific policies and programs that address the multiplicity of their vulnerabilities. However, it must be noted that the Sustainable Goal number 17 reemphasizes the role of partnership in the fulfillment of the global development agenda and the responsibility of all countries (in particular the richest one) to improve their productive and consumption patterns to protect the environment. In developed countries, the social protection system has proved to be a crucial factor in alleviating poverty and mitigating the intergenerational transmission of disadvantages. Differences in child poverty rates between EU countries are mainly attributed to the combined impact of cash benefits, social services, parental leave arrangements, and working conditions supporting family–work balance. As stressed by Papanastasiou, Papatheodorou and Petmesidou, among EU countries, generous dual-earner transfers and extensive family policy arrangements characterizing longstanding welfare states strongly contribute to children's well-being.

At the national and local level, governments should invest in children and youth as a priority. Sustained strong economic growth is useful to the reduction of vulnerabilities among children and youth. However, to reduce poverty and inequality this economic growth must be inclusive and the benefits equitably distributed in the societies. Otherwise, economic growth by itself will not automatically trickle down to improve their lives, as experience in the last decades in both developed and developing countries has shown. In addition, at all times, there must be a systematic and programmatic focus on health, education, social protection, and the provision of decent work. Nations must be committed to the provision of:

(a) Full employment and the raising of standards of living;
(b) Employment of workers in the occupations in which they can have the satisfaction of giving the fullest measure of their skill and attainments and make their greatest contribution to the common well-being.
(Declaration concerning the aims and purposes of the International Labour Organization [DECLARATION OF PHILADELPHIA], p. 2) [1]

Policies must establish and strengthen the various and intricate links between education and the labor market so that the training of the workforce is in keeping with the developmental goals of the countries. In addition, as we seek the ever-elusive economic growth, the developmental needs of the nation and its people are lost.

While not downplaying the importance of the parental background effects on the offspring's poverty risk, Papanastasiou, Papatheodorou. and Petmesidou propose that different welfare state regimes can play an equally important impact on the reproduction of poverty: In the countries of the social-democratic welfare state regime (i.e., the Nordic countries) a universal and (still) comparatively generous social protection system significantly minimizes the influence of a disadvantageous parental background on the offspring's poverty risk. Quoting Williams et al. (2013:3), Henry-Lee lists the following recommendations for more effective social protection programs (SP): (1) harmonize SP systems and policies across the region to better respond to increased regional mobility; (2) consolidate SP programs within countries to improve efficiency; (3) foster key human capital improvements among the poor to break intergenerational transmission of poverty; (4) improve monitoring and evaluation systems and data collection capacity to facilitate more responsive SP programs; and (5) increase

---

[1] Other international agreements and covenants, such as the Convention on the Rights of the Child also include provisions on the right to a minimum standard of living and social protection.

partnerships with civil society and private sector. Social protection programs must reflect the adherence to the right that everybody has the right to adequate food, clothing, shelter, education, health care, and security.

Dedoussopoulos and Papachristopoulou show that the institutional reforms in Greece, such as the increase of the flexibilization in working conditions, the lower minimum wage for the youth (compared to adults), and the relaxing precondition for dismissal compensations—imposed by the "rescue-deal" that the country has signed with its international lenders as a response to the debt crisis—have further deteriorated labor market integration of young people. Thus, the authors argue that policy in Greece has contributed greatly to the increase of precarious jobs, with significant short-term and long-term impacts on the society and the economy of the country.

Adam examines whether and under what conditions social economy activities and social entrepreneurship constitute useful strategies against unemployment and social exclusion (in particular among youngsters), a view that is widely promoted by national and international organizations. She addresses this issue in relation to Greece and in comparison to Latin American experience. Adam argues that in Greece, a series of deficiencies/inconsistencies in policy implementation, following new legal frameworks to regulate social entrepreneurship, have prevented social enterprises from delivering on their promises. Drawing upon the Latin American experience, she proposes improved managements and promotion of the so-called "solidarity economy" (i.e., cooperatives, mutual-benefit societies, social enterprises, and other similar economic efforts).

All authors agree that the resources targeted to children and youth be used with greater efficiency and effectiveness. Thus, in the case of China, Fang calls for the lifting of the barriers imposed by the *hukou* system on migrant workers and develop a social protection system that makes citizen rights fully accessible to them. Again, Fang reminds us that all programs and policies targeting children and youth must be informed by sound data/evidence. In the execution of the programs, there must be harmonization of efforts, equity, transparency, and accountability. Minujin, Born, Lombardía, and Delamónica propose a set of policies that could promote inclusion of adolescents and youngsters (A&Y), such as higher and more equitable investment in education, specific employment programs and policies focused on A&Y, addressing of gender issues in schools, valuing and supporting the (unpaid) care economy, and promoting competencies, connections, and confidence among A&Y. The authors argue that in order for these policies to be effective, they have to be combined with the proper macroeconomic and productive policies that promote full employment and decent jobs.

At the individual level, education is generally acknowledged as a key "liberating tool" from monetary poverty. There is a need to improve skills and facilitate integration into the formal labor market, as well as to strengthen the psychosocial well-being of youth and, consequently, of society. The nexus between poverty eradication and decent work cannot be overstated and individuals must have access to "decent work" and decent wages to break the vicious cycle between child poverty and youth unemployment and precarious employment. Children of poor households are often forced to work at early age (and thus to drop out of school) in order to contribute to family income. Consequently, due to their lower education compared to the rest of the labor force, they face profound obstacles in obtaining a decent and well-paid job. This not only violates children's rights (i.e., to education) but obstructs their future potential earnings and increase the risk to become poor as adults. Thus, parental and community support are also crucial for the reduction of child poverty, youth unemployment, and social exclusion. The contributions to this book reveal that individual policies alone cannot be effective in this matter. Child poverty and youth unemployment are structural problems of modern societies. Policy interventions to alleviate these phenomena need to be effectively incorporated to broad social and macroeconomic policies that promote economic growth, full employment, and social inclusion. By all indications, long-term strategies are essential to tackle the intergenerational transmission of disadvantages, which is a critical priority in combating the structural causes of present and future poverty. This constitutes a major challenge to various stakeholders at international, national, and local level. Within this framework, participation of children, adolescents, and youngsters in decisions that affect their lives is of crucial importance. However, the global consensus on austerity and the post-2015 sustainable development agenda serve incompatible goals, leaving no room for optimism concerting the eradication of child poverty and youth unemployment.

While the book provides some critical data and enhances the literature on child poverty, youth unemployment, and social inclusion, the authors advise that more longitudinal data would better inform the policy process. At all stages, policies must be formulated based on on-time and appropriate data. Improved monitoring and evaluation of policies is needed to better the targeting the needs of childhood and youth.

Overall, we hope the book will prove to be an important one which reminds academicians, students of development studies, childhood and youth advocates, policy makers, and implementers that the reduction of child poverty, youth unemployment, and social exclusion must be based on the principles of social justice, equity, and participatory governance. All humans must be considered equal citizens in whatever country they reside and nations are duty bound to provide an enabling environment for the fulfillment of the full potential of all citizens.

References

Williams, Asha, Cheston, Timothy, Coudouel, Aline, Subran, Ludovic 2013 "Tailoring social protection to small island developing states; Lessons learned from the Caribbean", *Social Protection & Labour Discussion Paper No. 1306* (Washington DC: The World Bank). In < http://hdl.handle.net/10986/16102> accessed 2 March 2016.

***ibidem**.eu*